WYRD.

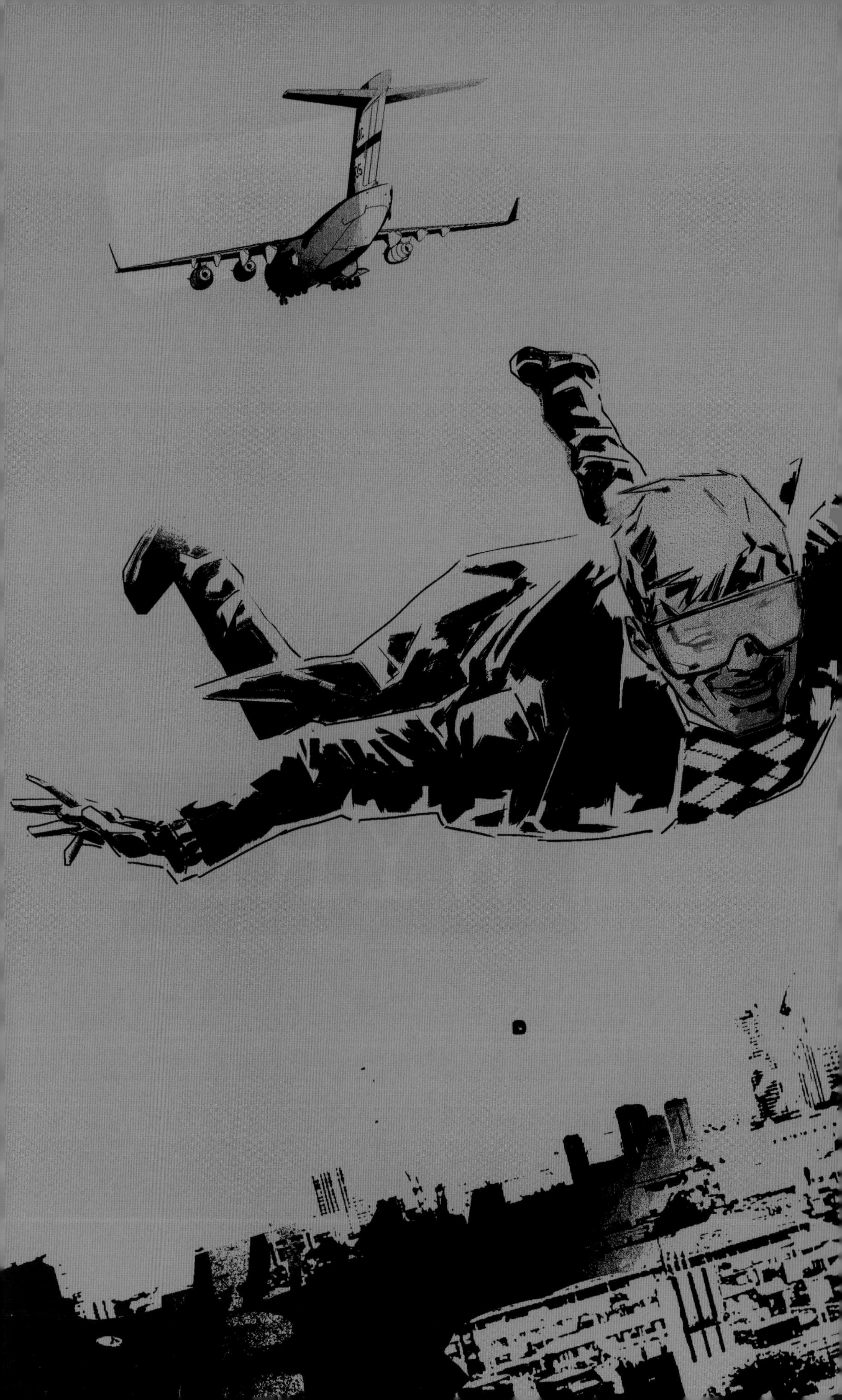

WYRD.

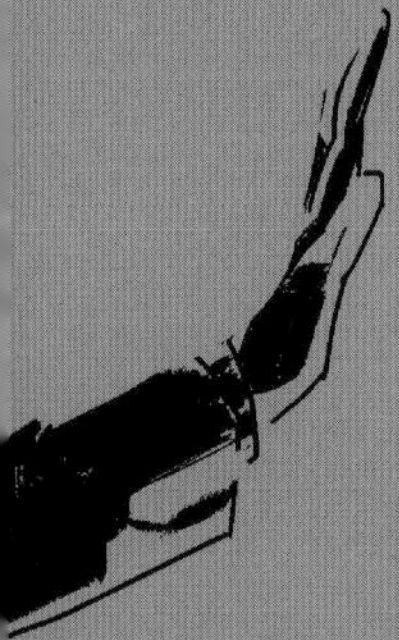

Curt Pires Antonio Fuso
Storytellers

Stefano Simeone
Colors

Micah Myers
Lettering

DARK HORSE BOOKS

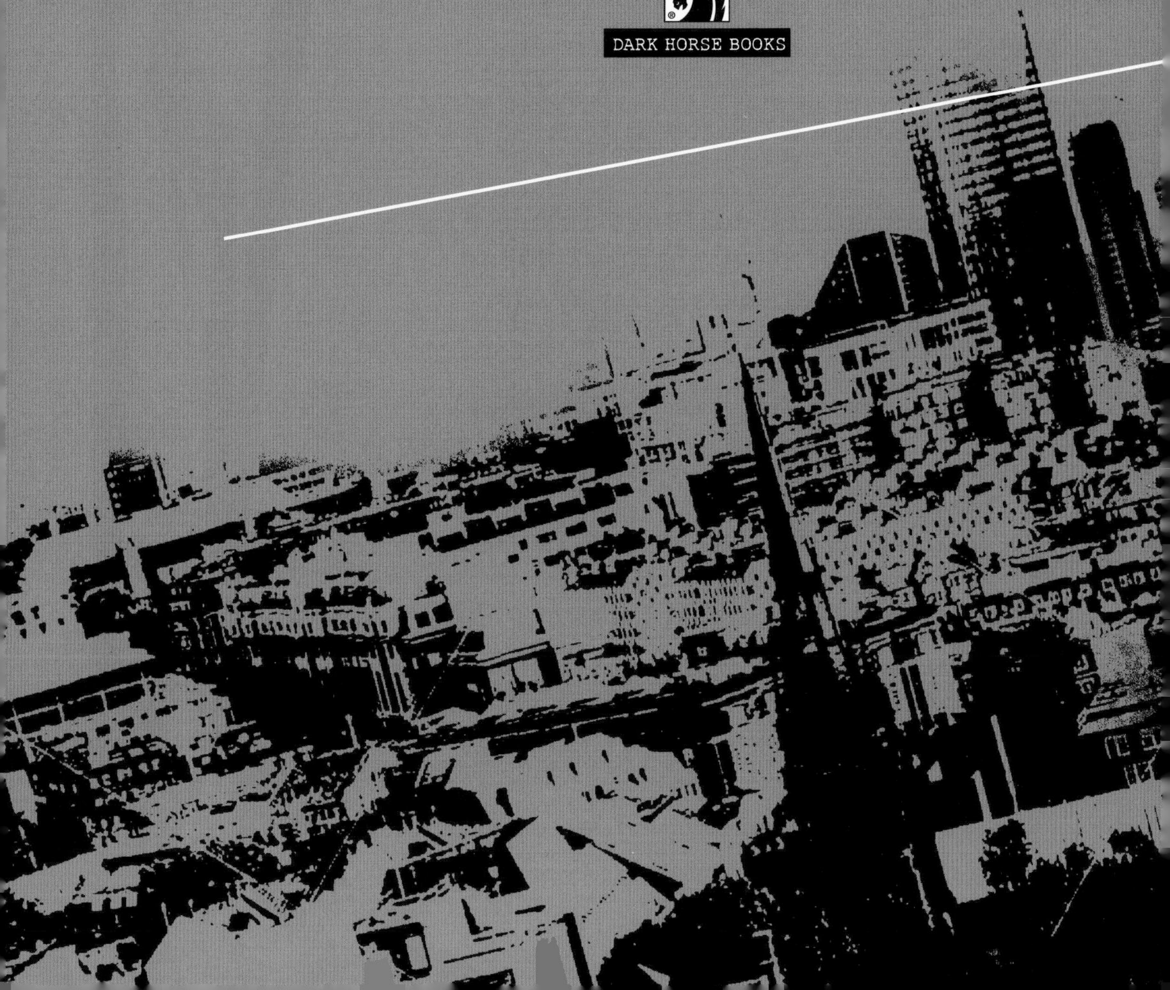

Publisher
Mike Richardson

Editor
Dave Marshall

Assistant Editor
Konner Knudsen

Designer
Brennan Thome

Digital Art Technician
Josie Christensen

This volume collects issues #1
through #4 of the Dark Horse
comic-book series *Wyrd*.

Library of Congress Control Number:2019943802

Published by Dark Horse Books / A division of Dark Horse Comics LLC
10956 SE Main Street / Milwaukie, OR 97222

darkhorse.com

First Edition: March 2020 / ISBN 978-1-50670-917-8

1 3 5 7 9 10 8 6 4 2
Printed in China

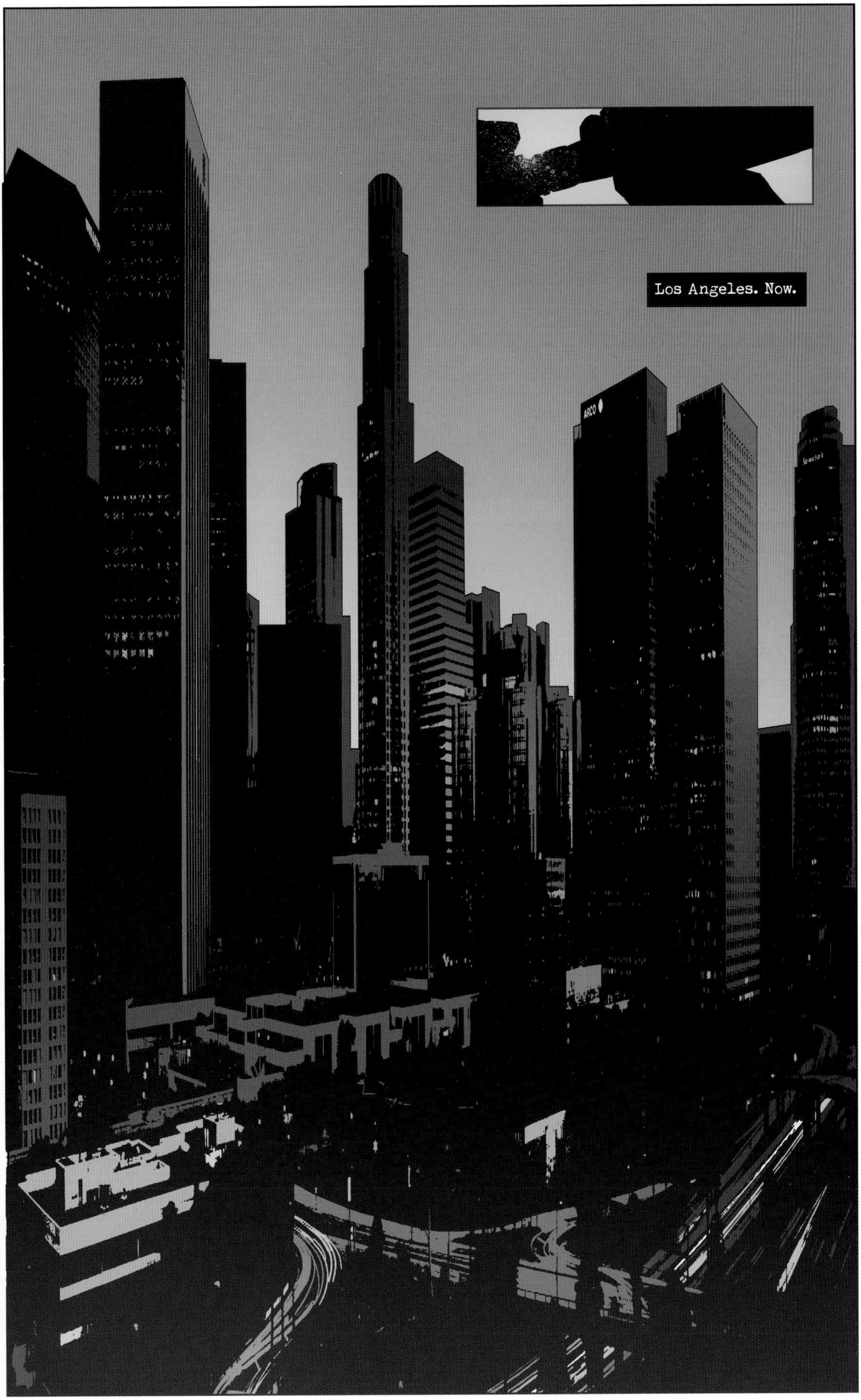
Los Angeles. Now.
ARCO

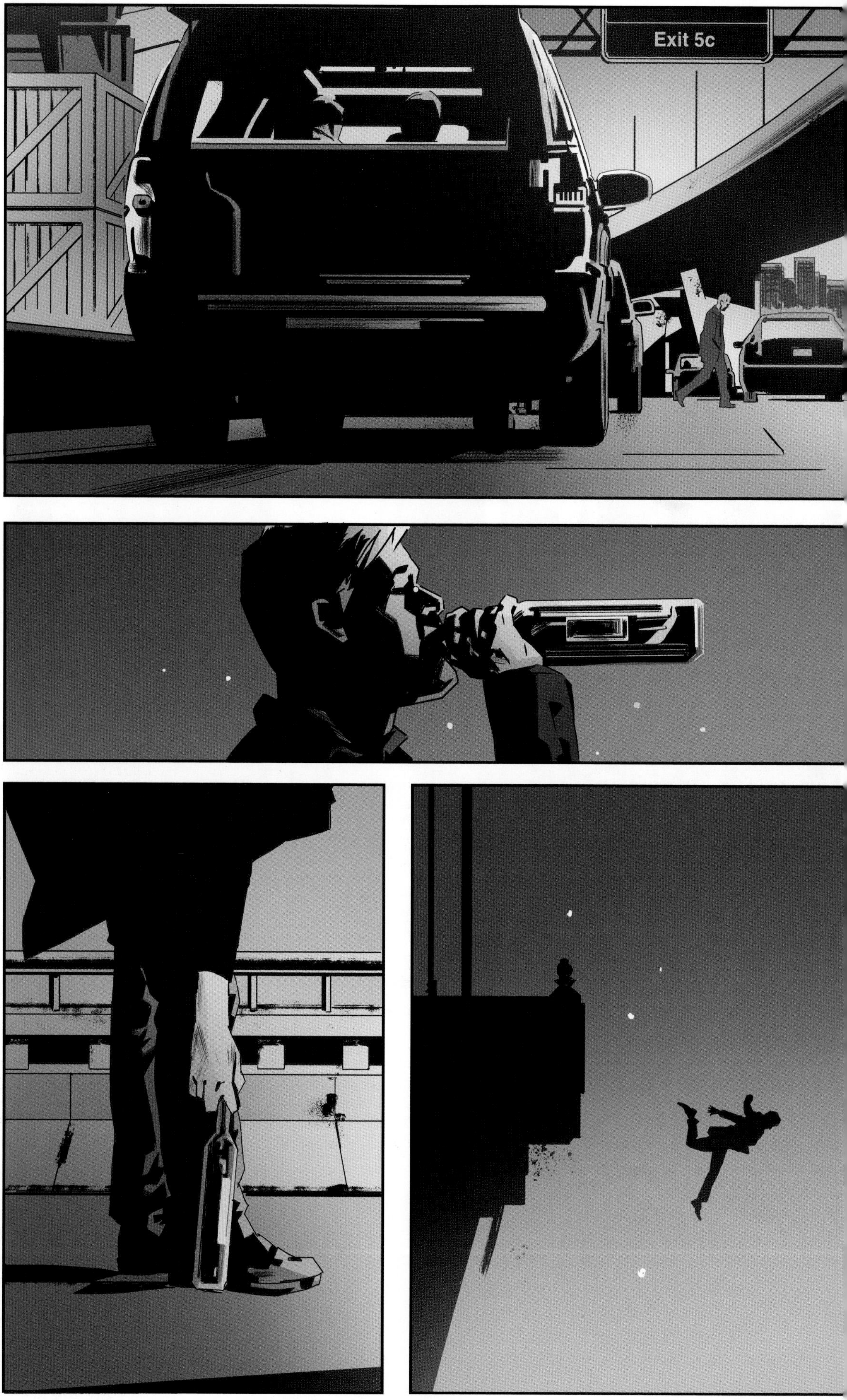
Exit 5c

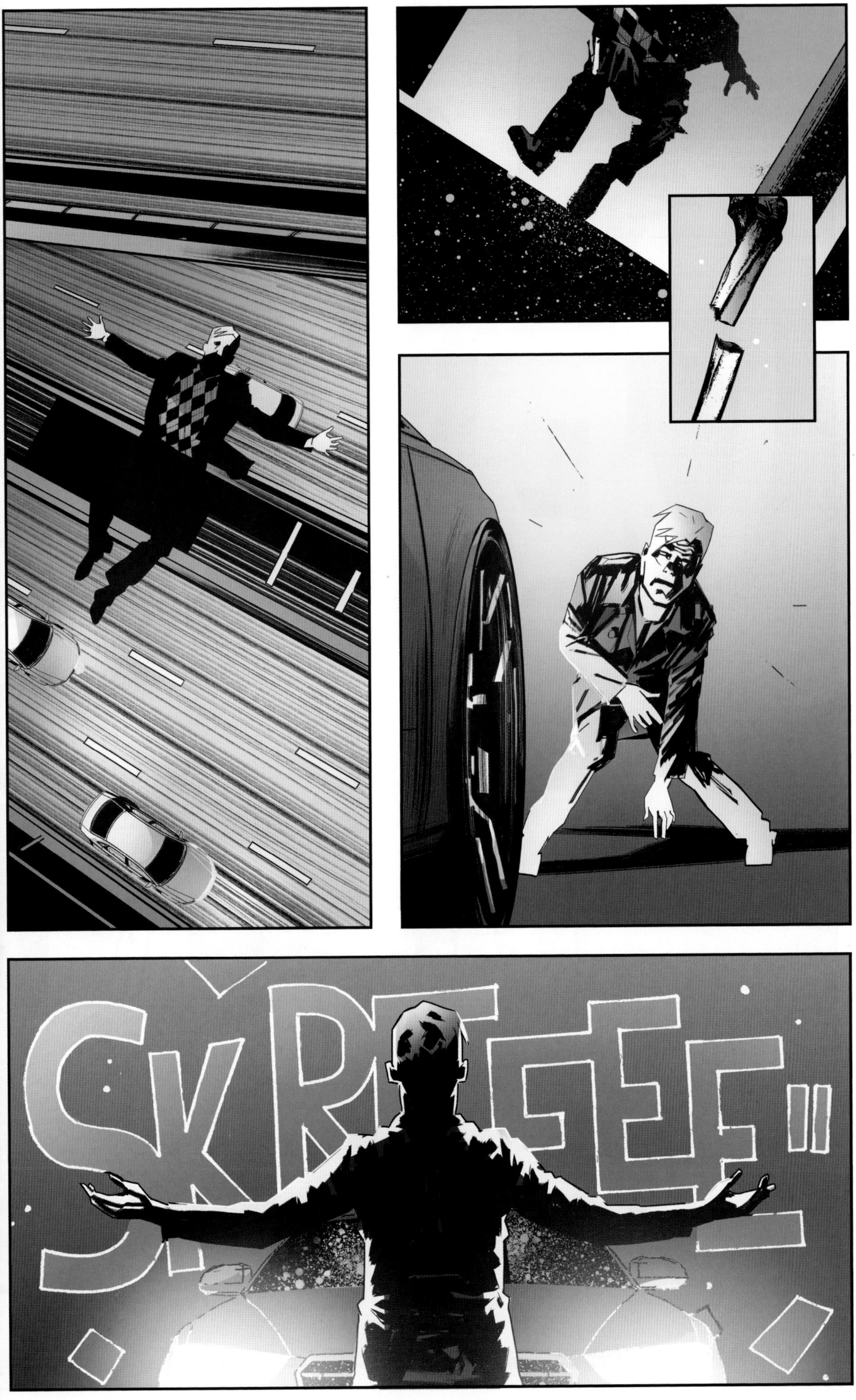

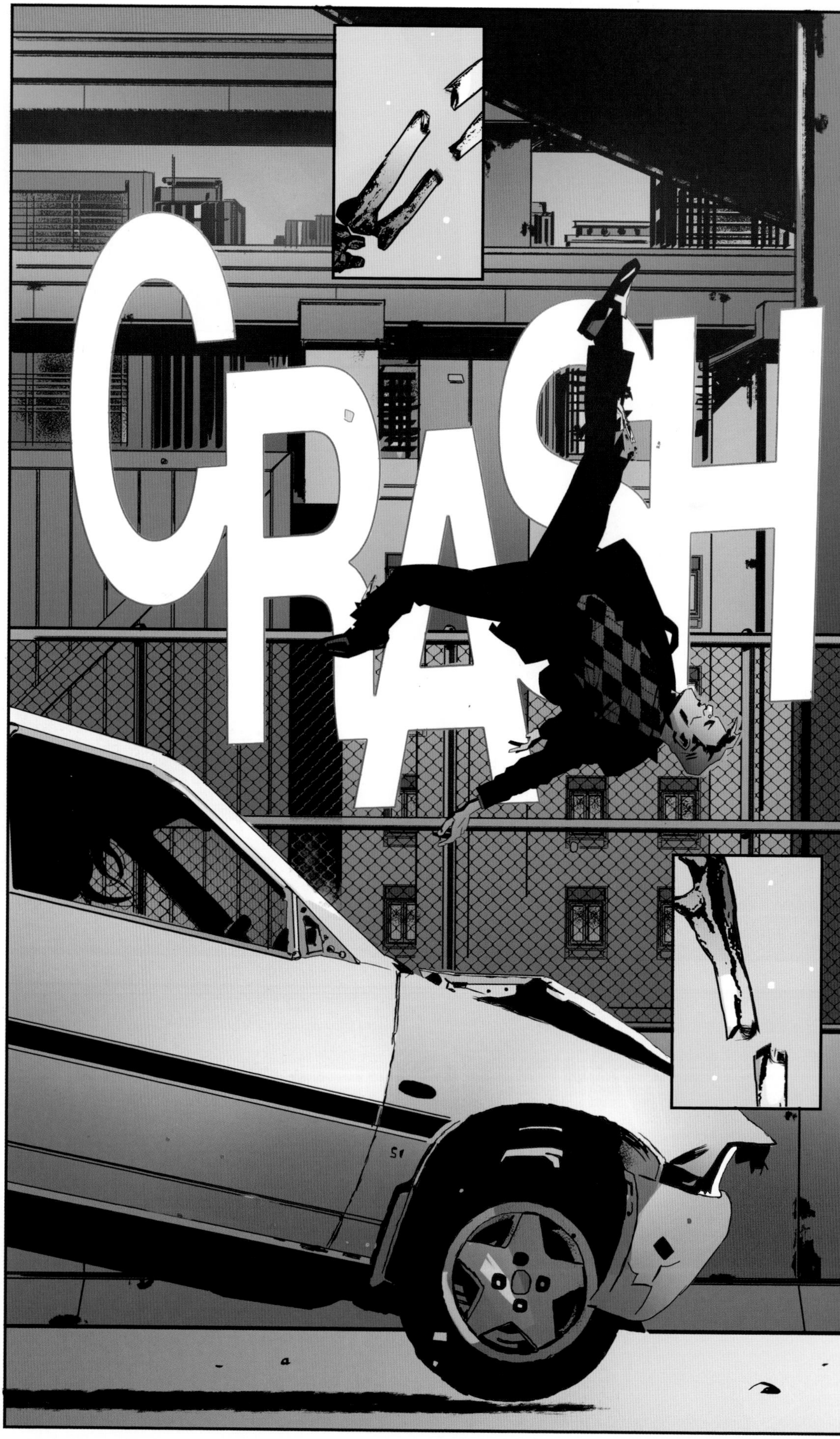
CRASH

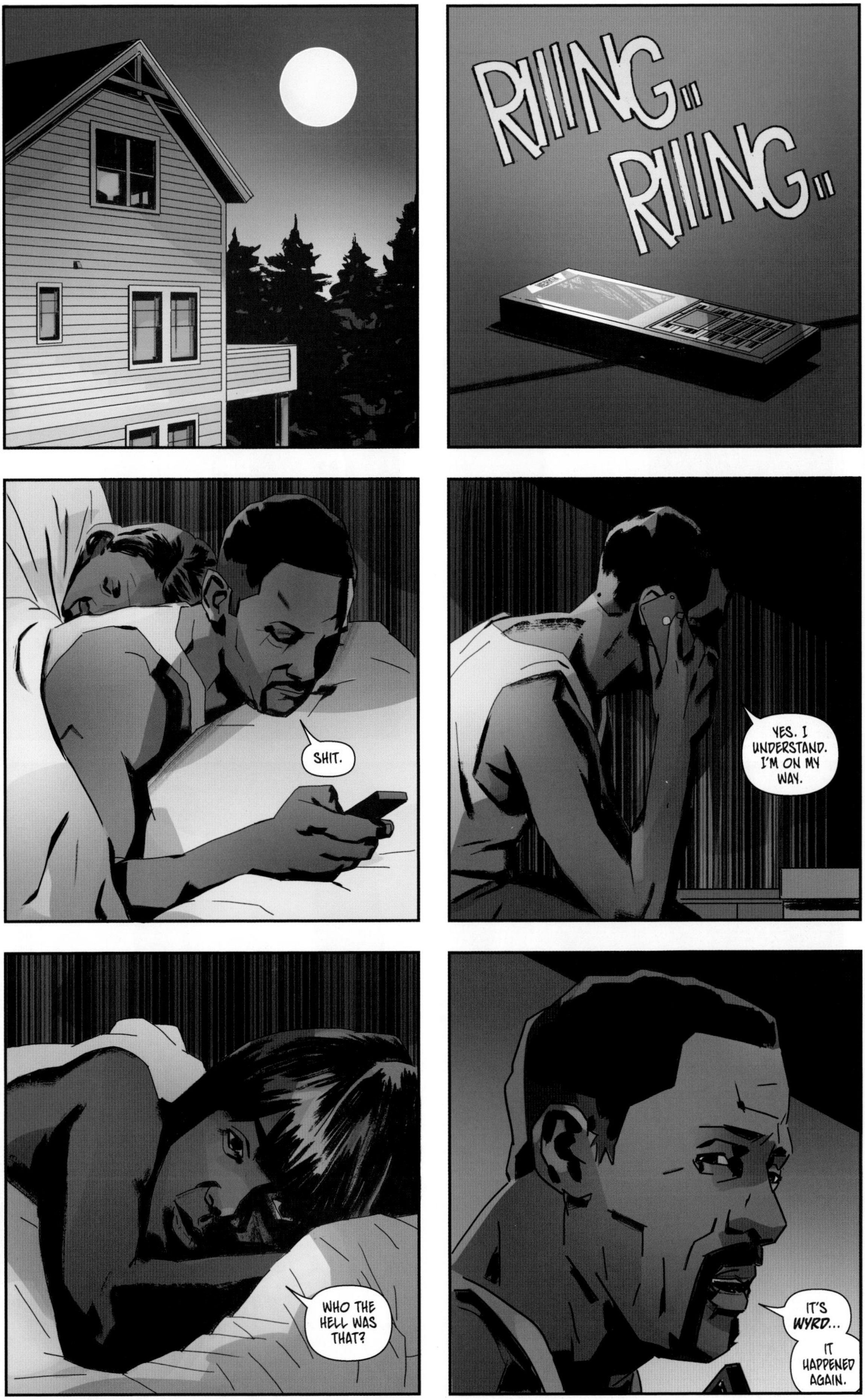
RIIING...
RIIING...
SHIT.
YES. I UNDERSTAND. I'M ON MY WAY.
WHO THE HELL WAS THAT?
IT'S WYRD...
IT HAPPENED AGAIN.

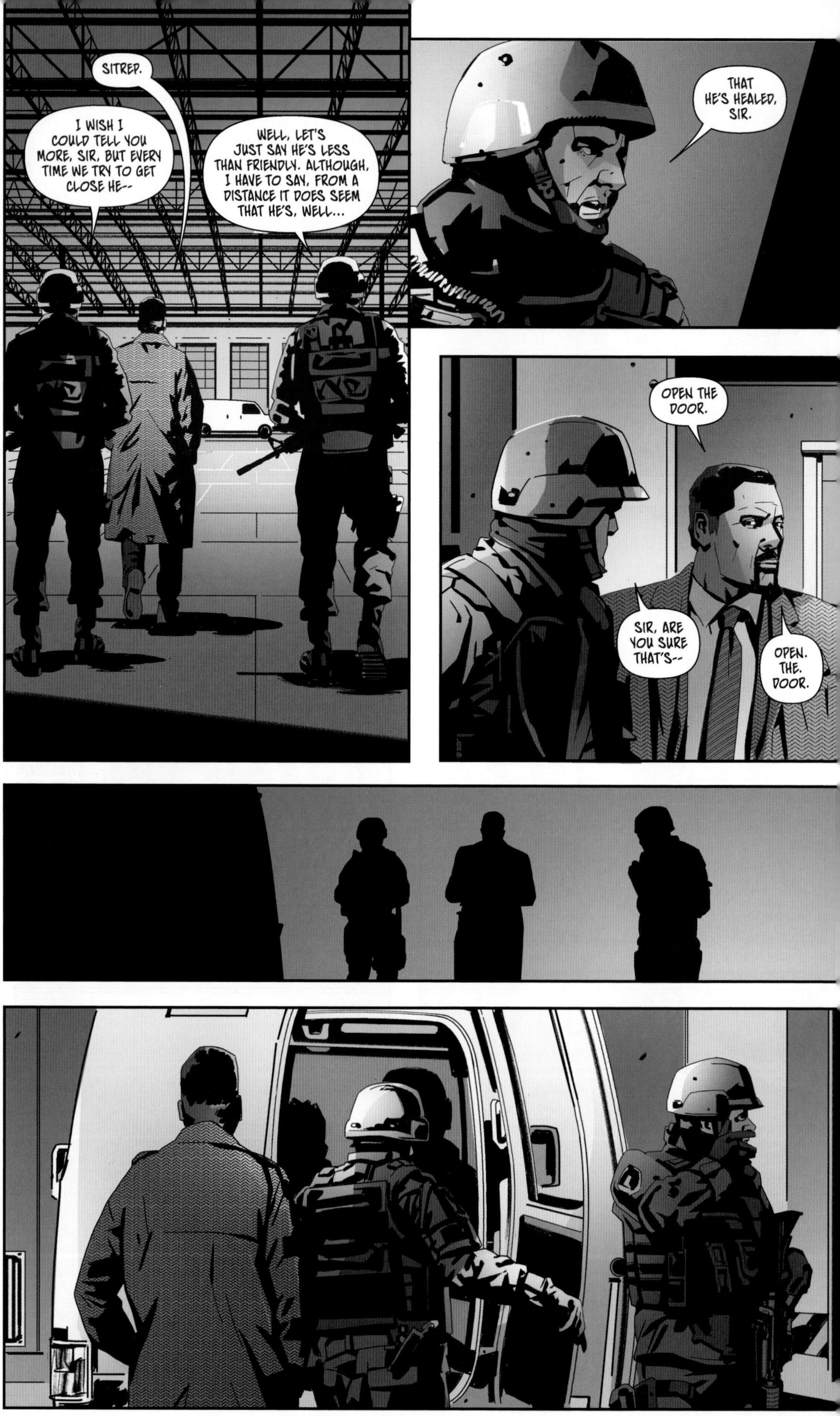
SITREP.
I WISH I COULD TELL YOU MORE, SIR, BUT EVERY TIME WE TRY TO GET CLOSE HE--
WELL, LET'S JUST SAY HE'S LESS THAN FRIENDLY. ALTHOUGH, I HAVE TO SAY, FROM A DISTANCE IT DOES SEEM THAT HE'S, WELL...
THAT HE'S HEALED, SIR.
OPEN THE DOOR.
SIR, ARE YOU SURE THAT'S--
OPEN. THE. DOOR.

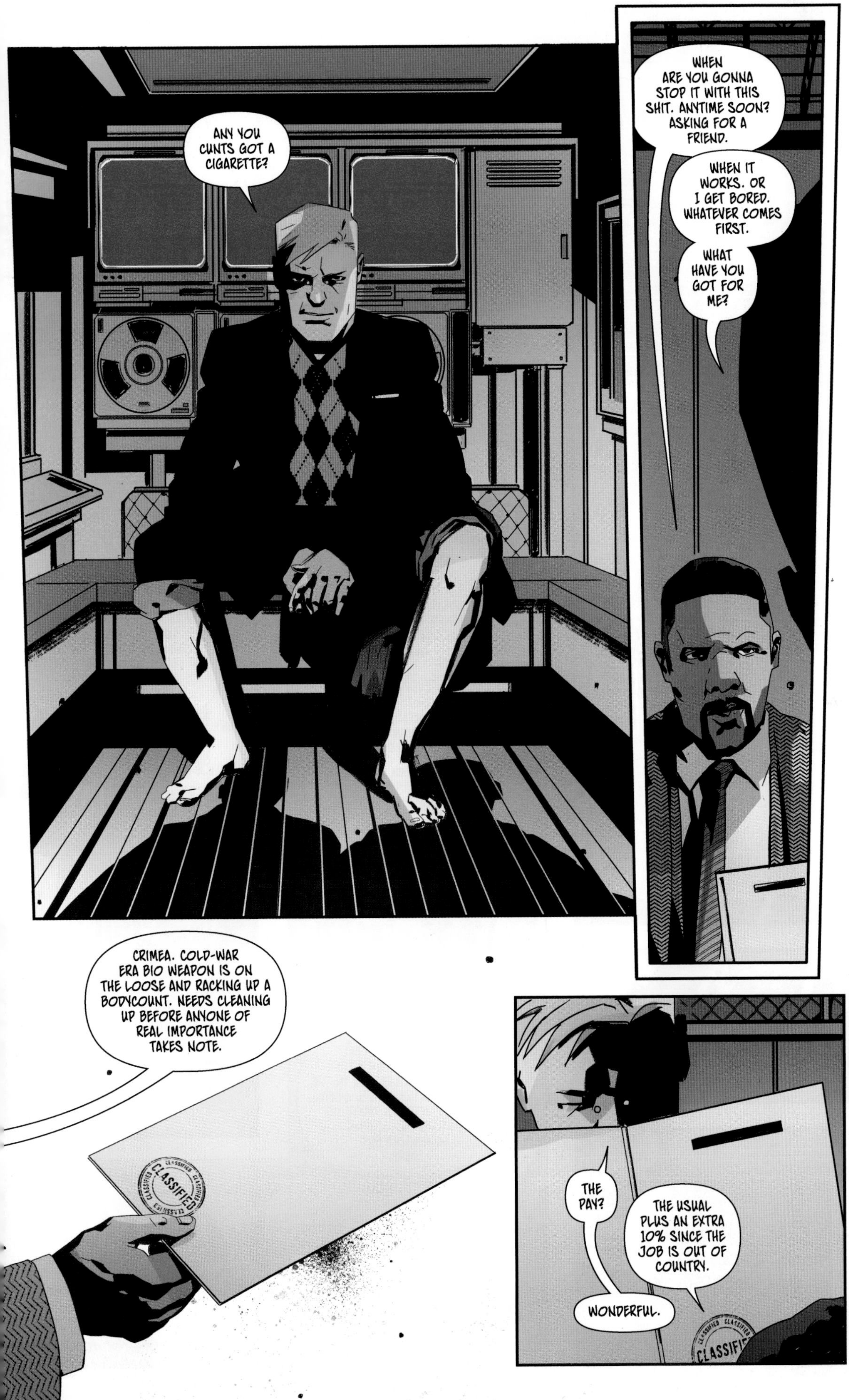
ANY YOU CUNTS GOT A CIGARETTE?
WHEN ARE YOU GONNA STOP IT WITH THIS SHIT. ANYTIME SOON? ASKING FOR A FRIEND.
WHEN IT WORKS. OR I GET BORED. WHATEVER COMES FIRST.
WHAT HAVE YOU GOT FOR ME?
CRIMEA. COLD-WAR ERA BIO WEAPON IS ON THE LOOSE AND RACKING UP A BODYCOUNT. NEEDS CLEANING UP BEFORE ANYONE OF REAL IMPORTANCE TAKES NOTE.
CLASSIFIED
THE PAY?
THE USUAL PLUS AN EXTRA 10% SINCE THE JOB IS OUT OF COUNTRY.
WONDERFUL.
CLASSIFIED

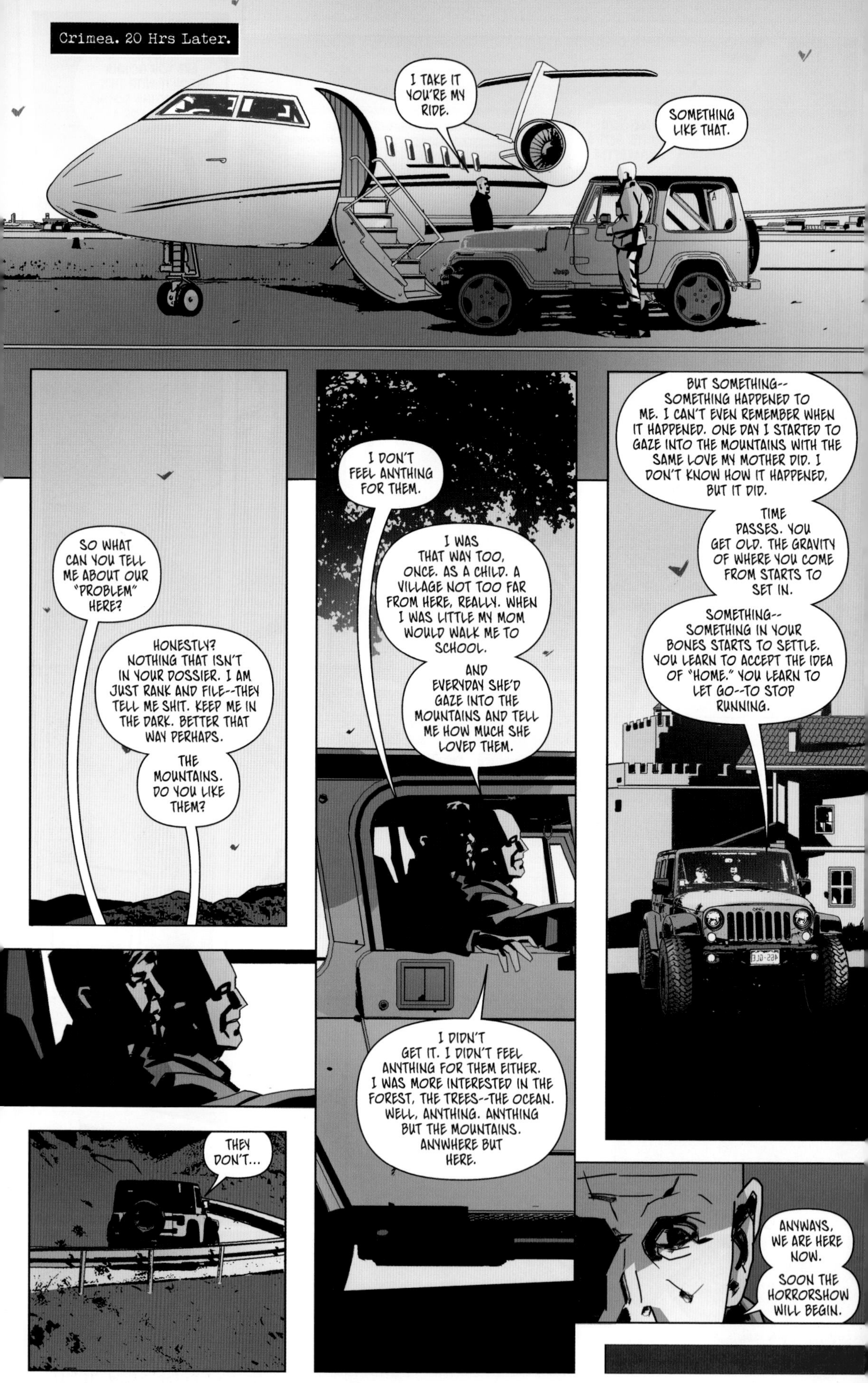
Crimea. 20 Hrs Later.
I TAKE IT YOU'RE MY RIDE.
SOMETHING LIKE THAT.
SO WHAT CAN YOU TELL ME ABOUT OUR "PROBLEM" HERE?
HONESTLY? NOTHING THAT ISN'T IN YOUR DOSSIER. I AM JUST RANK AND FILE--THEY TELL ME SHIT. KEEP ME IN THE DARK. BETTER THAT WAY PERHAPS.
THE MOUNTAINS. DO YOU LIKE THEM?
I DON'T FEEL ANYTHING FOR THEM.
I WAS THAT WAY TOO, ONCE. AS A CHILD. A VILLAGE NOT TOO FAR FROM HERE, REALLY. WHEN I WAS LITTLE MY MOM WOULD WALK ME TO SCHOOL.
AND EVERYDAY SHE'D GAZE INTO THE MOUNTAINS AND TELL ME HOW MUCH SHE LOVED THEM.
I DIDN'T GET IT. I DIDN'T FEEL ANYTHING FOR THEM EITHER. I WAS MORE INTERESTED IN THE FOREST, THE TREES--THE OCEAN. WELL, ANYTHING. ANYTHING BUT THE MOUNTAINS. ANYWHERE BUT HERE.
BUT SOMETHING--SOMETHING HAPPENED TO ME. I CAN'T EVEN REMEMBER WHEN IT HAPPENED. ONE DAY I STARTED TO GAZE INTO THE MOUNTAINS WITH THE SAME LOVE MY MOTHER DID. I DON'T KNOW HOW IT HAPPENED, BUT IT DID.
TIME PASSES. YOU GET OLD. THE GRAVITY OF WHERE YOU COME FROM STARTS TO SET IN.
SOMETHING--SOMETHING IN YOUR BONES STARTS TO SETTLE. YOU LEARN TO ACCEPT THE IDEA OF "HOME." YOU LEARN TO LET GO--TO STOP RUNNING.
THEY DON'T...
ANYWAYS, WE ARE HERE NOW.
SOON THE HORRORSHOW WILL BEGIN.

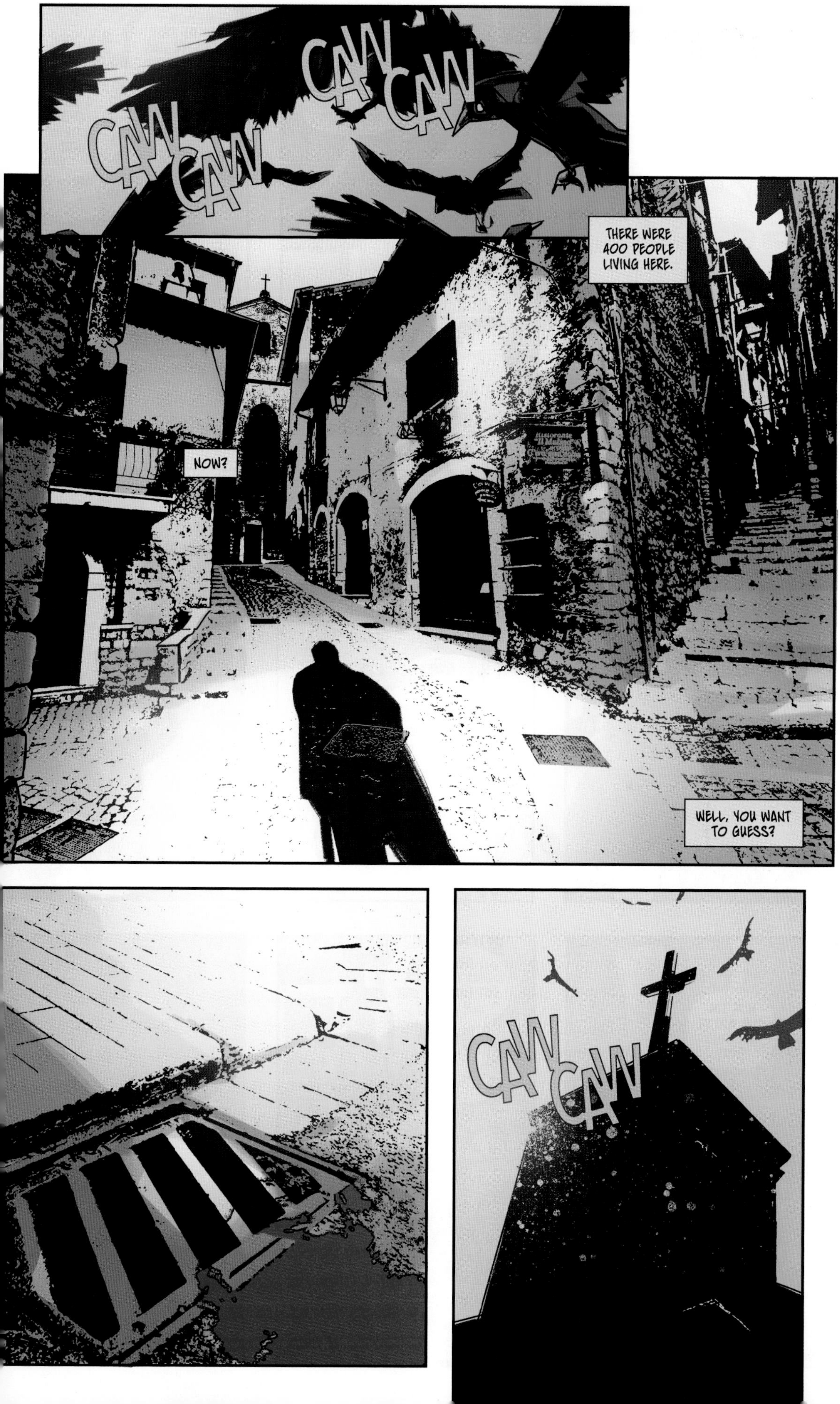
CAW CAW
CAW CAW
THERE WERE 400 PEOPLE LIVING HERE.
NOW?
WELL, YOU WANT TO GUESS?
CAW CAW

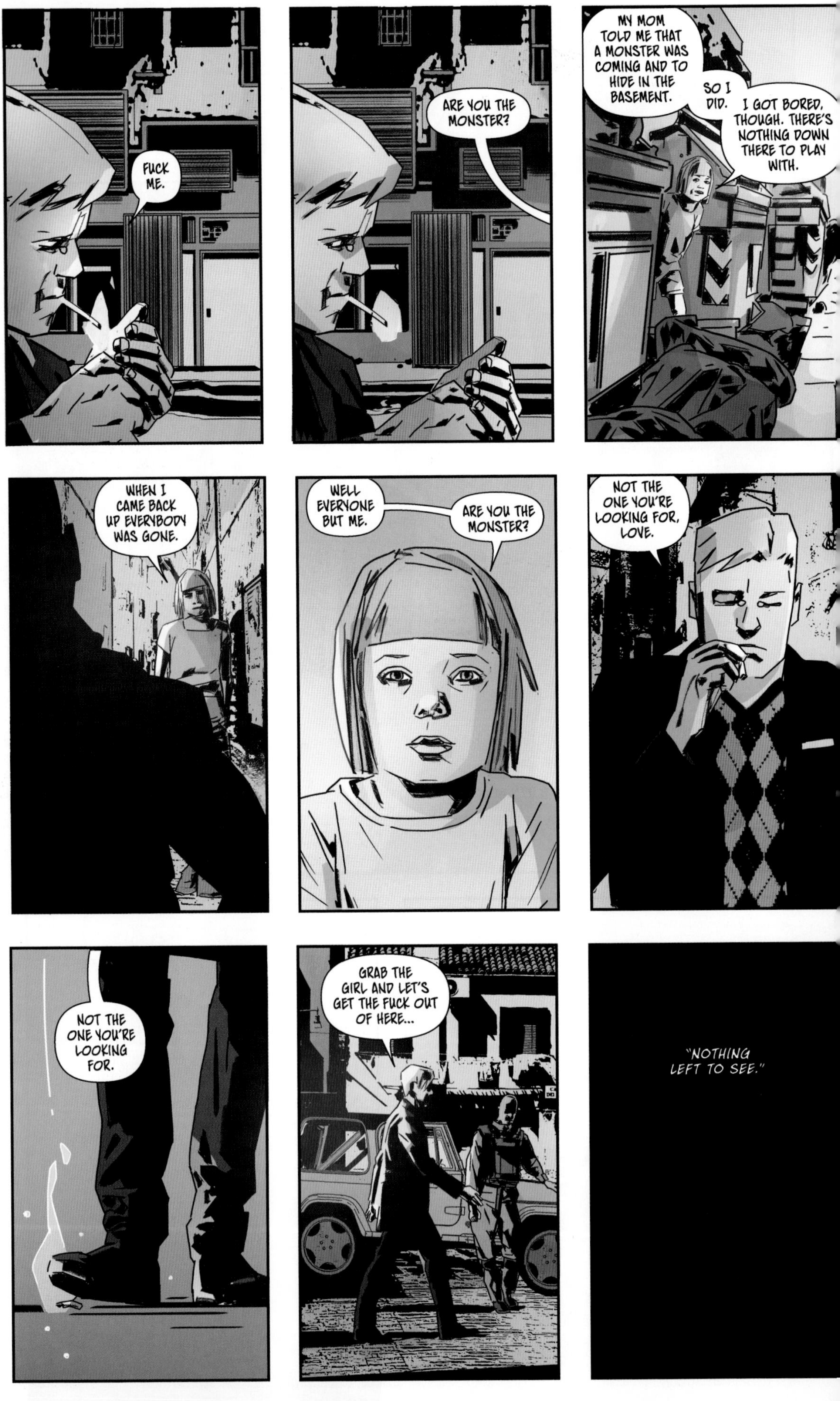

FUCK ME.
ARE YOU THE MONSTER?
MY MOM TOLD ME THAT A MONSTER WAS COMING AND TO HIDE IN THE BASEMENT.
SO I DID.
I GOT BORED, THOUGH. THERE'S NOTHING DOWN THERE TO PLAY WITH.
WHEN I CAME BACK UP EVERYBODY WAS GONE.
WELL EVERYONE BUT ME.
ARE YOU THE MONSTER?
NOT THE ONE YOU'RE LOOKING FOR, LOVE.
NOT THE ONE YOU'RE LOOKING FOR.
GRAB THE GIRL AND LET'S GET THE FUCK OUT OF HERE...
"NOTHING LEFT TO SEE."

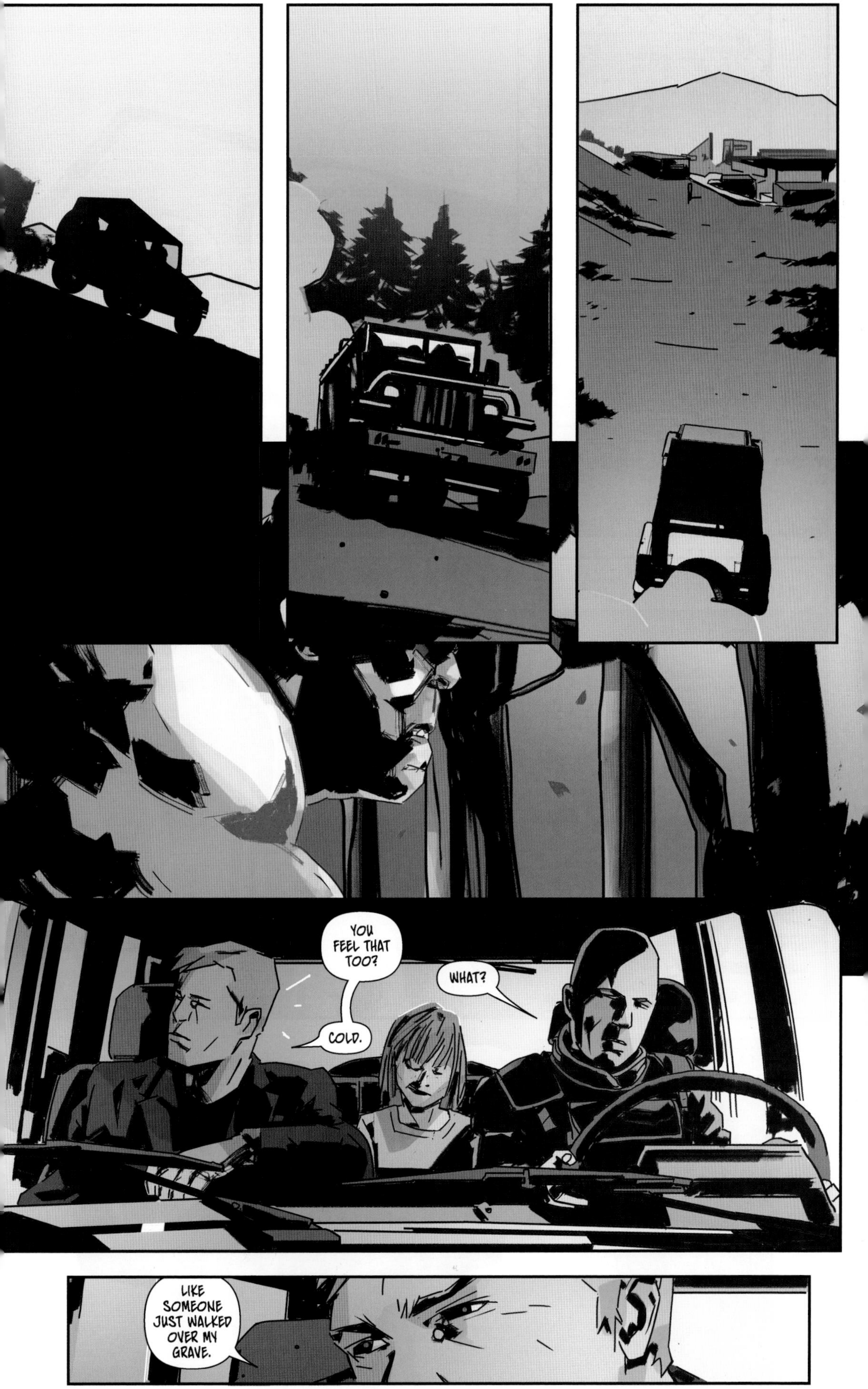
YOU FEEL THAT TOO?
WHAT?
COLD.
LIKE SOMEONE JUST WALKED OVER MY GRAVE.

STOP,
DANGEROUS
TO LIFE

СТОЙ,
ОПАСНО
ДЛЯ ЖИЗНИ

YOUR QUARTERS ARE JUST THROUGH THE DOOR AND TO THE LEFT. IF YOU FOLLOW ME I CAN SHOW YOU THE FILES WE'VE ASSEMBLED ON THE--

THAT WON'T BE NECESSARY. SEND THE FILES AND ALL ASSOCIATED MATERIALS TO MY QUARTERS.

ALONGSIDE A COUPLE BOTTLES OF WHATEVER THE MOST POTENT AND VILE SPIRIT THAT YOU'VE GOT TO OFFER.

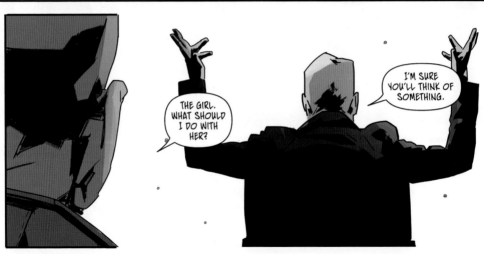

THE GIRL. WHAT SHOULD I DO WITH HER?

I'M SURE YOU'LL THINK OF SOMETHING.

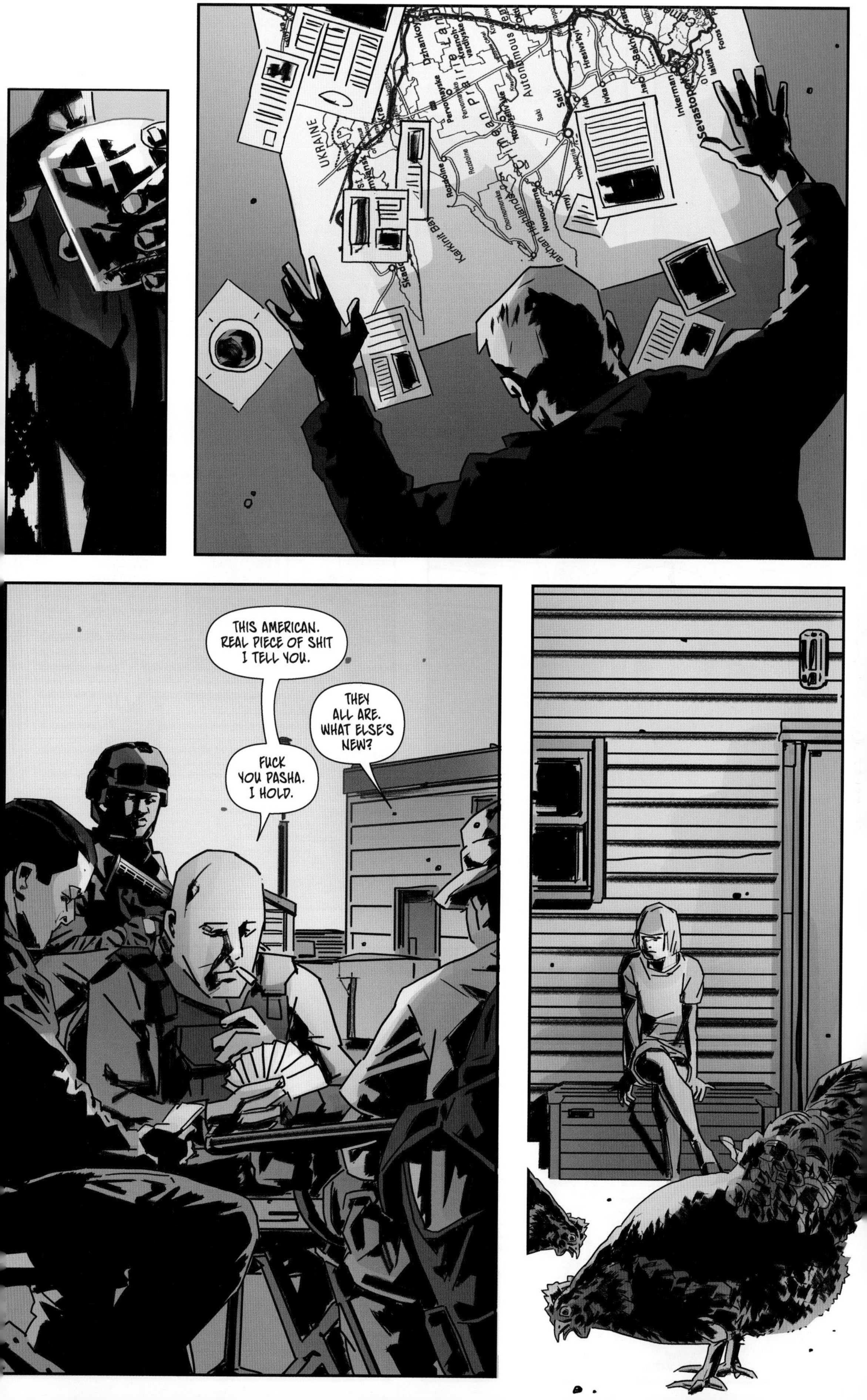
UKRAINE
Dzhankoy
Autonomous
Saki
Inkerman
Rozdolne
Karkinit Bay
THIS AMERICAN. REAL PIECE OF SHIT I TELL YOU.
FUCK YOU PASHA. I HOLD.
THEY ALL ARE. WHAT ELSE'S NEW?

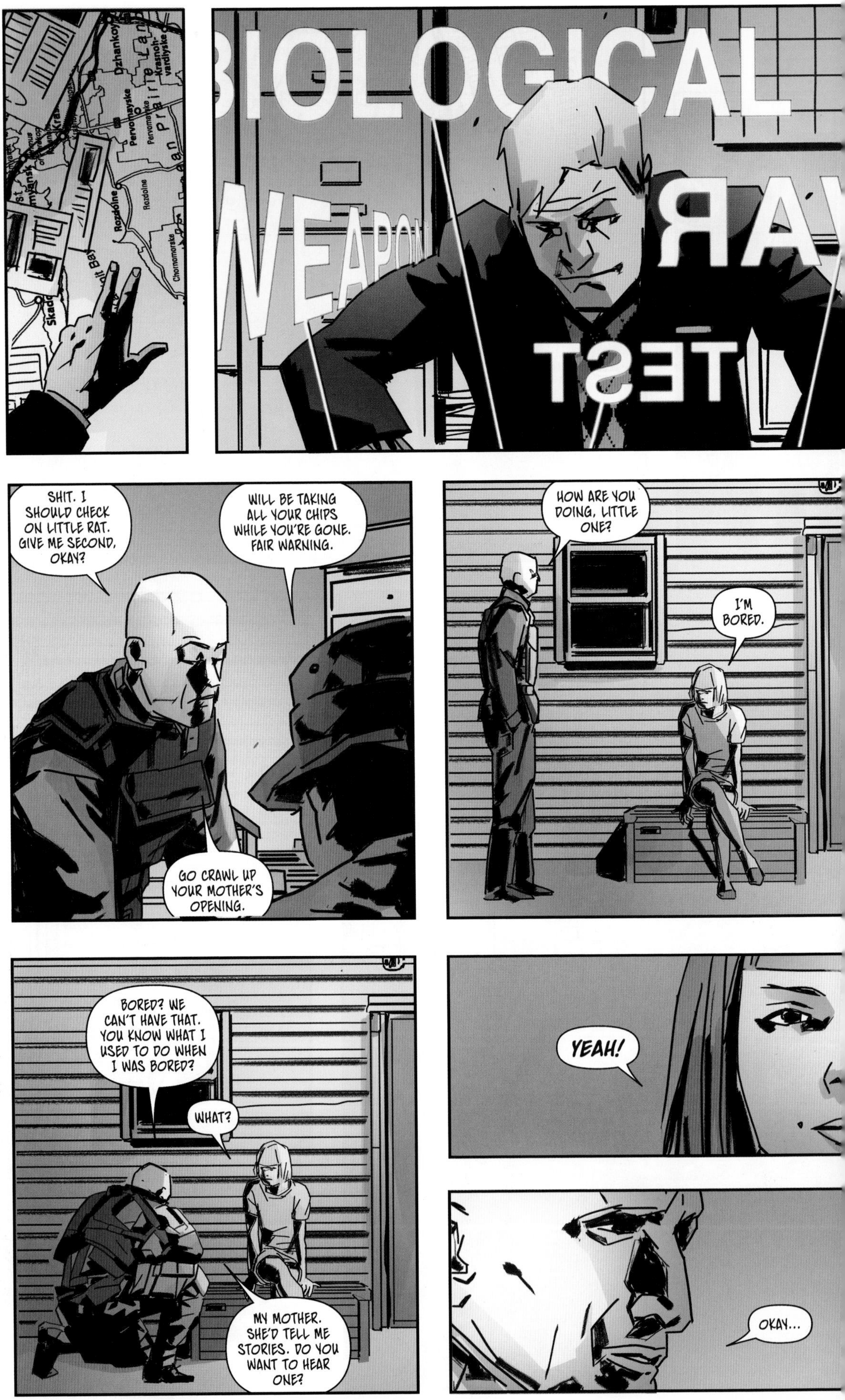
Dzhankoy
Pervomayske
Rozdolne
Chornomorske
BIOLOGICAL
WEAPON
WAR
TEST
SHIT. I SHOULD CHECK ON LITTLE RAT. GIVE ME SECOND, OKAY?
WILL BE TAKING ALL YOUR CHIPS WHILE YOU'RE GONE. FAIR WARNING.
GO CRAWL UP YOUR MOTHER'S OPENING.
HOW ARE YOU DOING, LITTLE ONE?
I'M BORED.
BORED? WE CAN'T HAVE THAT. YOU KNOW WHAT I USED TO DO WHEN I WAS BORED?
WHAT?
MY MOTHER. SHE'D TELL ME STORIES. DO YOU WANT TO HEAR ONE?
YEAH!
OKAY...

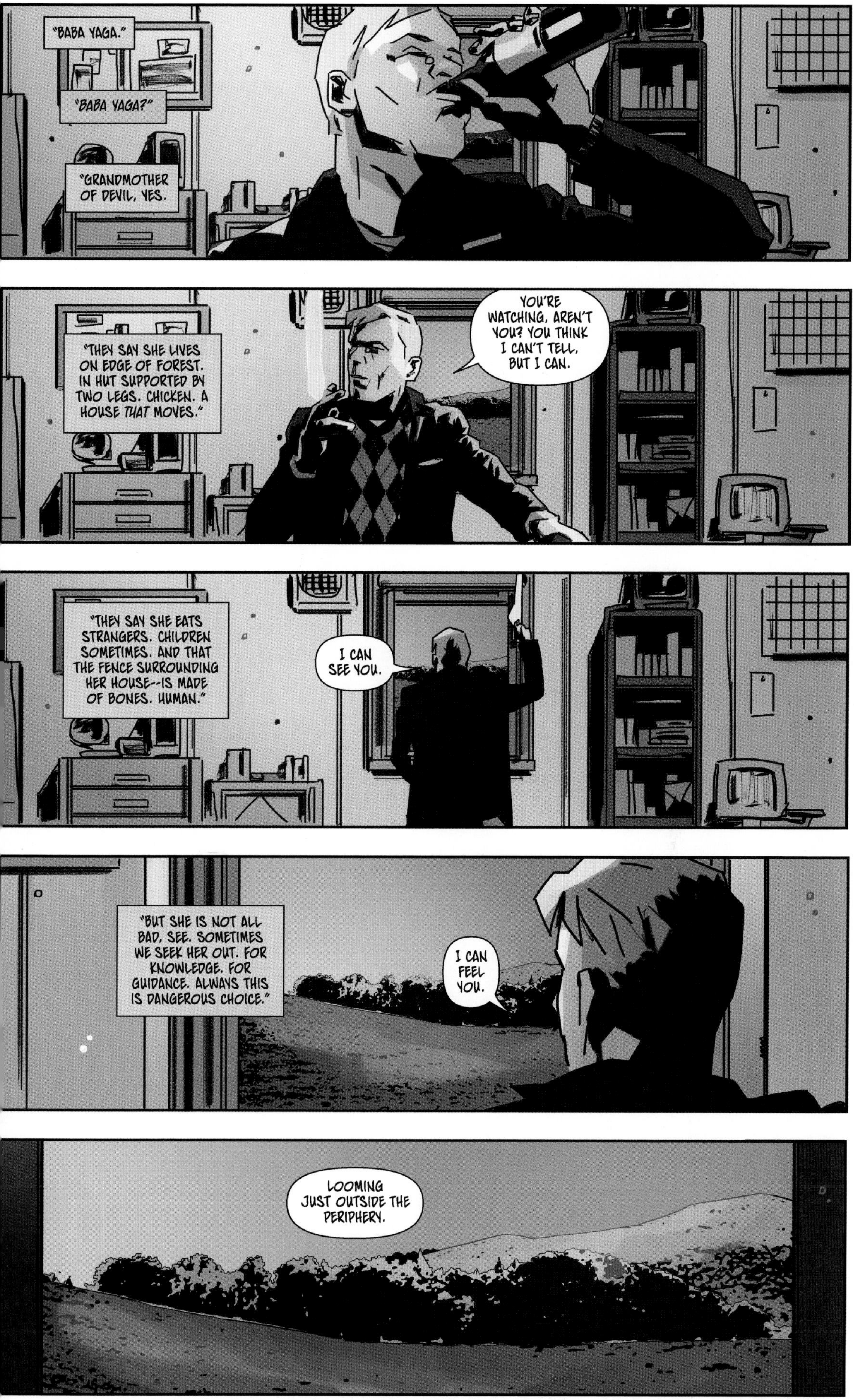
"BABA YAGA."
"BABA YAGA?"
"GRANDMOTHER OF DEVIL, YES.
"THEY SAY SHE LIVES ON EDGE OF FOREST. IN HUT SUPPORTED BY TWO LEGS. CHICKEN. A HOUSE *THAT* MOVES."
YOU'RE WATCHING, AREN'T YOU? YOU THINK I CAN'T TELL, BUT I CAN.
"THEY SAY SHE EATS STRANGERS. CHILDREN SOMETIMES. AND THAT THE FENCE SURROUNDING HER HOUSE--IS MADE OF BONES. HUMAN."
I CAN SEE YOU.
"BUT SHE IS NOT ALL BAD, SEE. SOMETIMES WE SEEK HER OUT. FOR KNOWLEDGE. FOR GUIDANCE. ALWAYS THIS IS DANGEROUS CHOICE."
I CAN FEEL YOU.
LOOMING JUST OUTSIDE THE PERIPHERY.

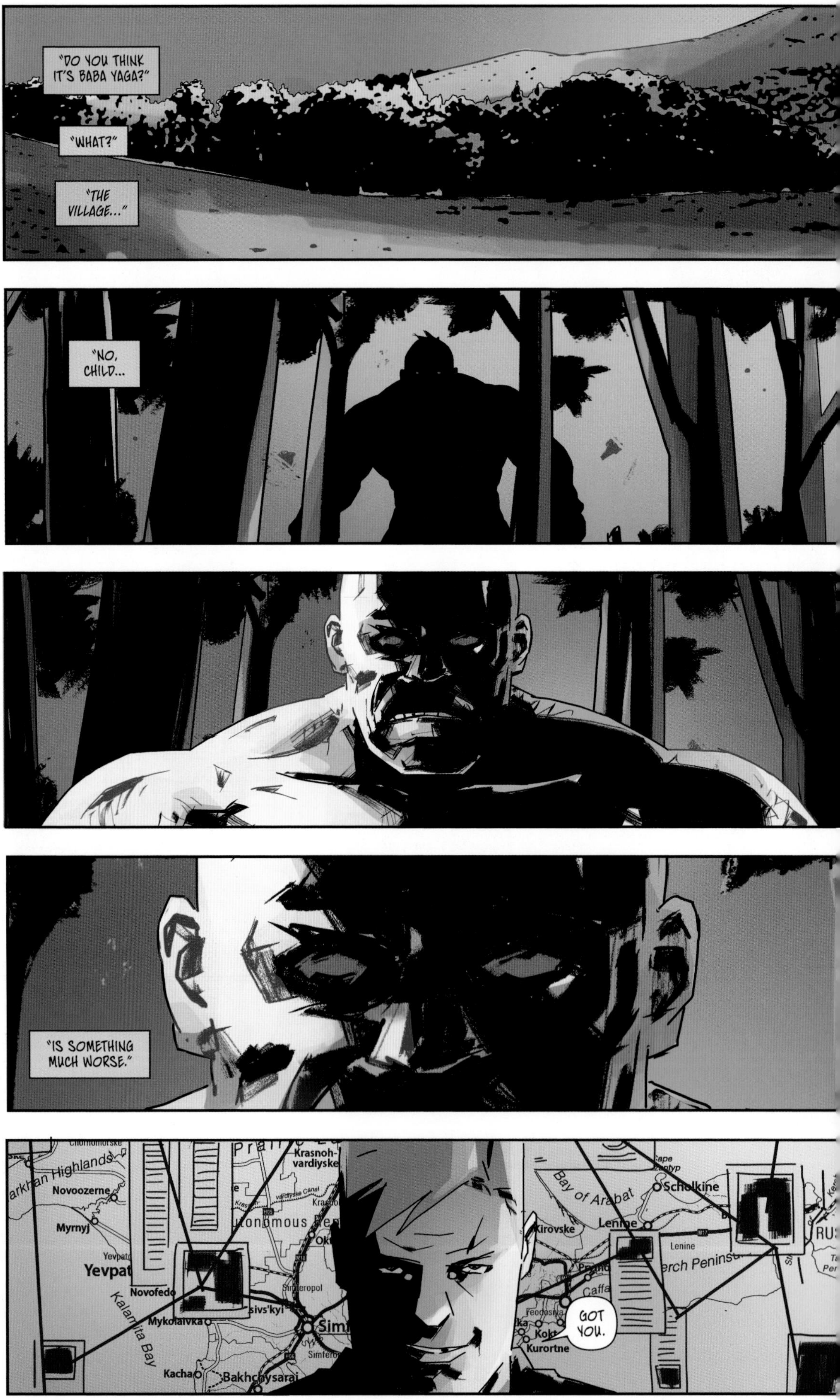
"DO YOU THINK IT'S BABA YAGA?"
"WHAT?"
"THE VILLAGE..."
"NO, CHILD...
"IS SOMETHING MUCH WORSE."
Novoozerne
Myrnyj
Yevpat
Novofedo
Mykolaivka
Simferopol
Kacha
Bakhchysarai
Krasnoh-vardiyske
Bay of Arabat
Scholkine
Kirovske
Lenine
Feodosiya
Kurortne
GOT YOU.

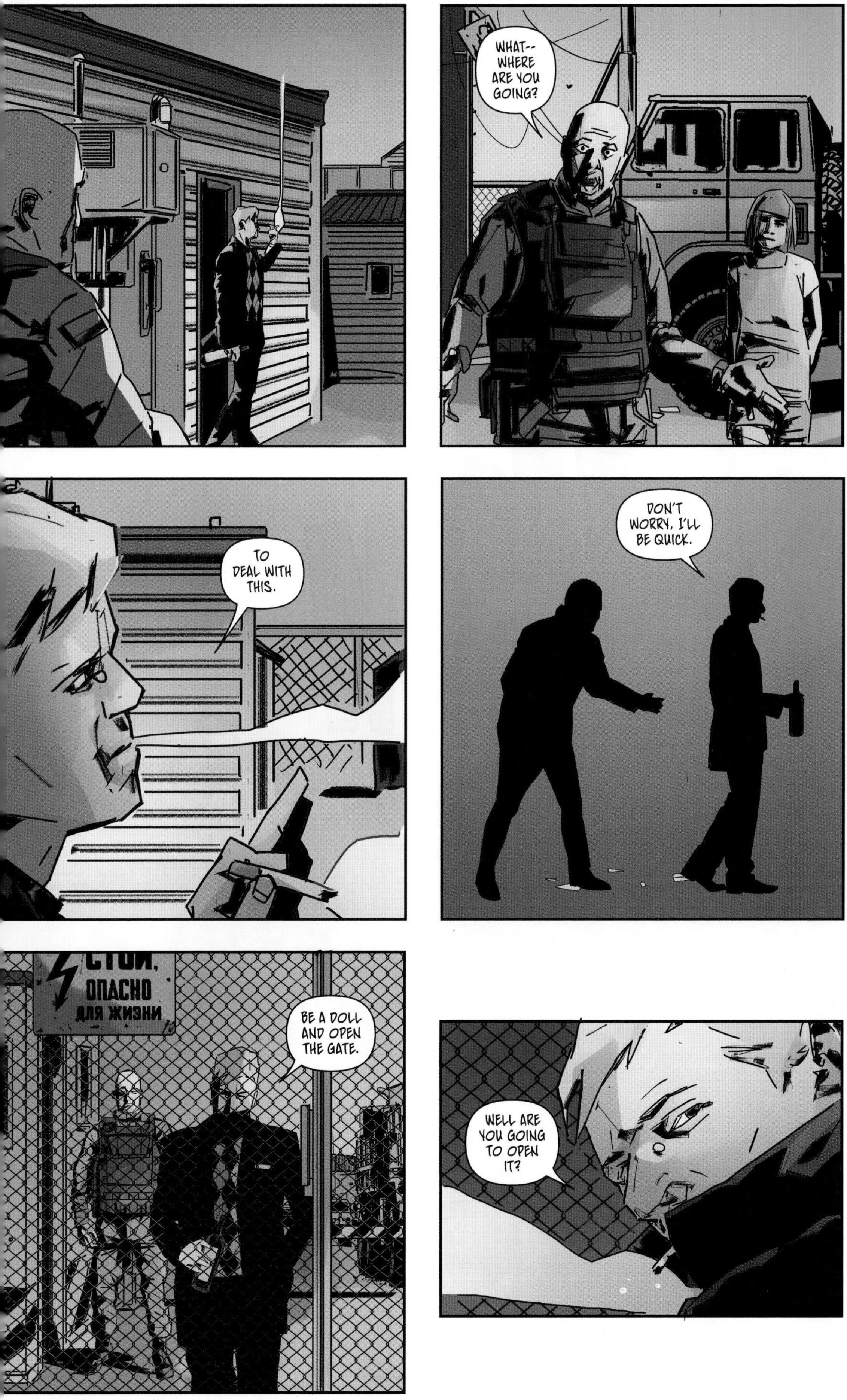
WHAT-- WHERE ARE YOU GOING?
TO DEAL WITH THIS.
DON'T WORRY, I'LL BE QUICK.
СТОЙ, ОПАСНО ДЛЯ ЖИЗНИ
BE A DOLL AND OPEN THE GATE.
WELL ARE YOU GOING TO OPEN IT?

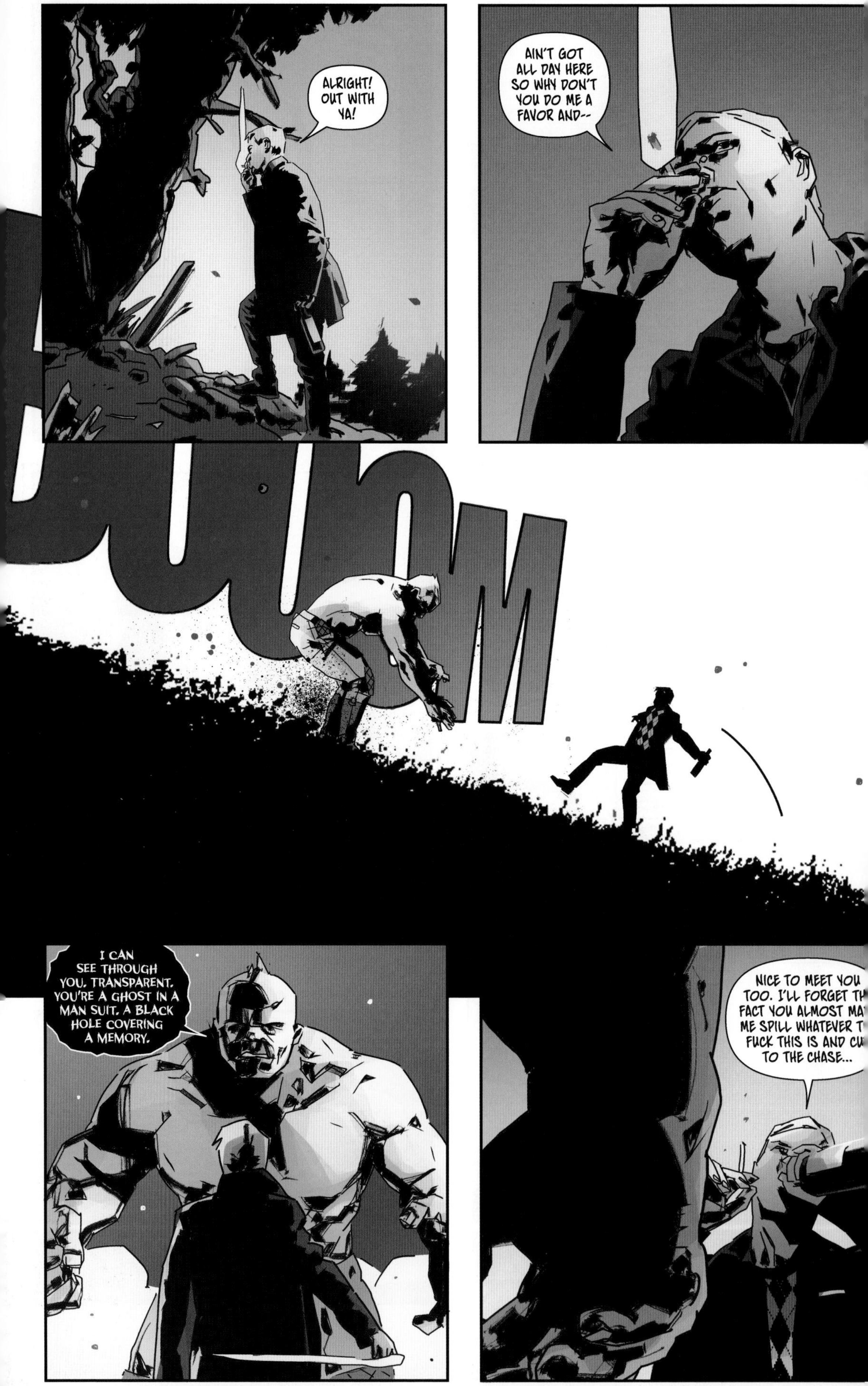
ALRIGHT! OUT WITH YA!
AIN'T GOT ALL DAY HERE SO WHY DON'T YOU DO ME A FAVOR AND--
I CAN SEE THROUGH YOU. TRANSPARENT. YOU'RE A GHOST IN A MAN SUIT. A BLACK HOLE COVERING A MEMORY.
NICE TO MEET YOU TOO. I'LL FORGET TH FACT YOU ALMOST MA ME SPILL WHATEVER T FUCK THIS IS AND CU TO THE CHASE...

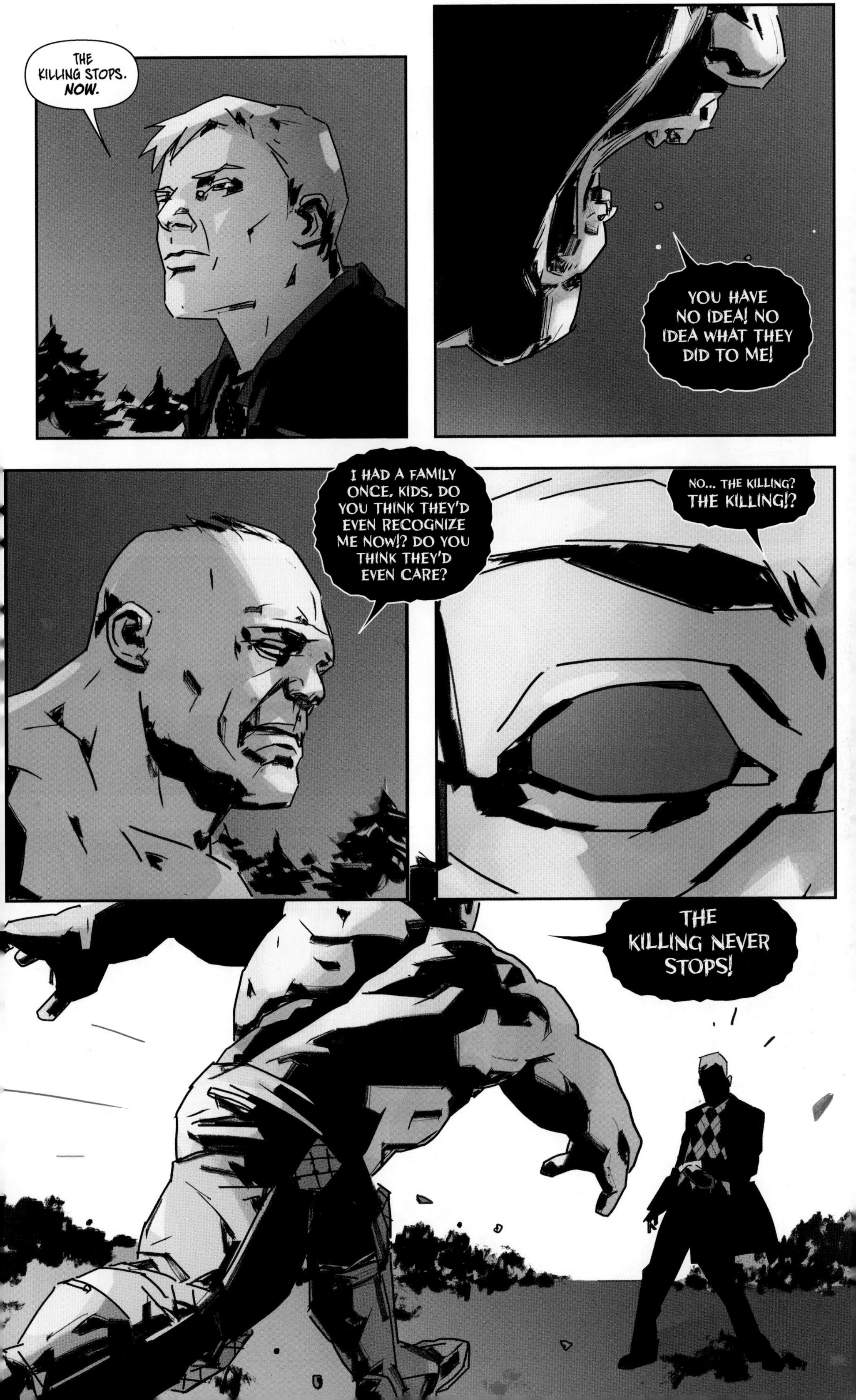
THE KILLING STOPS. NOW.
YOU HAVE NO IDEA! NO IDEA WHAT THEY DID TO ME!
I HAD A FAMILY ONCE. KIDS. DO YOU THINK THEY'D EVEN RECOGNIZE ME NOW!? DO YOU THINK THEY'D EVEN CARE?
NO... THE KILLING? THE KILLING!?
THE KILLING NEVER STOPS!

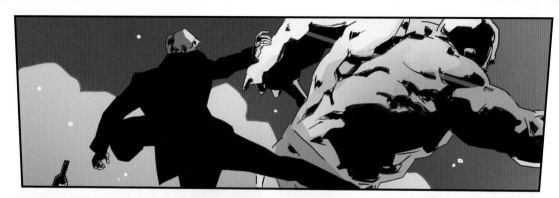

US Super Soldier.

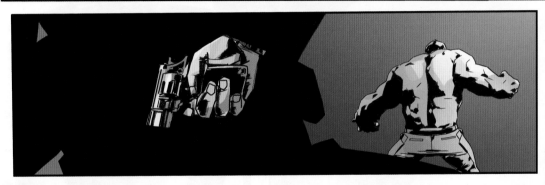

Brinkmanship.

Patriot.

Sacrifice.

Failure.

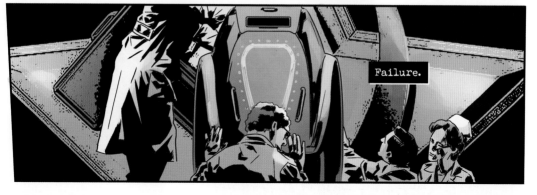

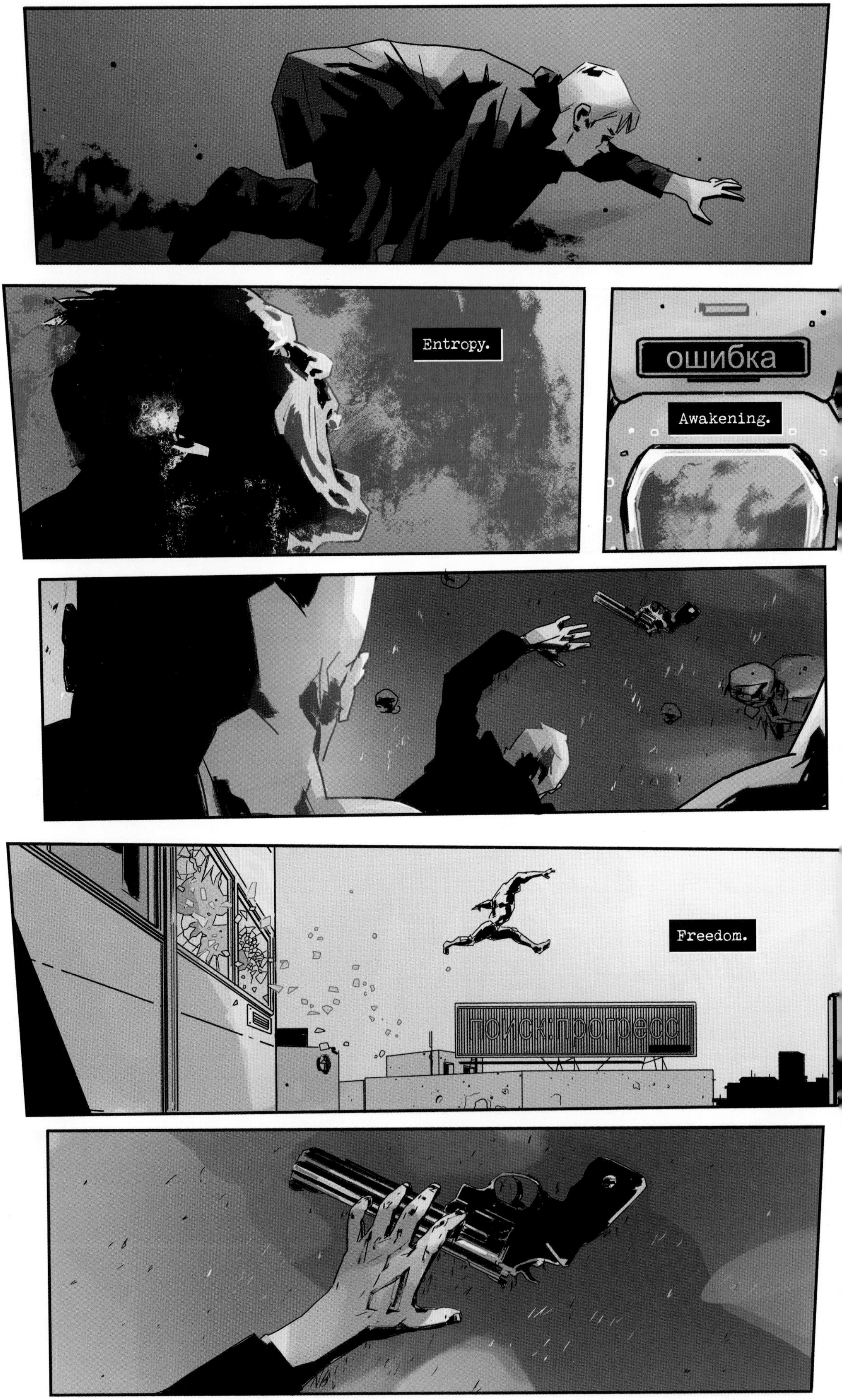
Entropy.
ошибка
Awakening.
Freedom.
поиск:прогресс

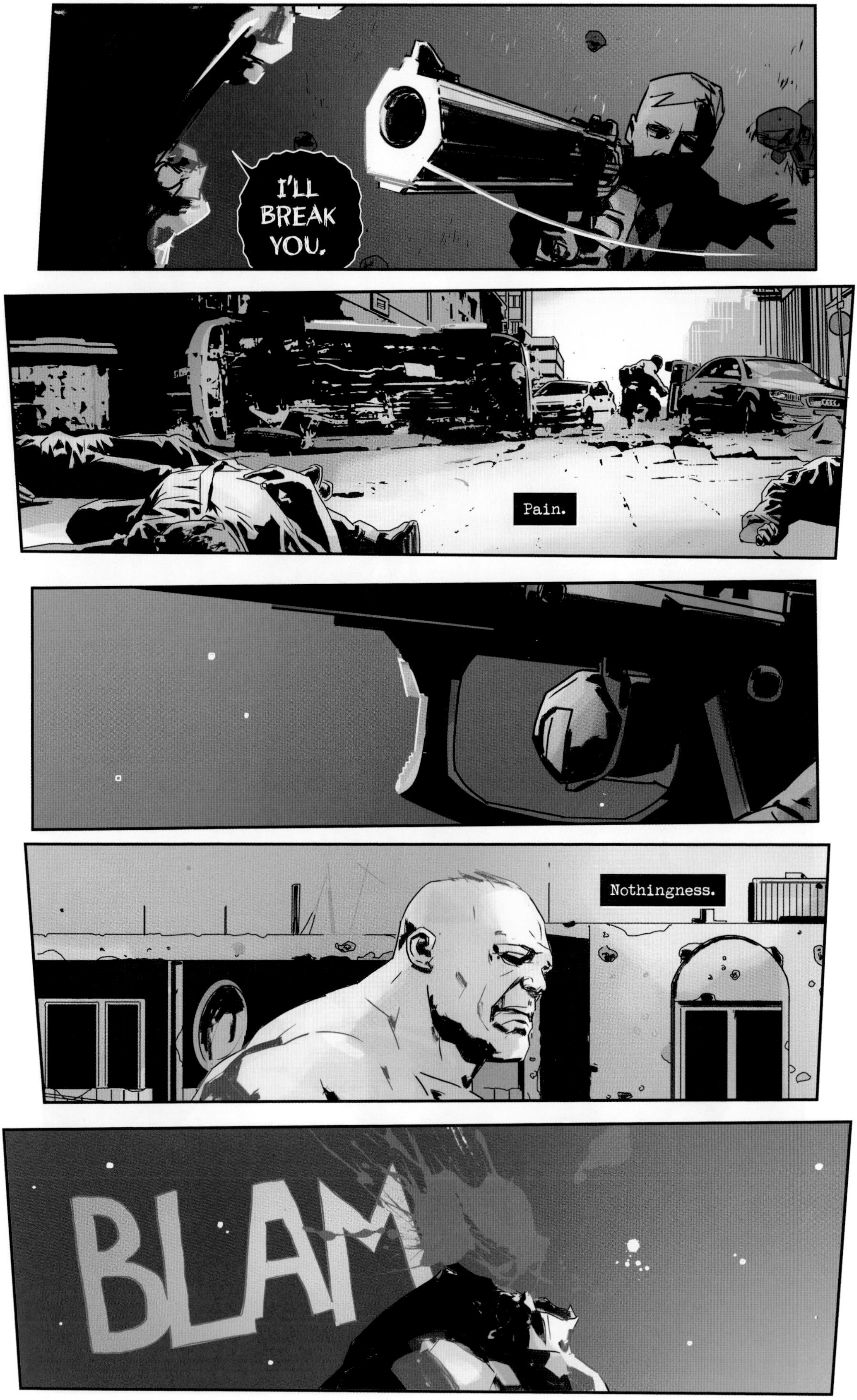
I'LL BREAK YOU.
Pain.
Nothingness.
BLAM

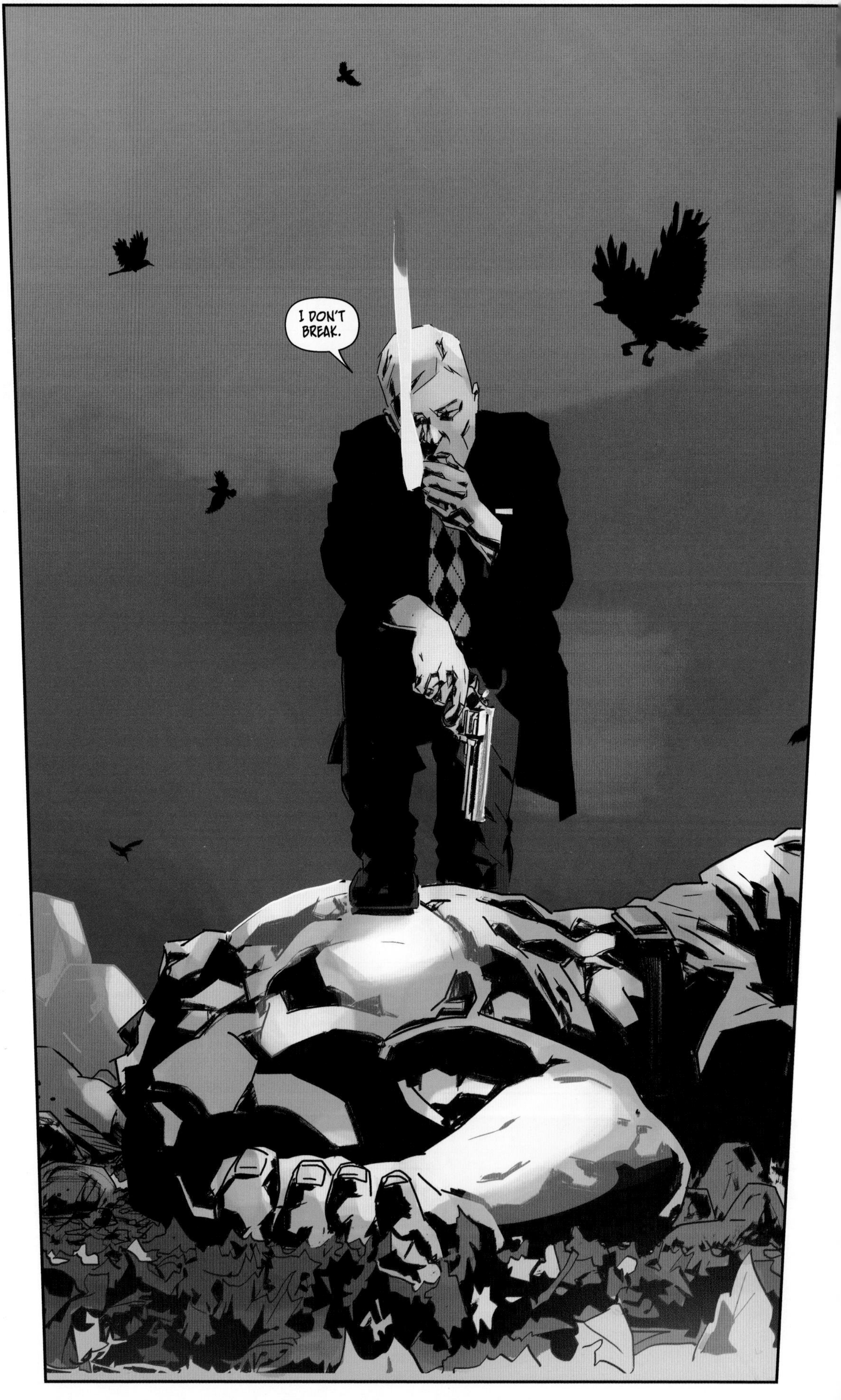
I DON'T BREAK.

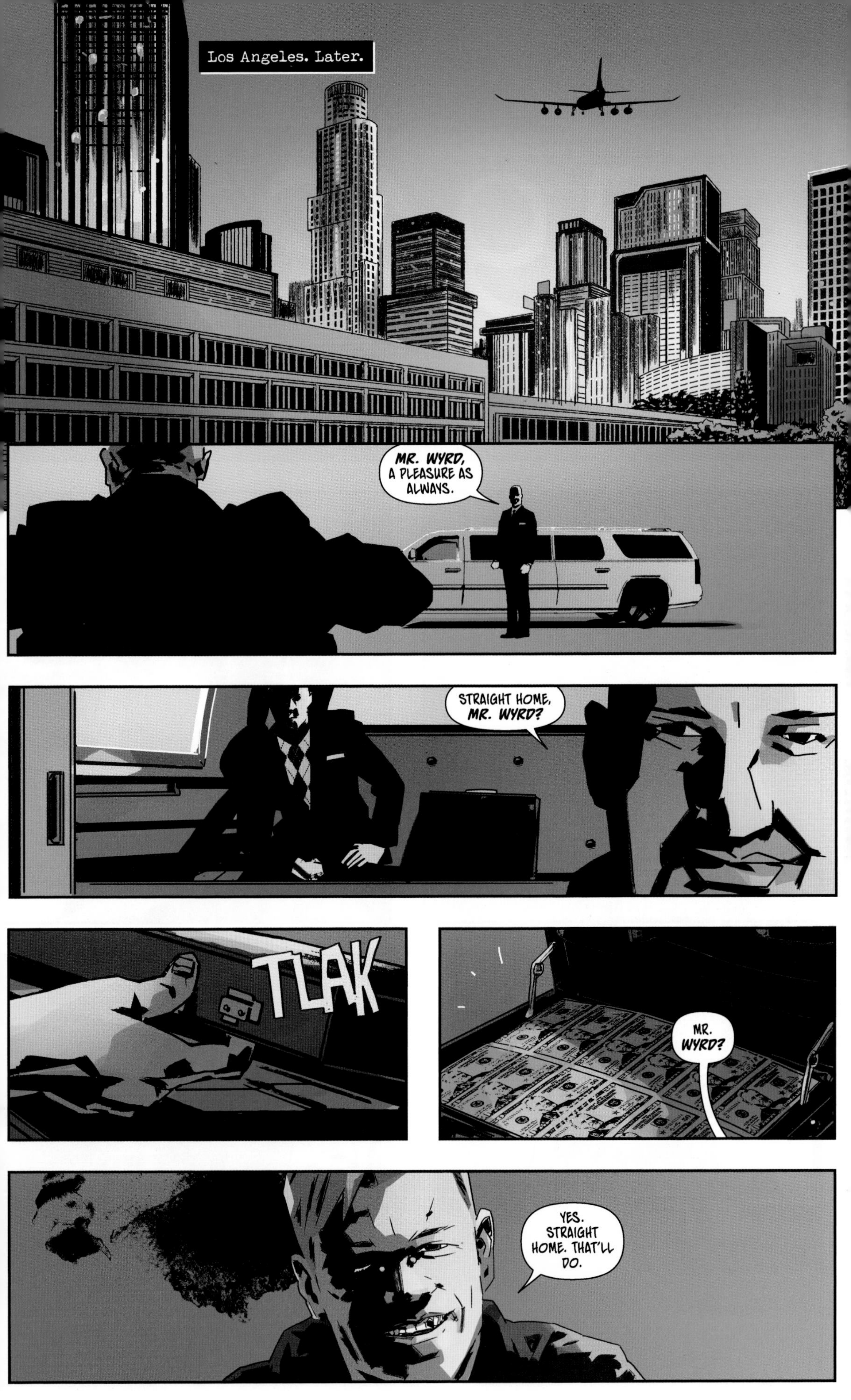
Los Angeles. Later.
MR. WYRD, A PLEASURE AS ALWAYS.
STRAIGHT HOME, MR. WYRD?
TLAK
MR. WYRD?
YES. STRAIGHT HOME. THAT'LL DO.

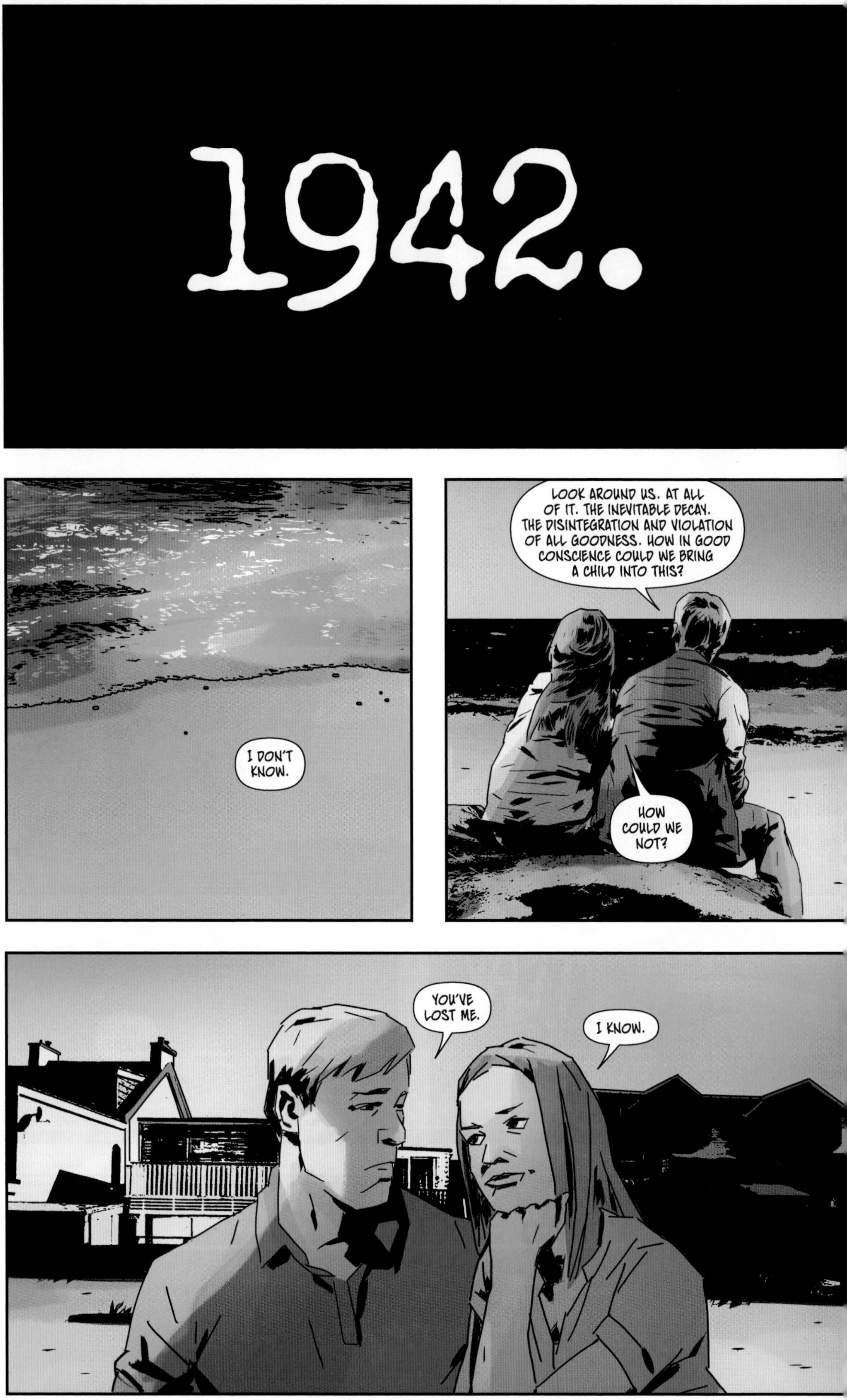
1942.
I DON'T KNOW.
LOOK AROUND US. AT ALL OF IT. THE INEVITABLE DECAY. THE DISINTEGRATION AND VIOLATION OF ALL GOODNESS. HOW IN GOOD CONSCIENCE COULD WE BRING A CHILD INTO THIS?
HOW COULD WE NOT?
YOU'VE LOST ME.
I KNOW.

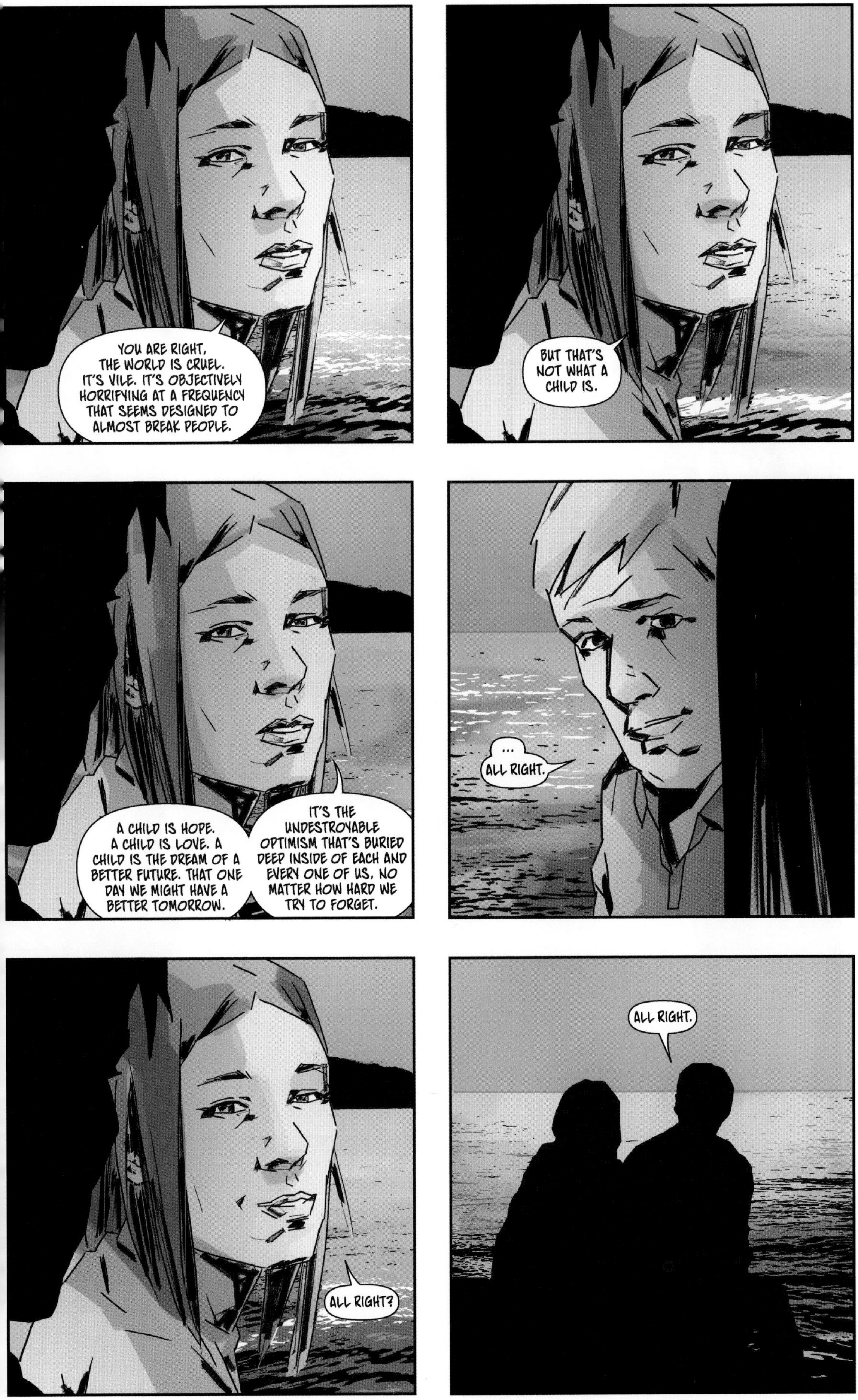
YOU ARE RIGHT, THE WORLD IS CRUEL. IT'S VILE. IT'S OBJECTIVELY HORRIFYING AT A FREQUENCY THAT SEEMS DESIGNED TO ALMOST BREAK PEOPLE.
BUT THAT'S NOT WHAT A CHILD IS.
A CHILD IS HOPE. A CHILD IS LOVE. A CHILD IS THE DREAM OF A BETTER FUTURE. THAT ONE DAY WE MIGHT HAVE A BETTER TOMORROW.
IT'S THE UNDESTROYABLE OPTIMISM THAT'S BURIED DEEP INSIDE OF EACH AND EVERY ONE OF US, NO MATTER HOW HARD WE TRY TO FORGET.
... ALL RIGHT.
ALL RIGHT?
ALL RIGHT.

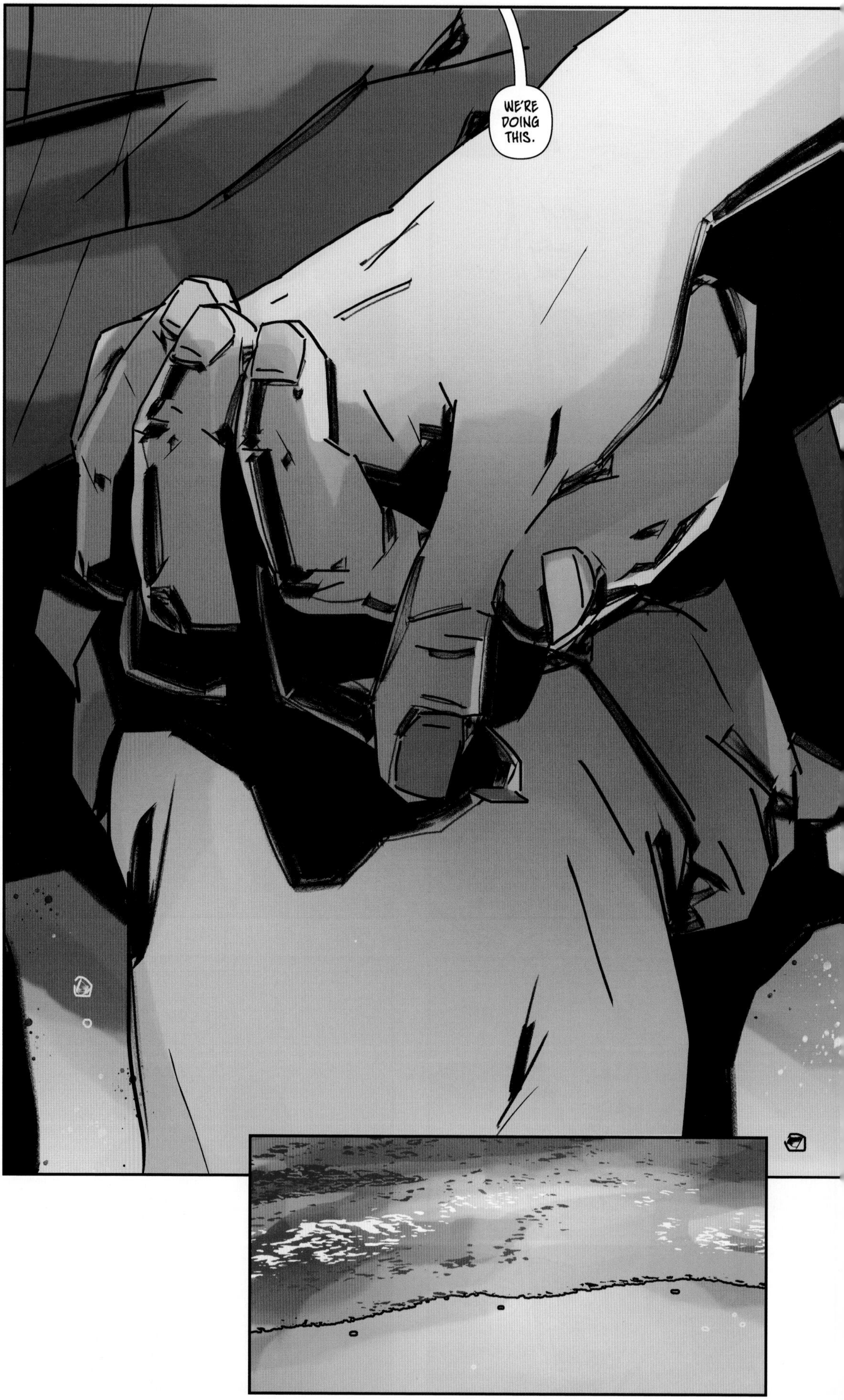
WE'RE DOING THIS.

Oxford University. The Past.

ARE YOU READY, BROTHER?

THERE CAN BE NO UNCERTAINTY. ONCE YOU STEP INSIDE THE CHURCH THERE IS NO TURNING BACK FROM THE RITUAL.

I DON'T-- I DON'T KNOW.

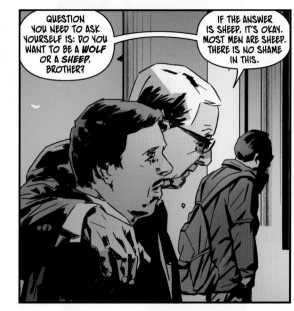

QUESTION YOU NEED TO ASK YOURSELF IS: DO YOU WANT TO BE A *WOLF* OR A *SHEEP*, BROTHER?

IF THE ANSWER IS SHEEP, IT'S OKAY. MOST MEN ARE SHEEP. THERE IS NO SHAME IN THIS.

BUT IF YOU RECKON YOURSELF A WOLF...WE HAVE BUSINESS TO ATTEND TO.

LET'S GO.

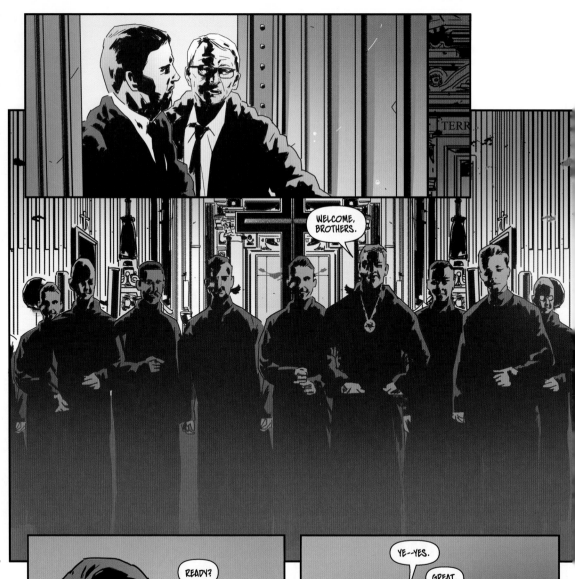

WELCOME, BROTHERS.

READY?

YE--YES.

GREAT.

BROTHER FERRIER, FETCH THE BEAST. LET US CONSECRATE THE RECRUIT!

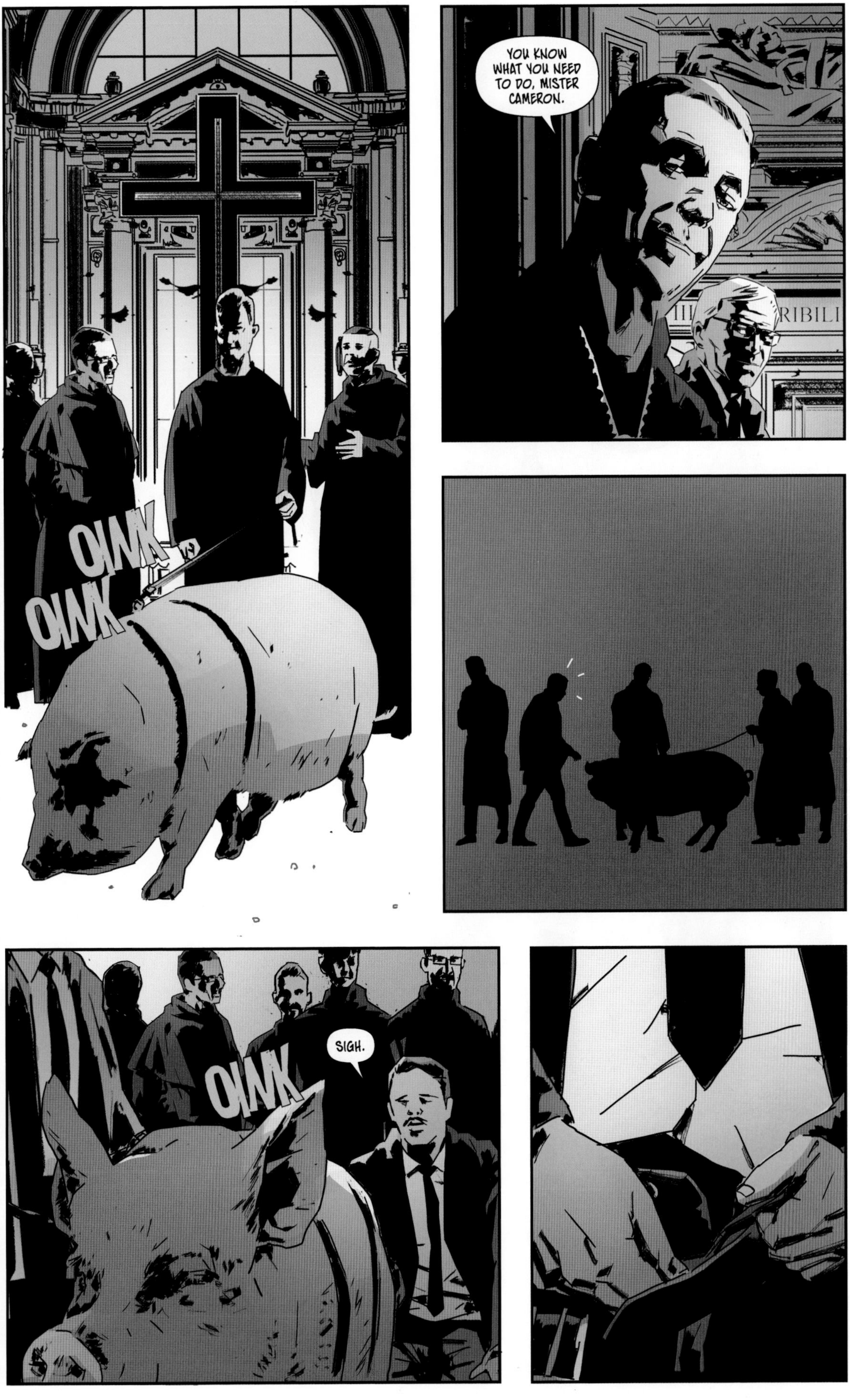
OINK
OINK
YOU KNOW WHAT YOU NEED TO DO, MISTER CAMERON.
OINK
SIGH.

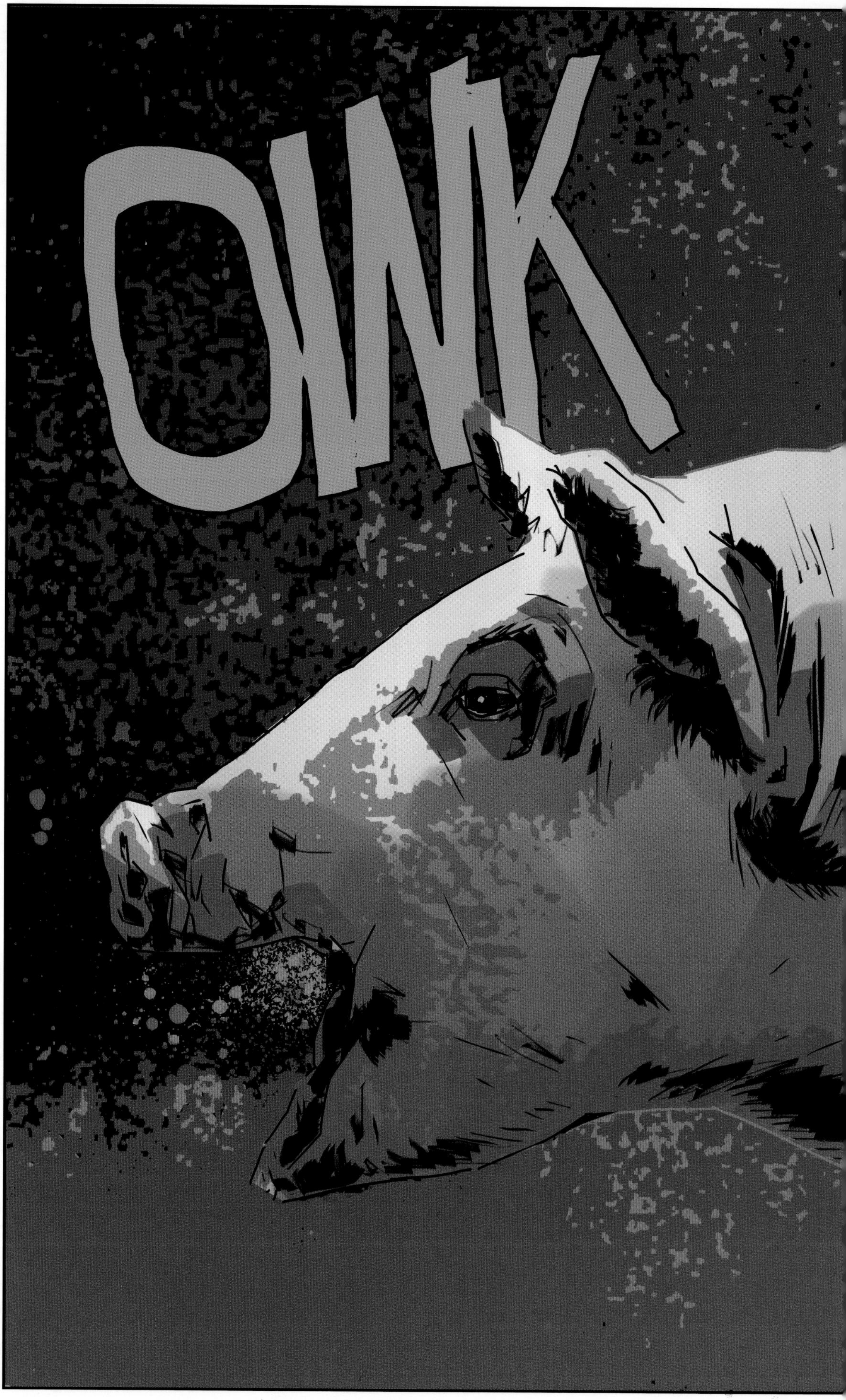
OINK

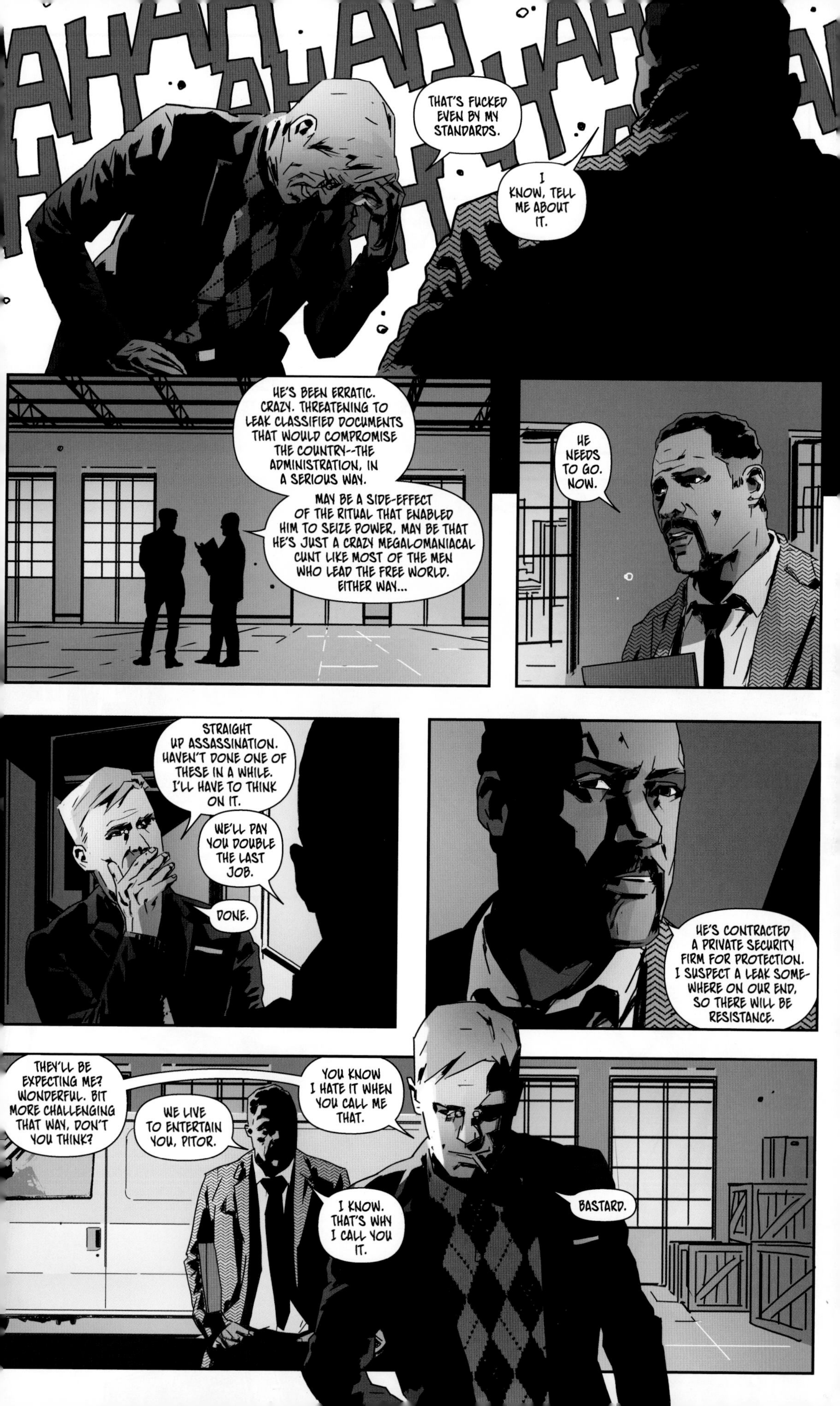
AHAHAHAHAHAHA
THAT'S FUCKED EVEN BY MY STANDARDS.
I KNOW, TELL ME ABOUT IT.
HE'S BEEN ERRATIC. CRAZY. THREATENING TO LEAK CLASSIFIED DOCUMENTS THAT WOULD COMPROMISE THE COUNTRY--THE ADMINISTRATION, IN A SERIOUS WAY.
MAY BE A SIDE-EFFECT OF THE RITUAL THAT ENABLED HIM TO SEIZE POWER, MAY BE THAT HE'S JUST A CRAZY MEGALOMANIACAL CUNT LIKE MOST OF THE MEN WHO LEAD THE FREE WORLD. EITHER WAY...
HE NEEDS TO GO. NOW.
STRAIGHT UP ASSASSINATION. HAVEN'T DONE ONE OF THESE IN A WHILE. I'LL HAVE TO THINK ON IT.
WE'LL PAY YOU DOUBLE THE LAST JOB.
DONE.
HE'S CONTRACTED A PRIVATE SECURITY FIRM FOR PROTECTION. I SUSPECT A LEAK SOMEWHERE ON OUR END, SO THERE WILL BE RESISTANCE.
THEY'LL BE EXPECTING ME? WONDERFUL. BIT MORE CHALLENGING THAT WAY, DON'T YOU THINK?
WE LIVE TO ENTERTAIN YOU, PITOR.
YOU KNOW I HATE IT WHEN YOU CALL ME THAT.
I KNOW. THAT'S WHY I CALL YOU IT.
BASTARD.

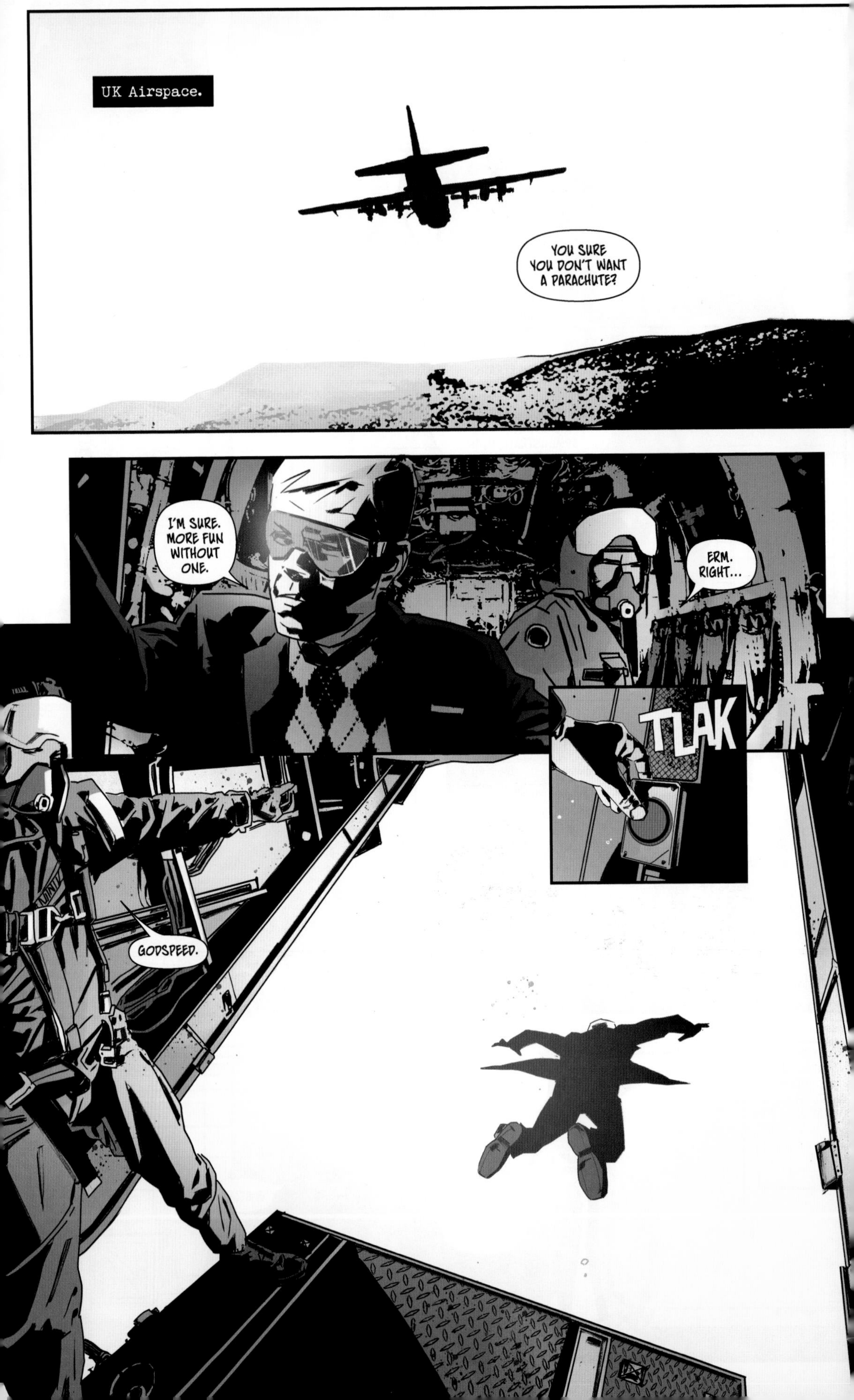
UK Airspace.
YOU SURE YOU DON'T WANT A PARACHUTE?
I'M SURE. MORE FUN WITHOUT ONE.
ERM. RIGHT...
TLAK
GODSPEED.

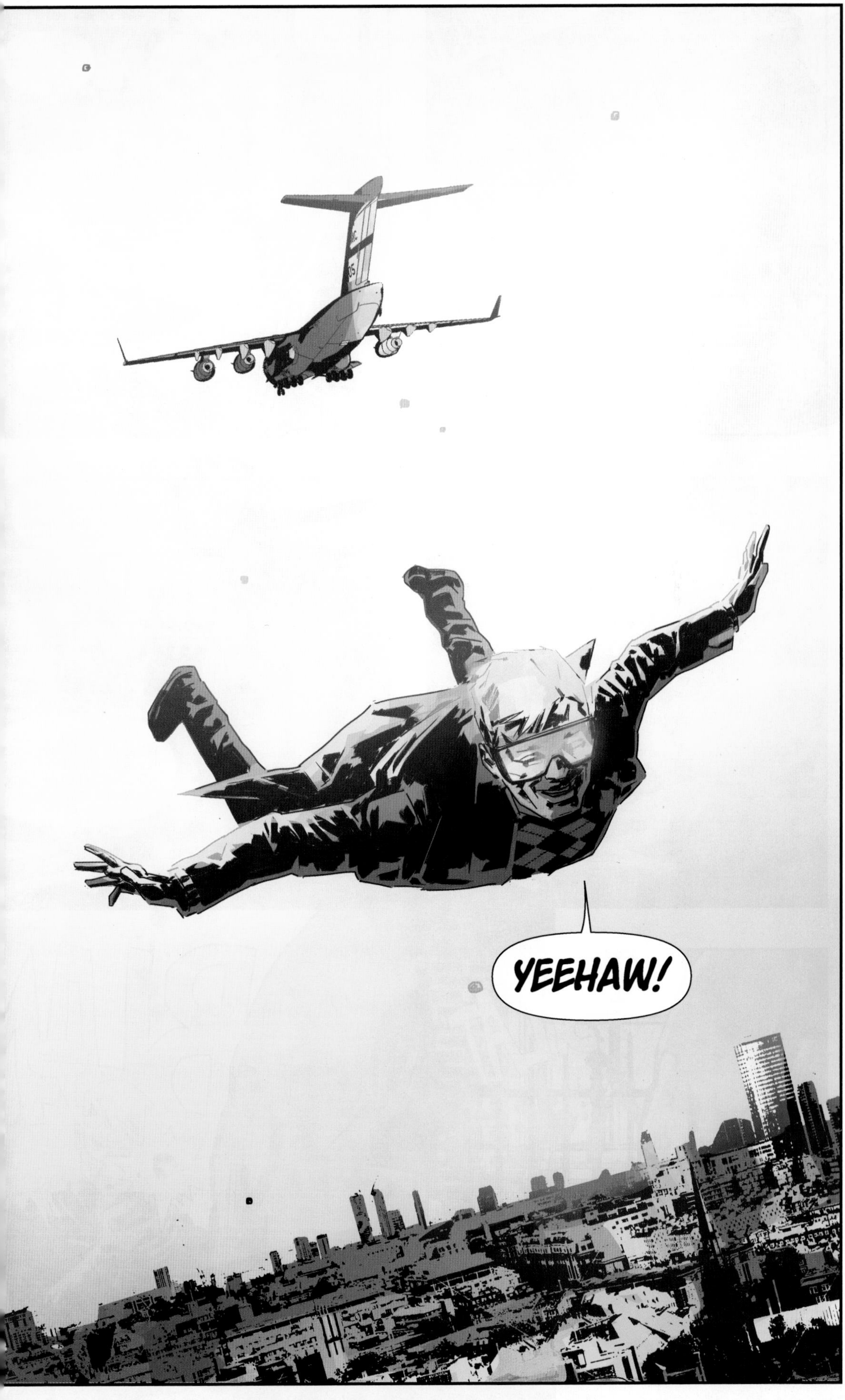
YEEHAW!

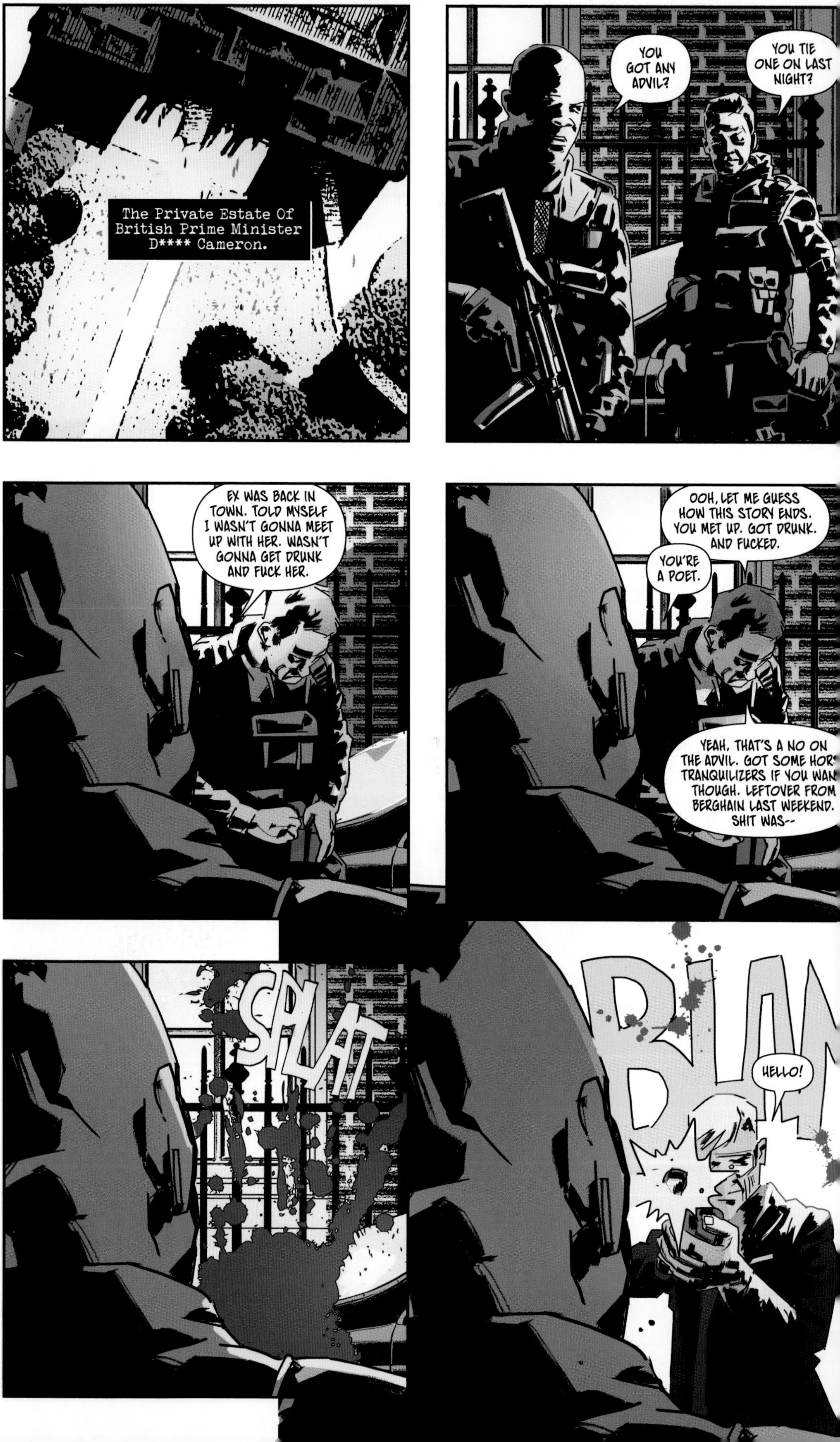
The Private Estate Of British Prime Minister D**** Cameron.
YOU GOT ANY ADVIL?
YOU TIE ONE ON LAST NIGHT?
EX WAS BACK IN TOWN. TOLD MYSELF I WASN'T GONNA MEET UP WITH HER. WASN'T GONNA GET DRUNK AND FUCK HER.
OOH, LET ME GUESS HOW THIS STORY ENDS. YOU MET UP. GOT DRUNK. AND FUCKED.
YOU'RE A POET.
YEAH, THAT'S A NO ON THE ADVIL. GOT SOME HOR TRANQUILIZERS IF YOU WAN THOUGH. LEFTOVER FROM BERGHAIN LAST WEEKEND. SHIT WAS--
SPLAT
HELLO!

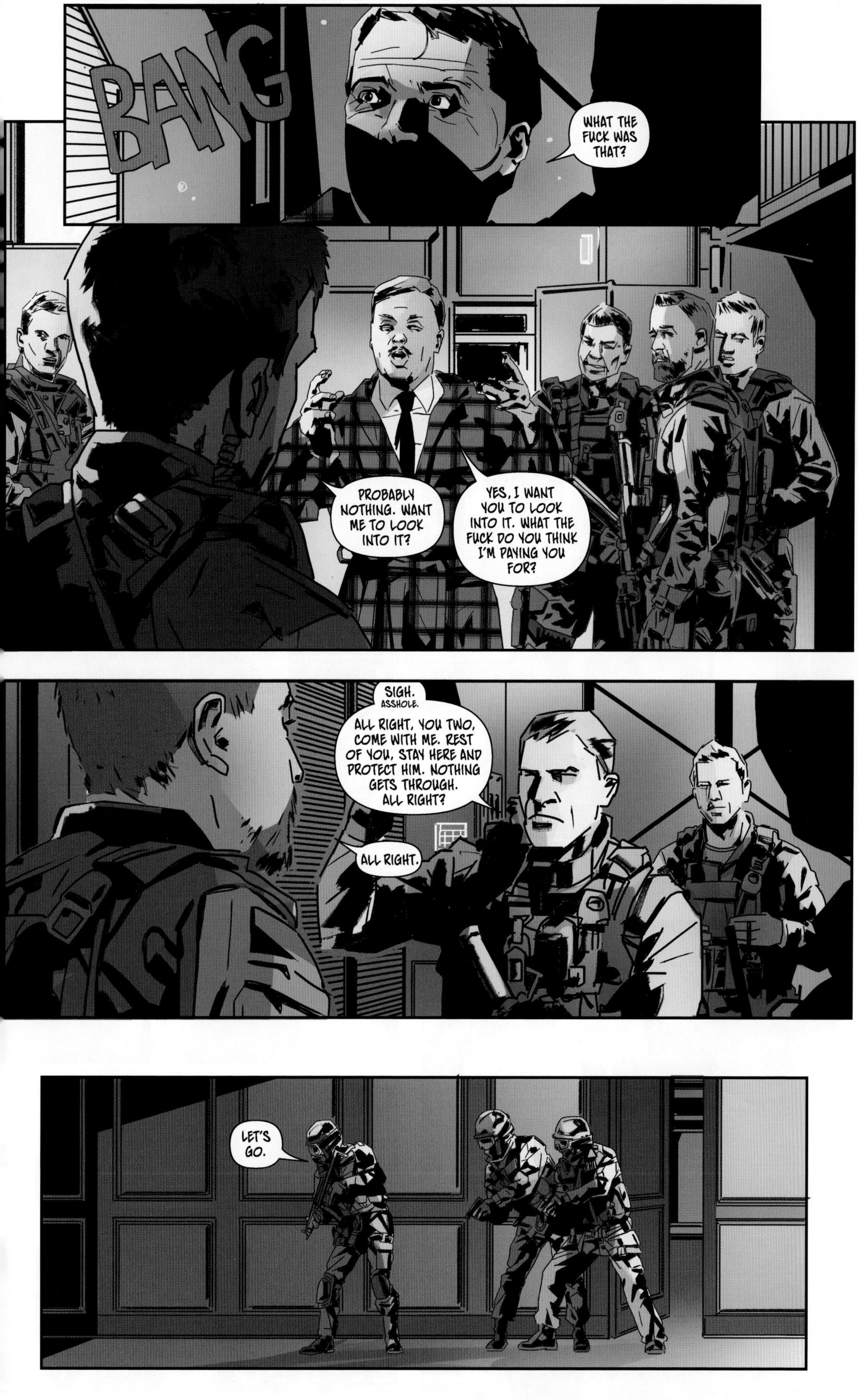
BANG
WHAT THE FUCK WAS THAT?
PROBABLY NOTHING. WANT ME TO LOOK INTO IT?
YES, I WANT YOU TO LOOK INTO IT. WHAT THE FUCK DO YOU THINK I'M PAYING YOU FOR?
SIGH. ASSHOLE.
ALL RIGHT, YOU TWO, COME WITH ME. REST OF YOU, STAY HERE AND PROTECT HIM. NOTHING GETS THROUGH. ALL RIGHT?
ALL RIGHT.
LET'S GO.

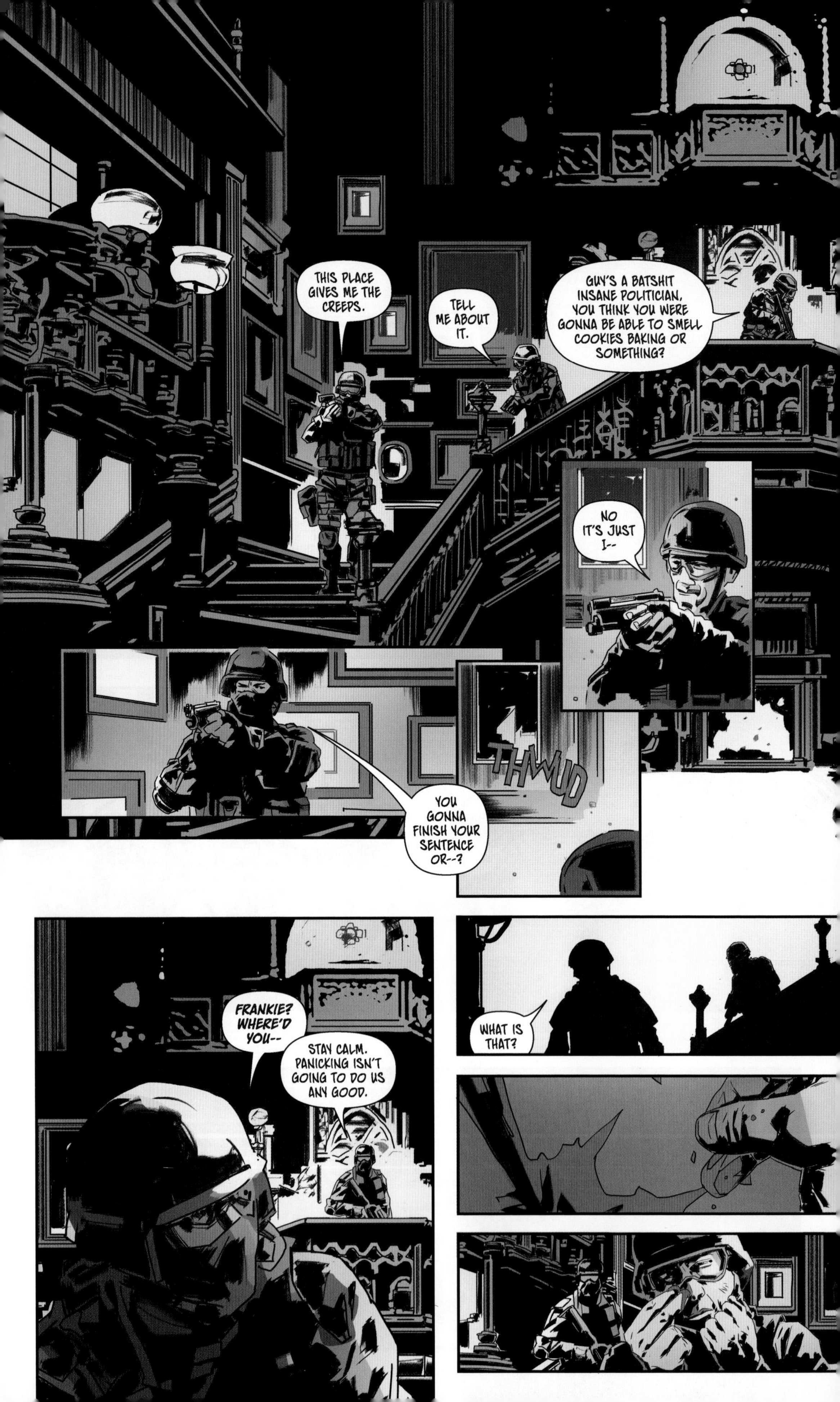
THIS PLACE GIVES ME THE CREEPS.
TELL ME ABOUT IT.
GUY'S A BATSHIT INSANE POLITICIAN, YOU THINK YOU WERE GONNA BE ABLE TO SMELL COOKIES BAKING OR SOMETHING?
NO IT'S JUST I--
THWUD
YOU GONNA FINISH YOUR SENTENCE OR--?
FRANKIE? WHERE'D YOU--
STAY CALM. PANICKING ISN'T GOING TO DO US ANY GOOD.
WHAT IS THAT?

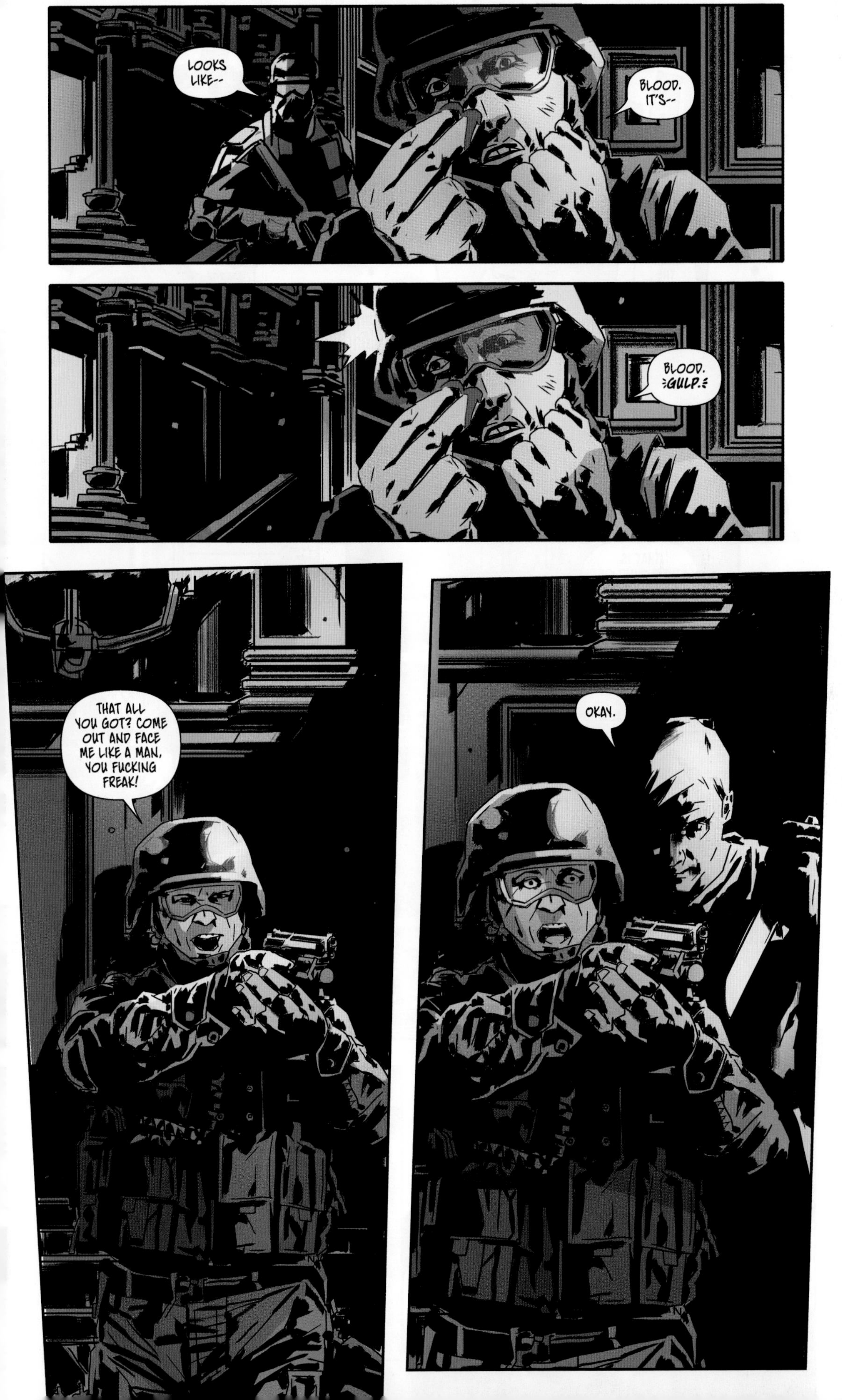
LOOKS LIKE--
BLOOD. IT'S--
BLOOD. GULP.
THAT ALL YOU GOT? COME OUT AND FACE ME LIKE A MAN, YOU FUCKING FREAK!
OKAY.

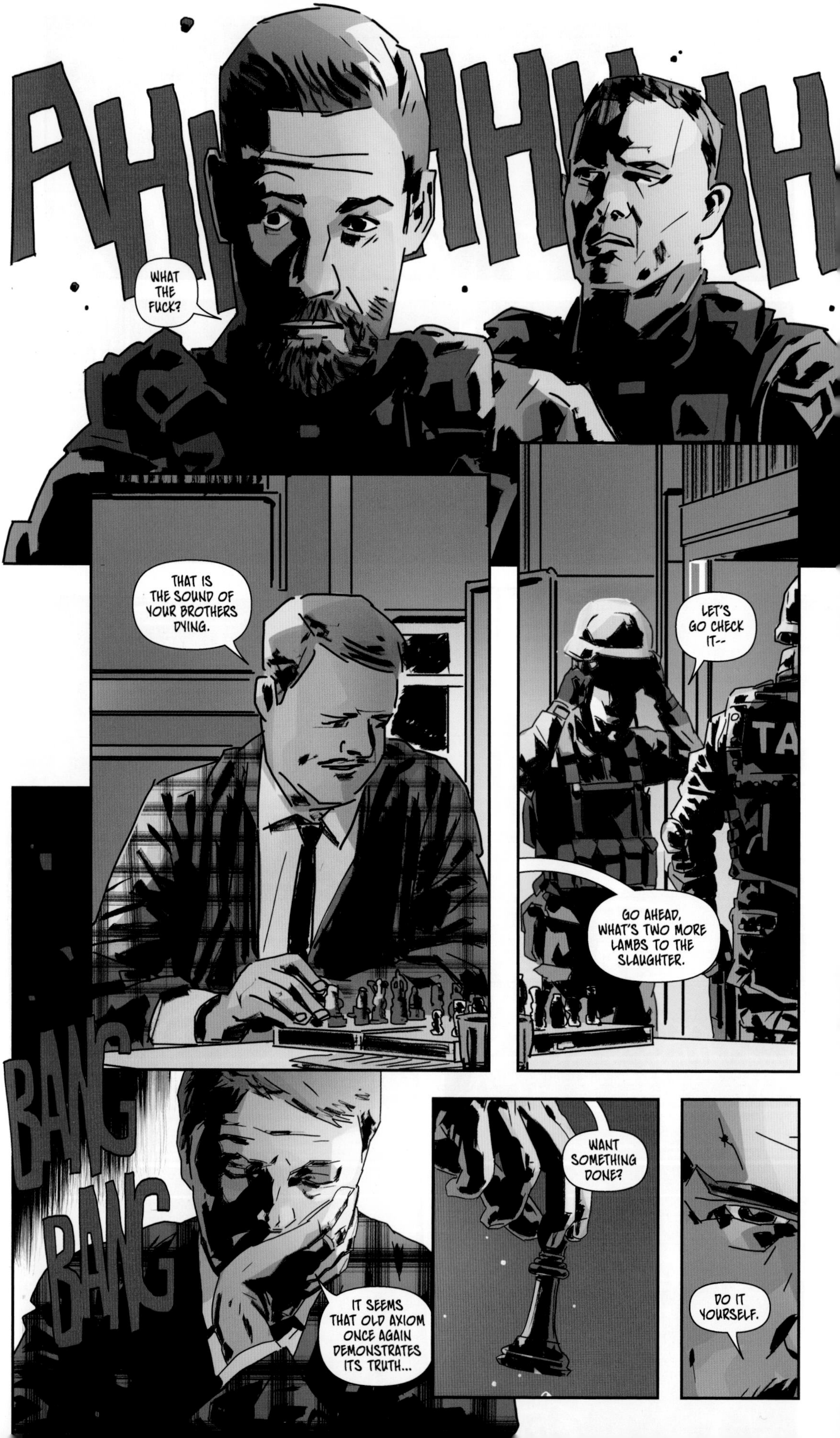
AHHHHHHH
WHAT THE FUCK?
THAT IS THE SOUND OF YOUR BROTHERS DYING.
LET'S GO CHECK IT--
GO AHEAD, WHAT'S TWO MORE LAMBS TO THE SLAUGHTER.
BANG
BANG
IT SEEMS THAT OLD AXIOM ONCE AGAIN DEMONSTRATES ITS TRUTH...
WANT SOMETHING DONE?
DO IT YOURSELF.

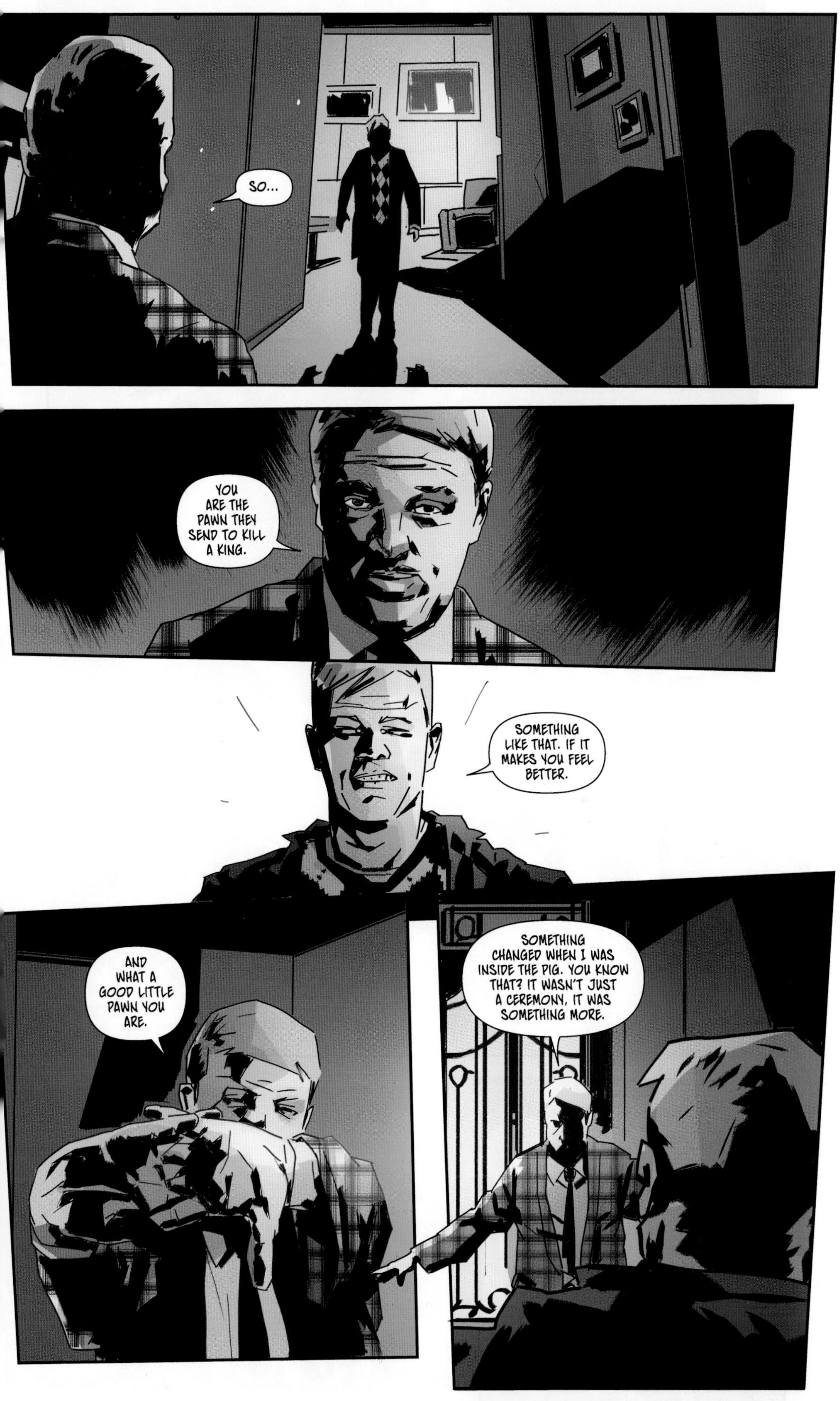
SO...
YOU ARE THE PAWN THEY SEND TO KILL A KING.
SOMETHING LIKE THAT. IF IT MAKES YOU FEEL BETTER.
AND WHAT A GOOD LITTLE PAWN YOU ARE.
SOMETHING CHANGED WHEN I WAS INSIDE THE PIG. YOU KNOW THAT? IT WASN'T JUST A CEREMONY, IT WAS SOMETHING MORE.

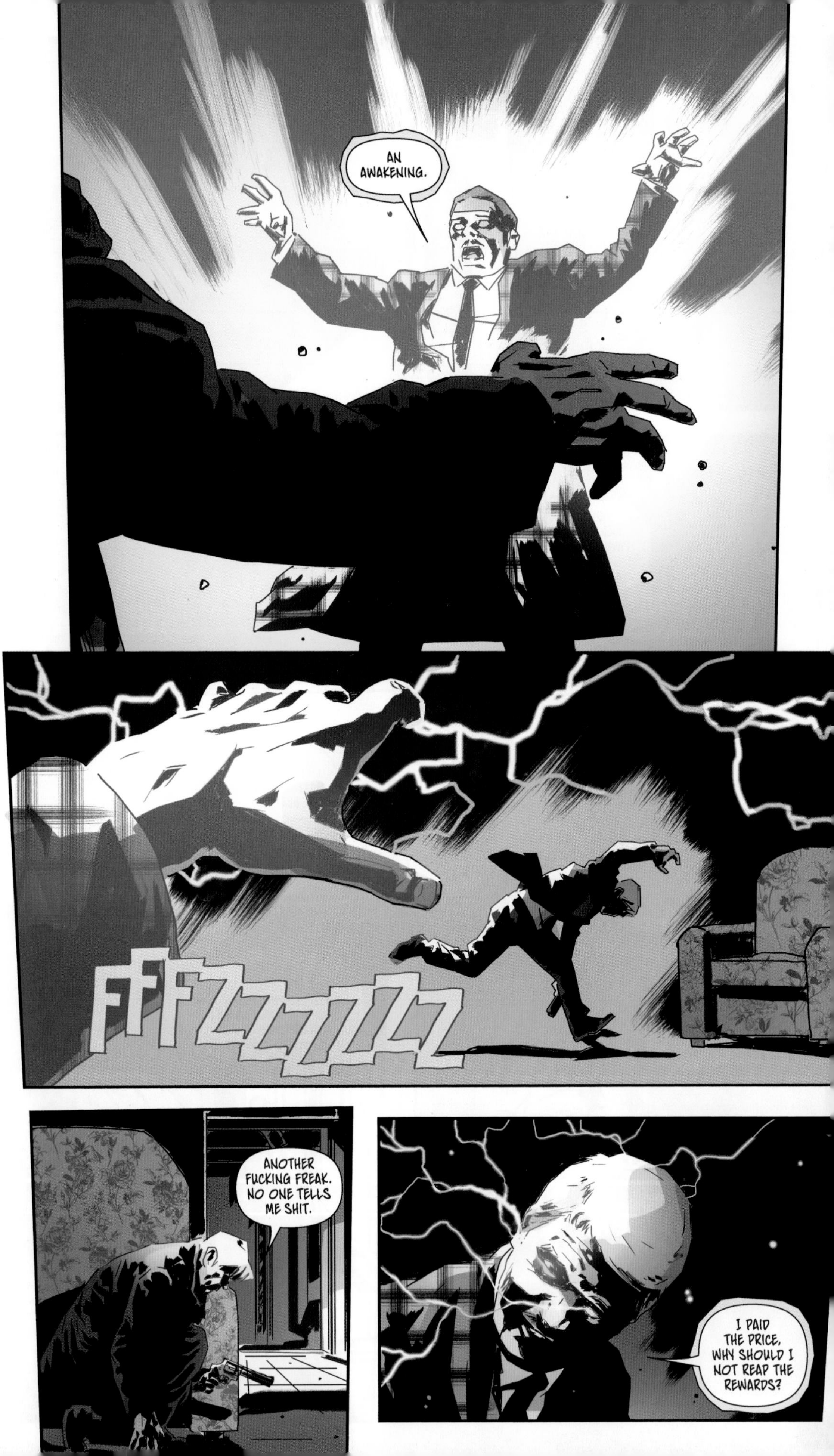
AN AWAKENING.
FFFZZZZZZZ
ANOTHER FUCKING FREAK. NO ONE TELLS ME SHIT.
I PAID THE PRICE, WHY SHOULD I NOT REAP THE REWARDS?

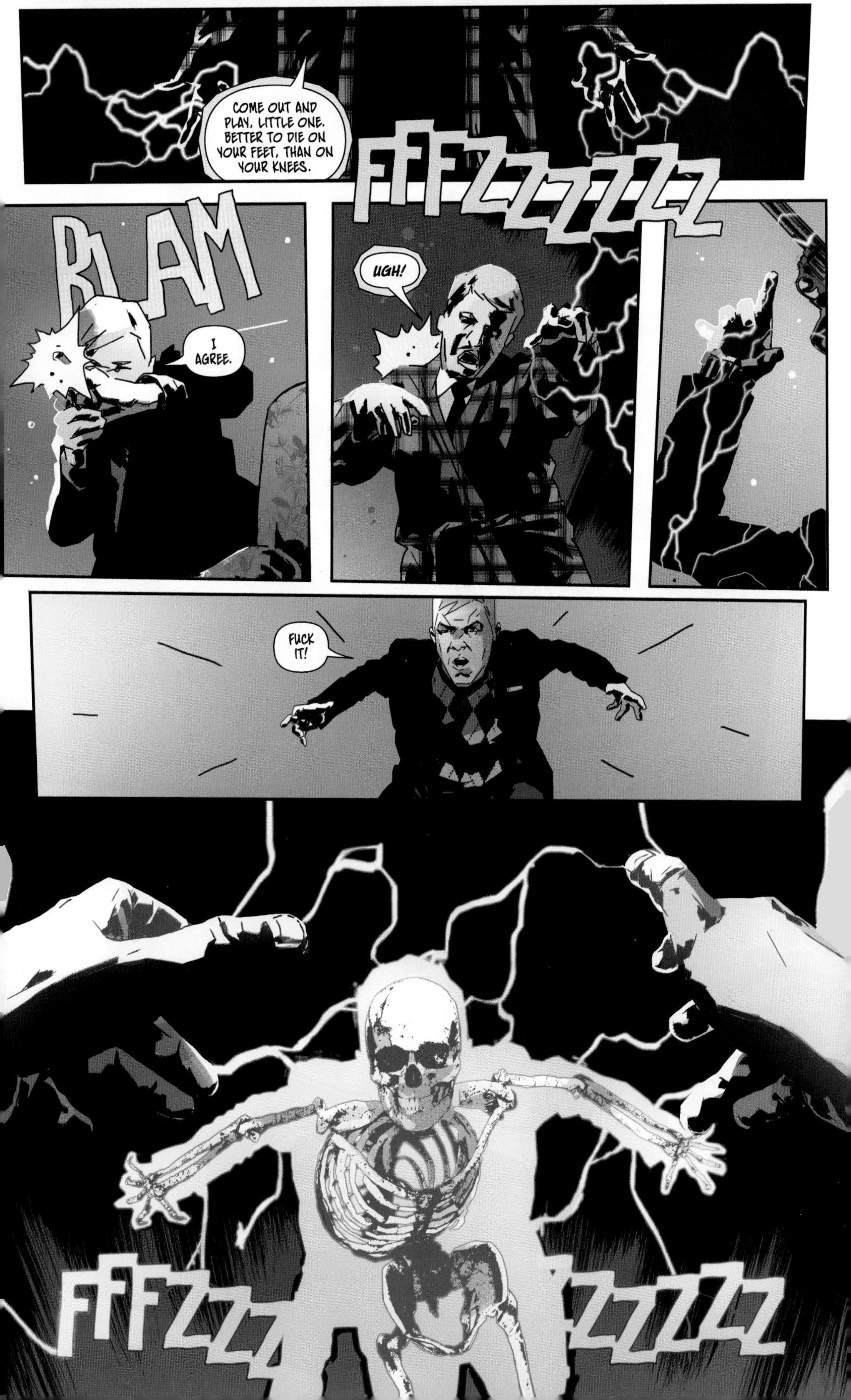
COME OUT AND PLAY, LITTLE ONE. BETTER TO DIE ON YOUR FEET, THAN ON YOUR KNEES.
FFFZZZZZZZ
BLAM
I AGREE.
UGH!
FUCK IT!
FFFZZZ
ZZZZZ

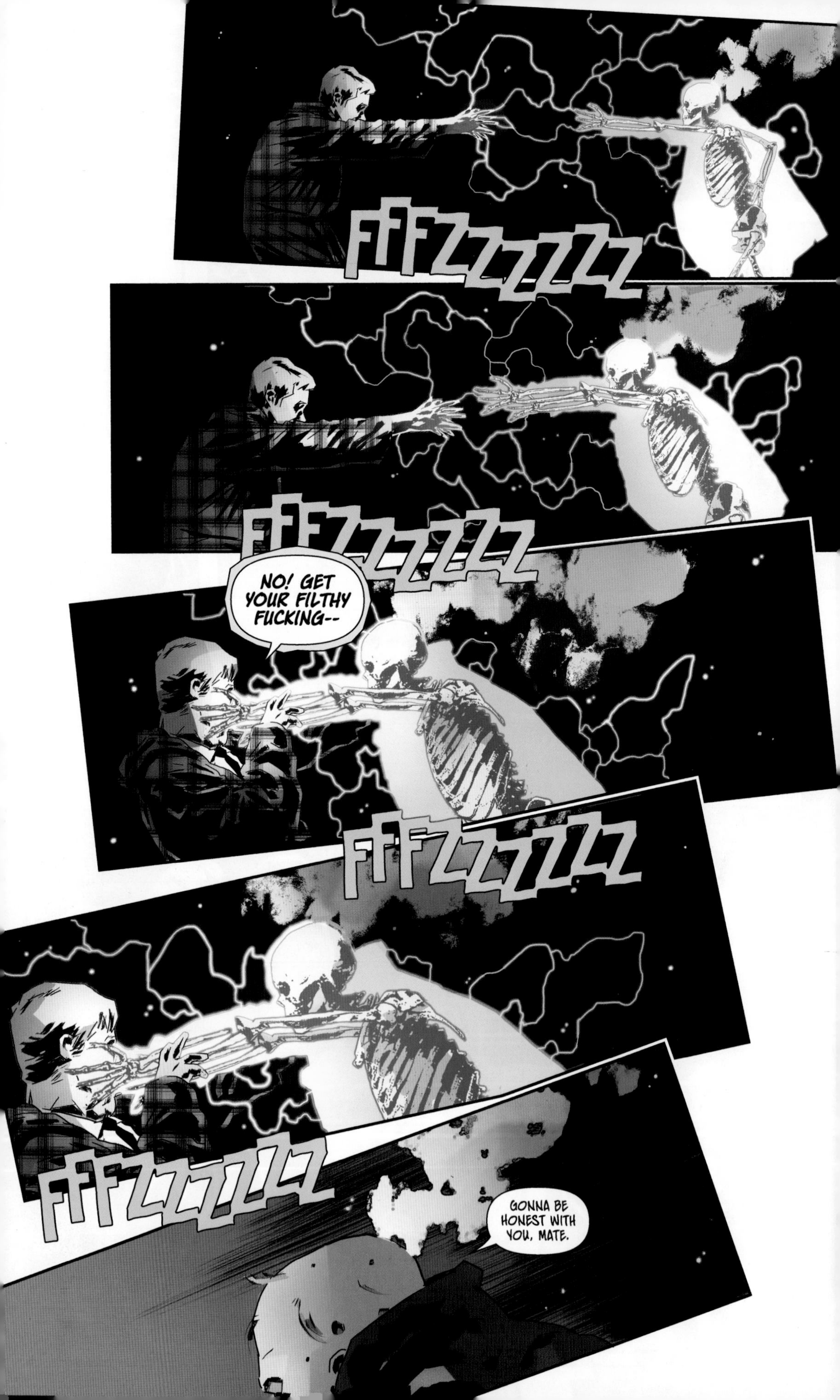
FFFZZZZZZZ
FFFZZZZZZZ
NO! GET YOUR FILTHY FUCKING--
FFFZZZZZZZ
FFFZZZZZZZ
GONNA BE HONEST WITH YOU, MATE.

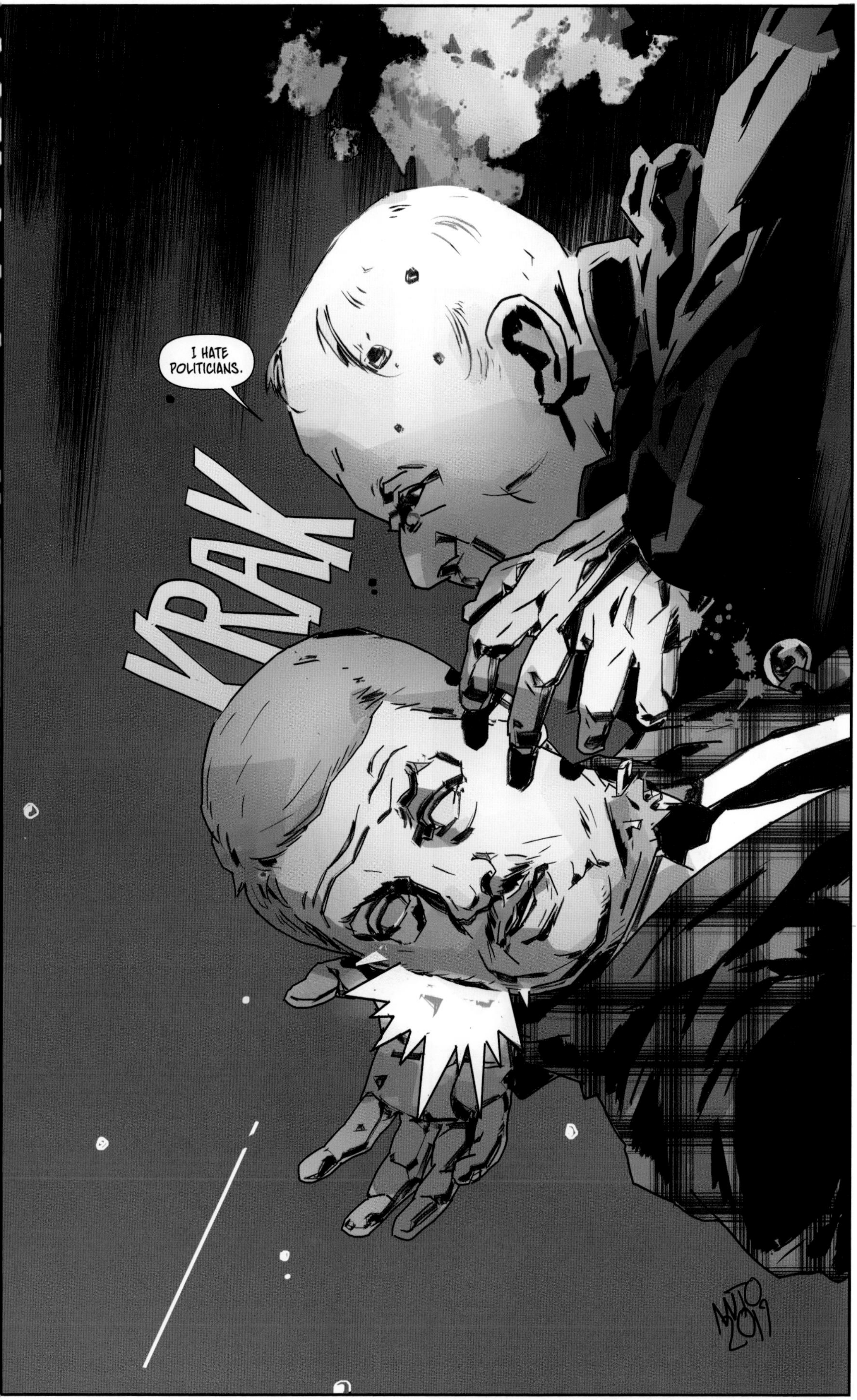
I HATE POLITICIANS.
KRAK

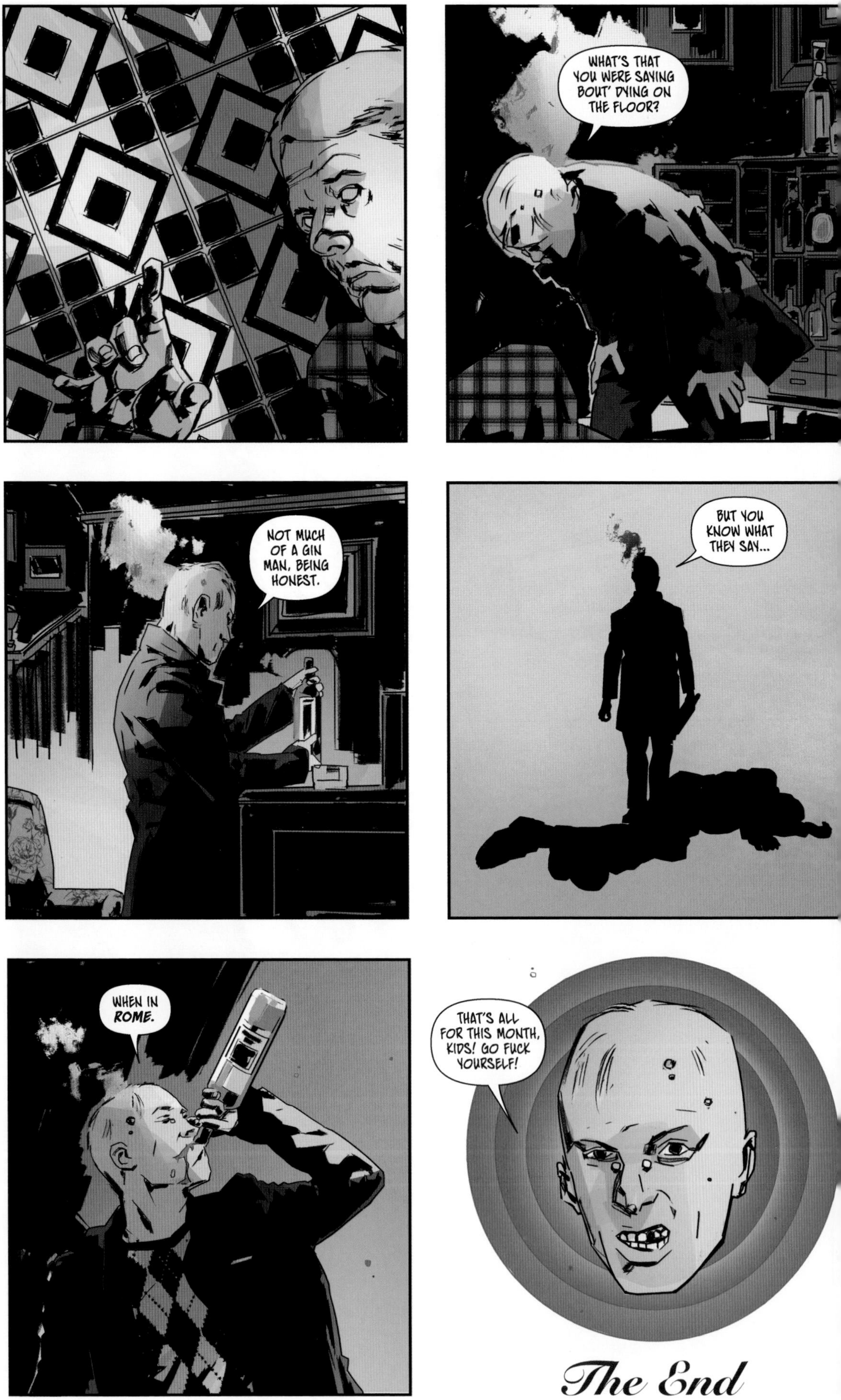
WHAT'S THAT YOU WERE SAYING BOUT' DYING ON THE FLOOR?
NOT MUCH OF A GIN MAN, BEING HONEST.
BUT YOU KNOW WHAT THEY SAY...
WHEN IN **ROME.**
THAT'S ALL FOR THIS MONTH, KIDS! GO FUCK YOURSELF!
The End

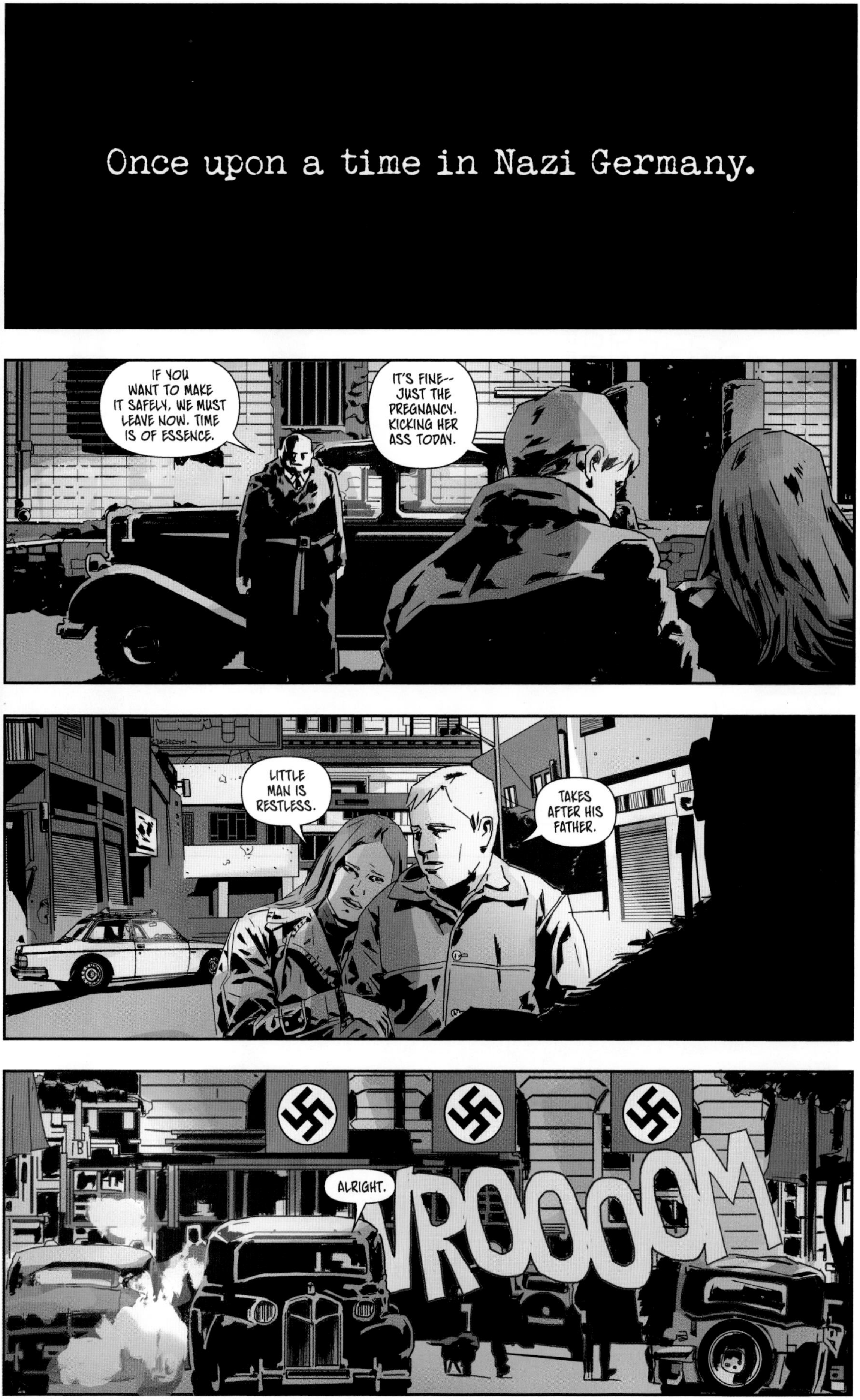
Once upon a time in Nazi Germany.
IF YOU WANT TO MAKE IT SAFELY, WE MUST LEAVE NOW. TIME IS OF ESSENCE.
IT'S FINE-- JUST THE PREGNANCY. KICKING HER ASS TODAY.
LITTLE MAN IS RESTLESS.
TAKES AFTER HIS FATHER.
ALRIGHT.
VROOOOM

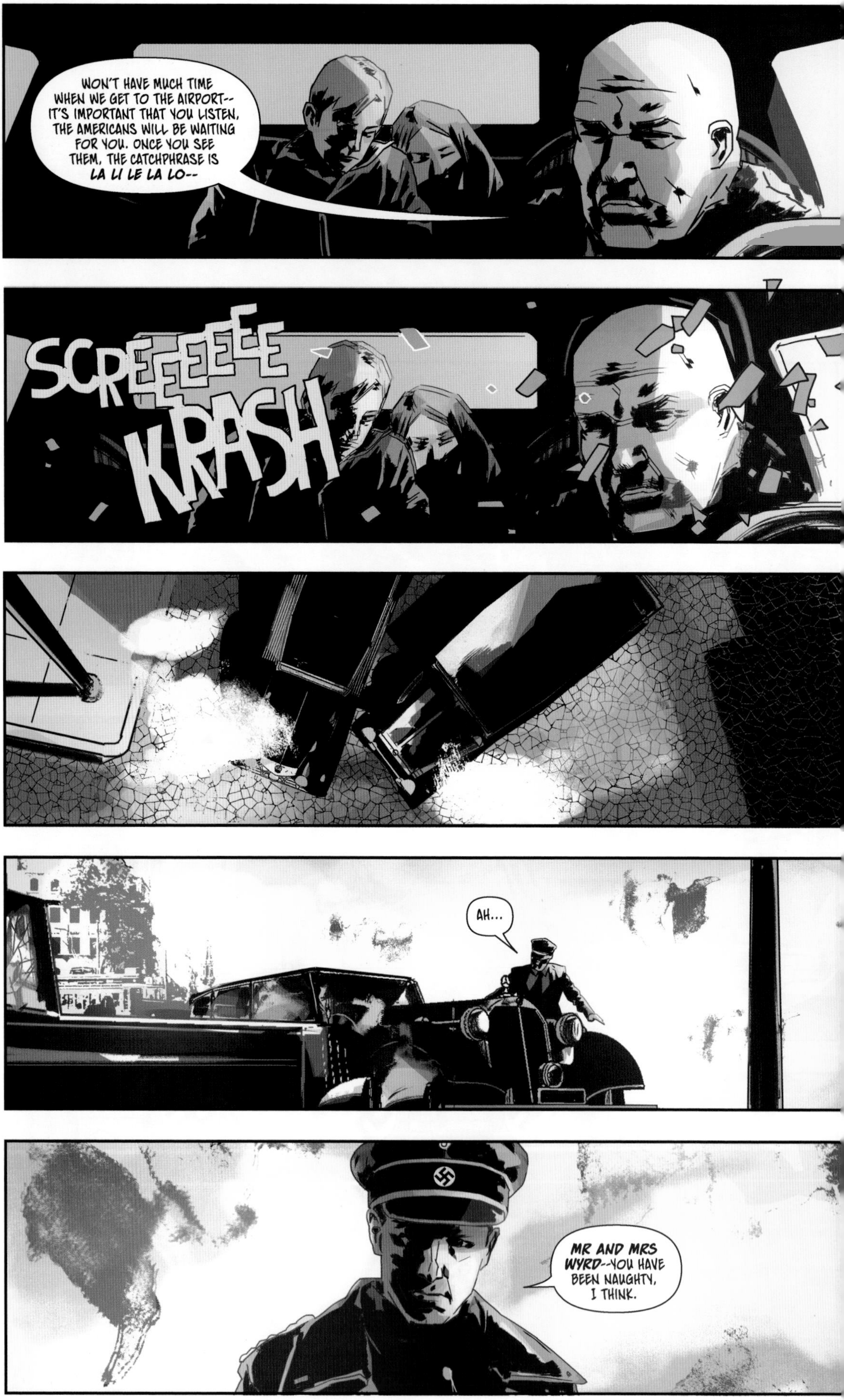
WON'T HAVE MUCH TIME WHEN WE GET TO THE AIRPORT-- IT'S IMPORTANT THAT YOU LISTEN. THE AMERICANS WILL BE WAITING FOR YOU. ONCE YOU SEE THEM, THE CATCHPHRASE IS *LA LI LE LA LO--*
SCREEEEEEE
KRASH
AH...
MR AND MRS WYRD--YOU HAVE BEEN NAUGHTY, I THINK.

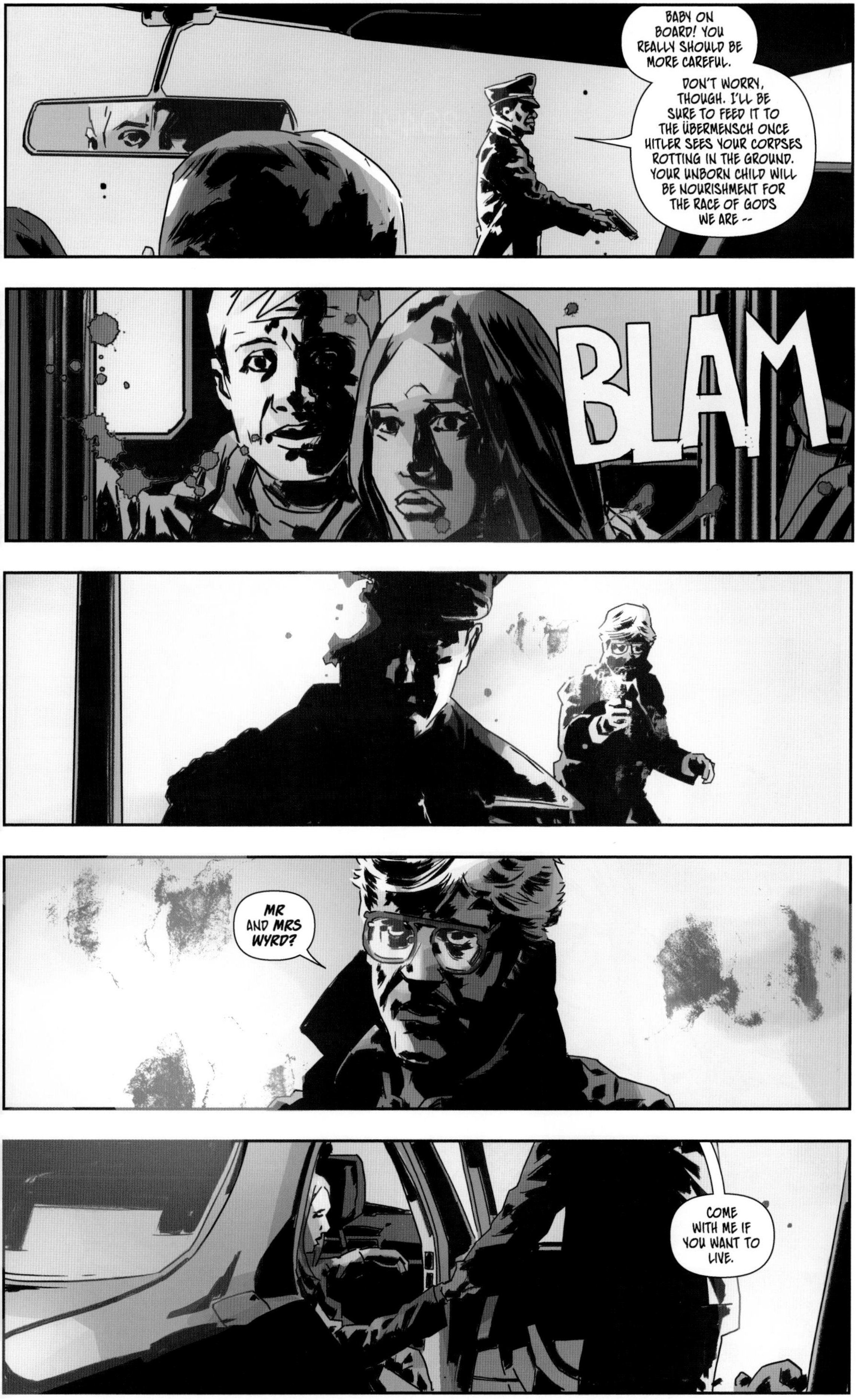
BABY ON BOARD! YOU REALLY SHOULD BE MORE CAREFUL.
DON'T WORRY, THOUGH. I'LL BE SURE TO FEED IT TO THE ÜBERMENSCH ONCE HITLER SEES YOUR CORPSES ROTTING IN THE GROUND. YOUR UNBORN CHILD WILL BE NOURISHMENT FOR THE RACE OF GODS WE ARE --
BLAM
MR AND MRS WYRD?
COME WITH ME IF YOU WANT TO LIVE.

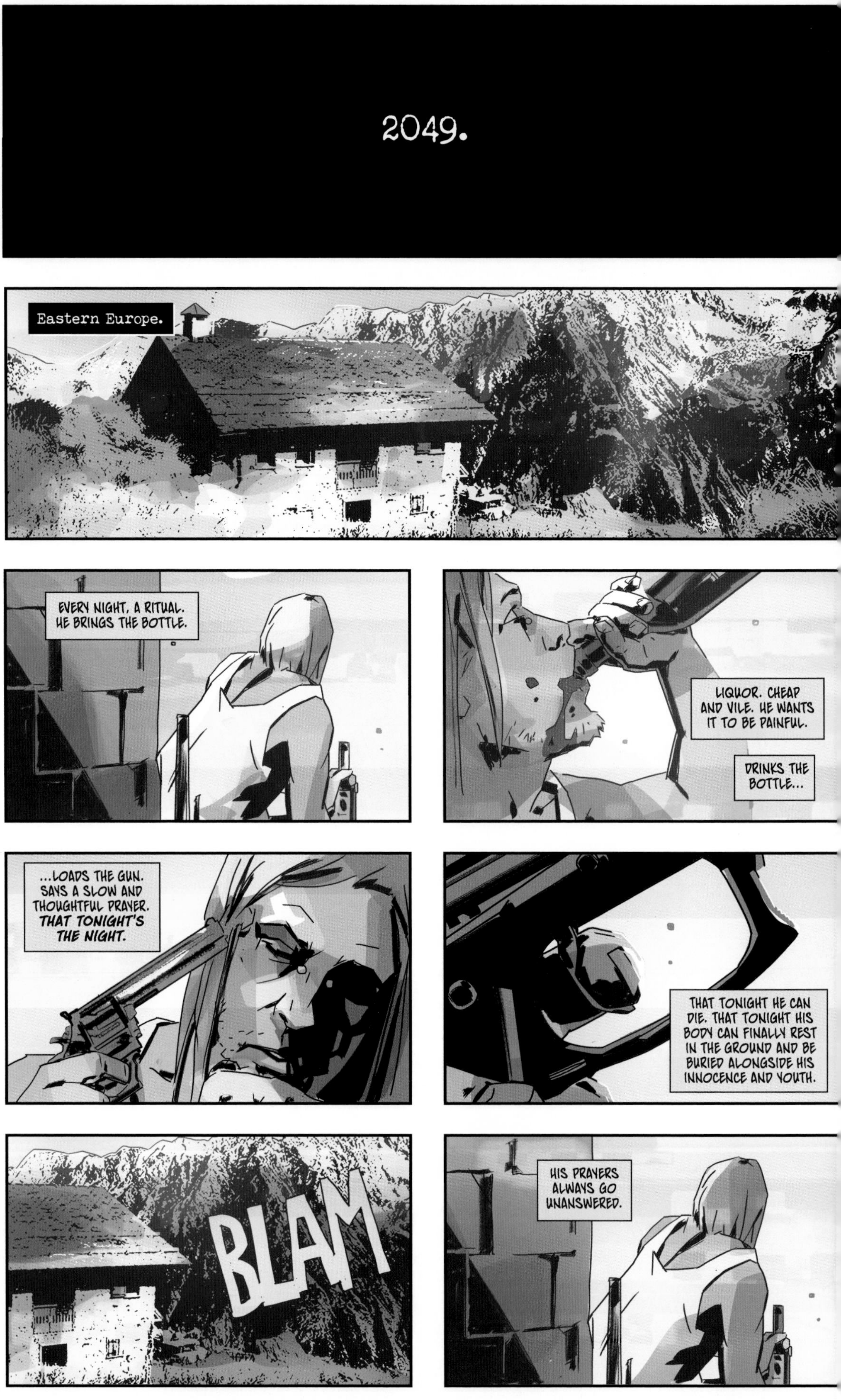
2049.
Eastern Europe.
EVERY NIGHT, A RITUAL. HE BRINGS THE BOTTLE.
LIQUOR. CHEAP AND VILE. HE WANTS IT TO BE PAINFUL.
DRINKS THE BOTTLE...
...LOADS THE GUN. SAYS A SLOW AND THOUGHTFUL PRAYER. THAT TONIGHT'S THE NIGHT.
THAT TONIGHT HE CAN DIE. THAT TONIGHT HIS BODY CAN FINALLY REST IN THE GROUND AND BE BURIED ALONGSIDE HIS INNOCENCE AND YOUTH.
BLAM
HIS PRAYERS ALWAYS GO UNANSWERED.

US Airspace.
YOU BOYS OKAY UP THERE?
YES SIR. SKY IS CLEAR, SHOULD BE SMOOTH SAILING FROM HERE ON OUT.
WHY DO YOU THINK THEY GOT ALL OF US HERE, ANYWAYS? FOUR ARMED GUARDS JUST FOR A CARGO TRANSFER. SEEMS A BIT OVERKILL TO ME.
I DON'T ASK QUESTIONS. I JUST SHOW UP, AND COLLECT MY PAYCHEQUE.
YEAH, SURE. BUT, I MEAN, THINK ABOUT IT-- WHATEVER'S IN THAT BOX-- WHATEVER'S WORTH PAYING FOUR OF US. HAS TO BE CRAZY RIGHT?
LIKE I SAID... I DON'T ASK QUESTIONS.
YOU'RE NO FUN. LET ME KNOW IF YOU EVER DECIDE TO REMOVE THE STICK FROM YOUR ASS. OKAY?
DEAL.
LEAST YOU'RE A GOOD SPORT ABOUT THAT.

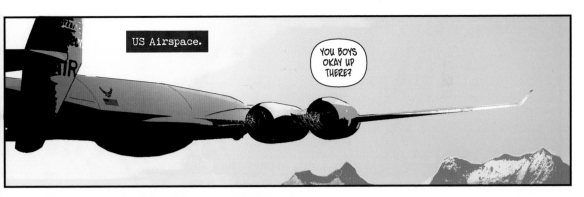

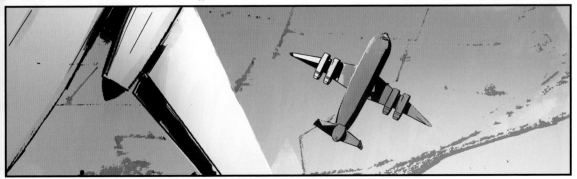

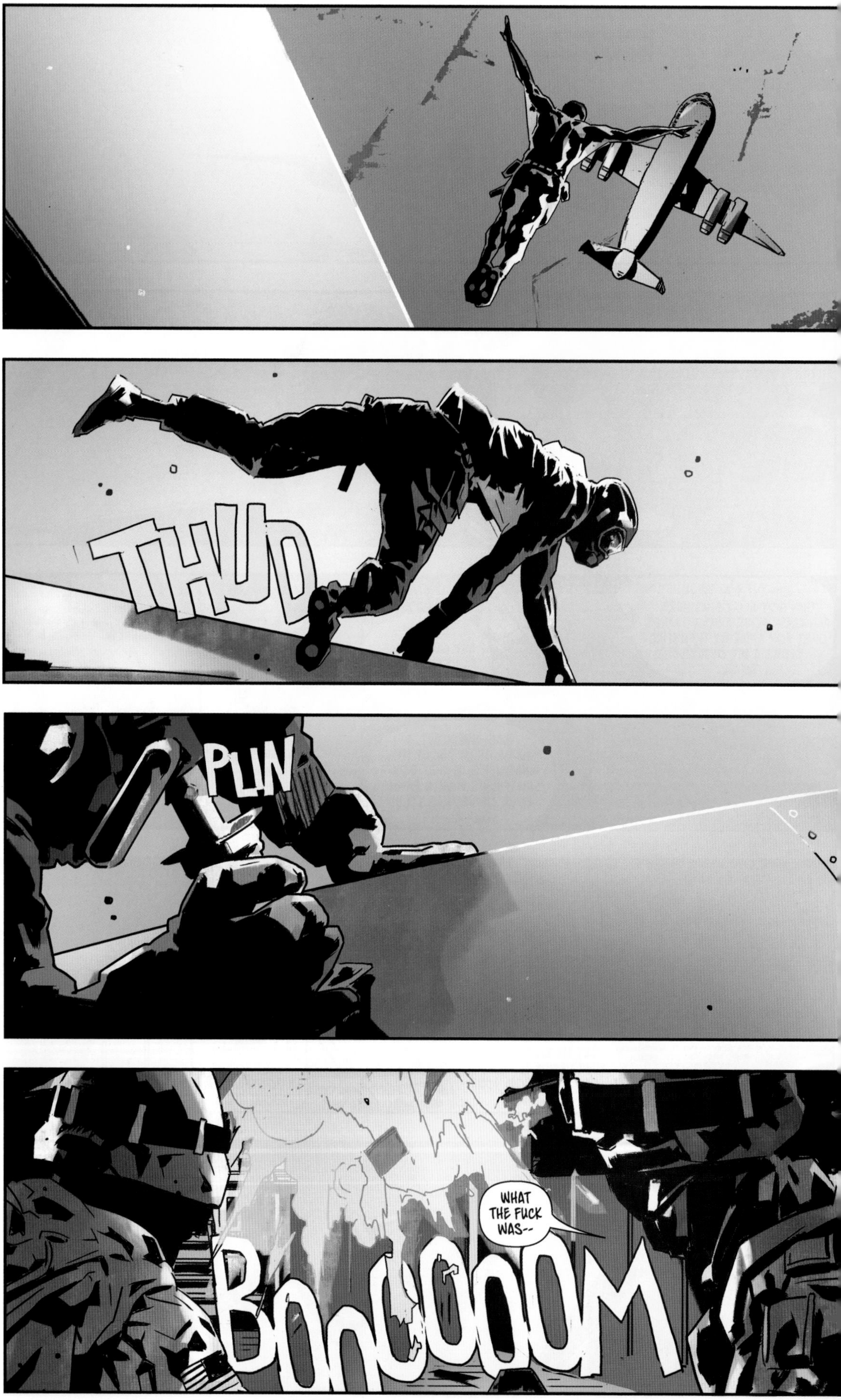
THUD
PLIN
WHAT THE FUCK WAS--
BOOOOOOM

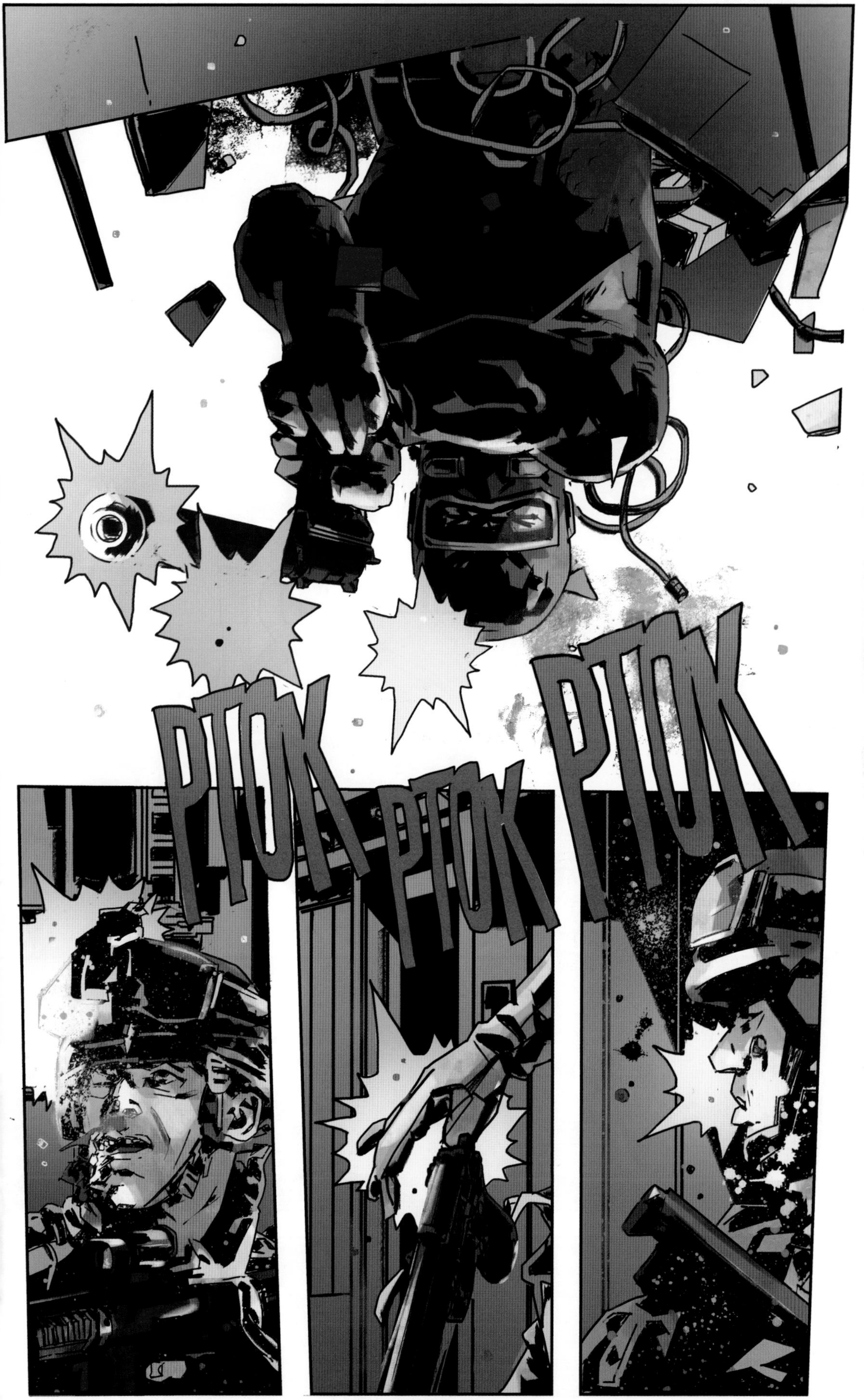
PTOK
PTOK
PTOK

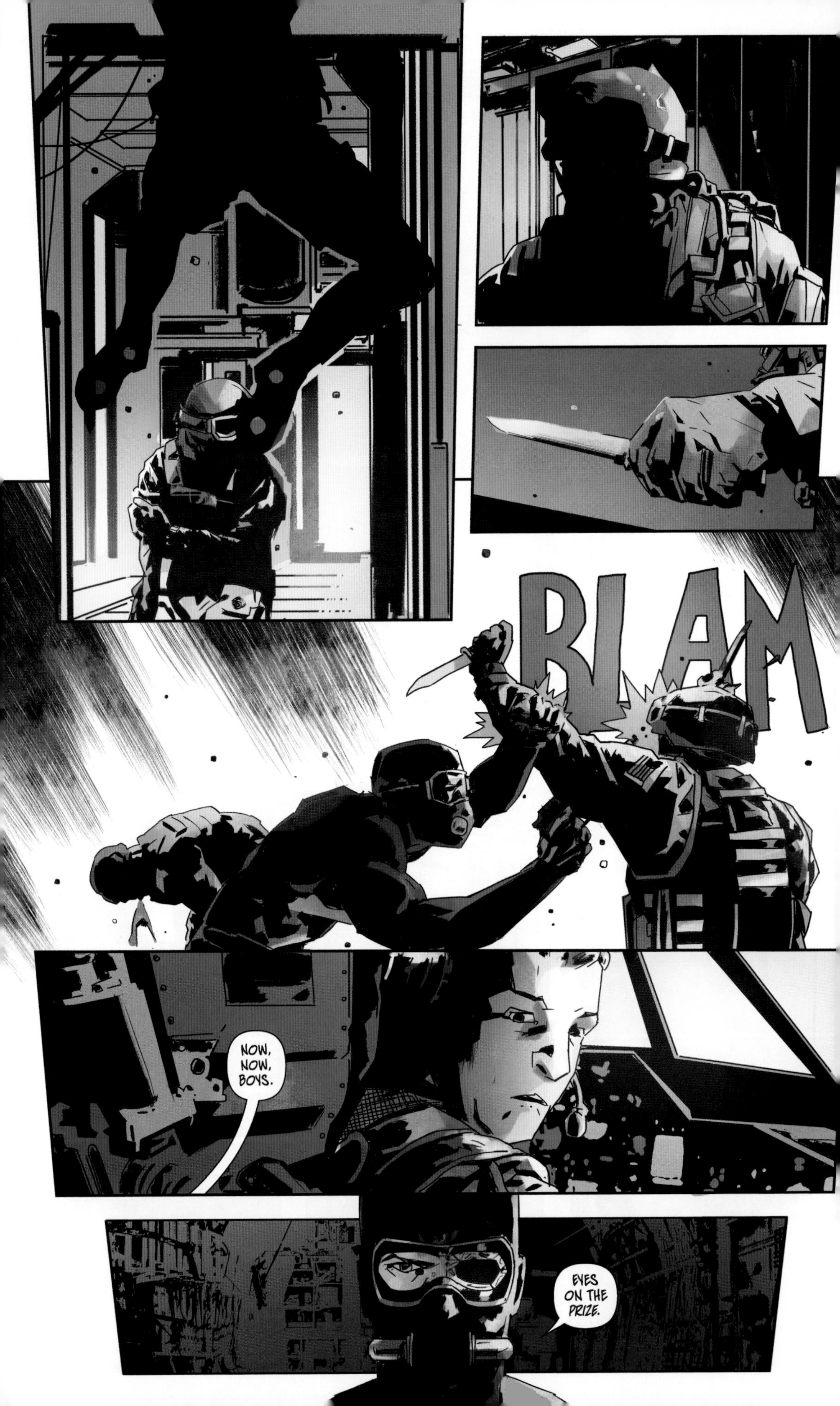
BLAM
NOW, NOW, BOYS.
EYES ON THE PRIZE.

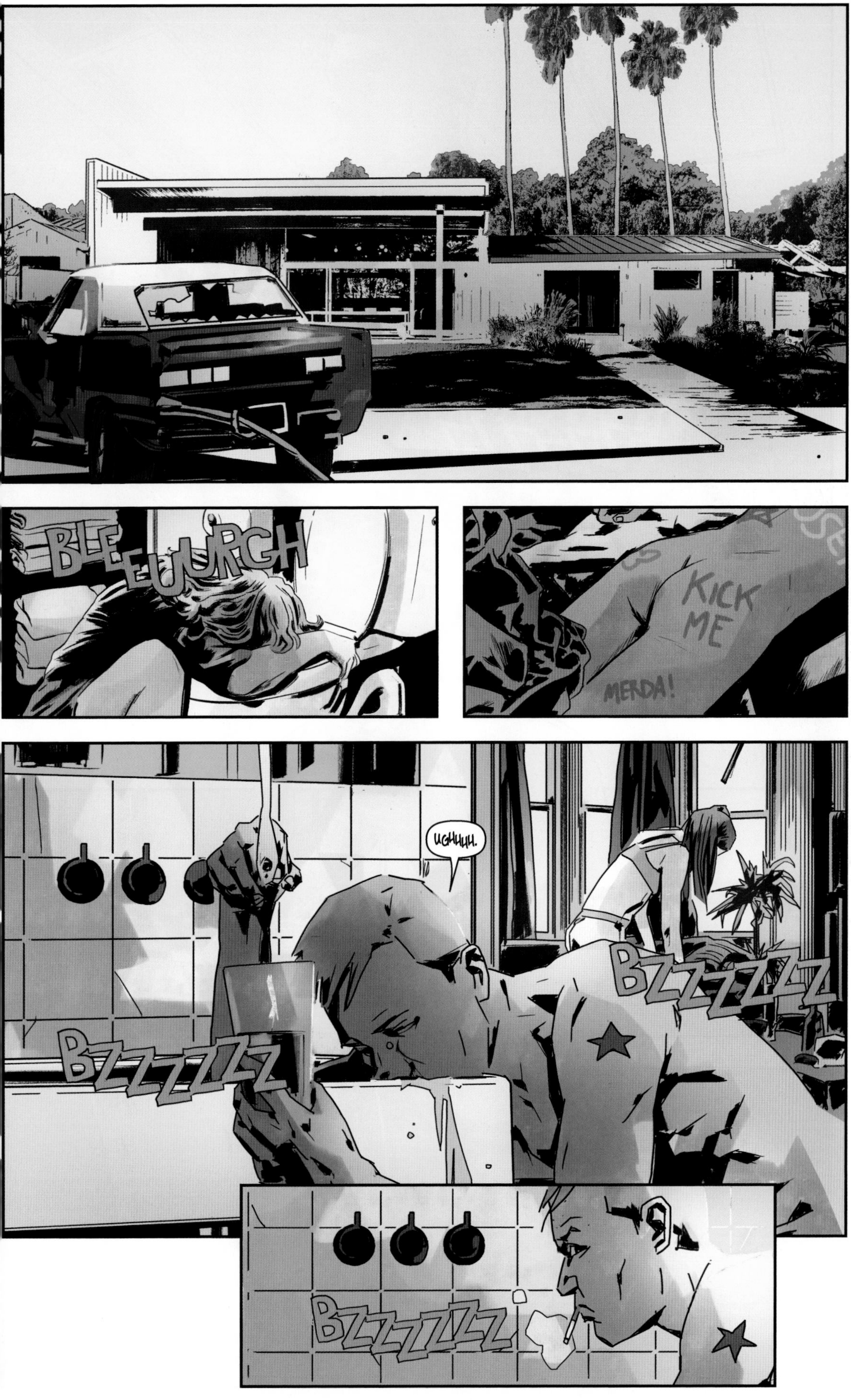
BLEEUURGH
KICK ME
MERDA!
UGHHHH.
BZZZZZZZ
BZZZZZZZ
BZZZZZZZ

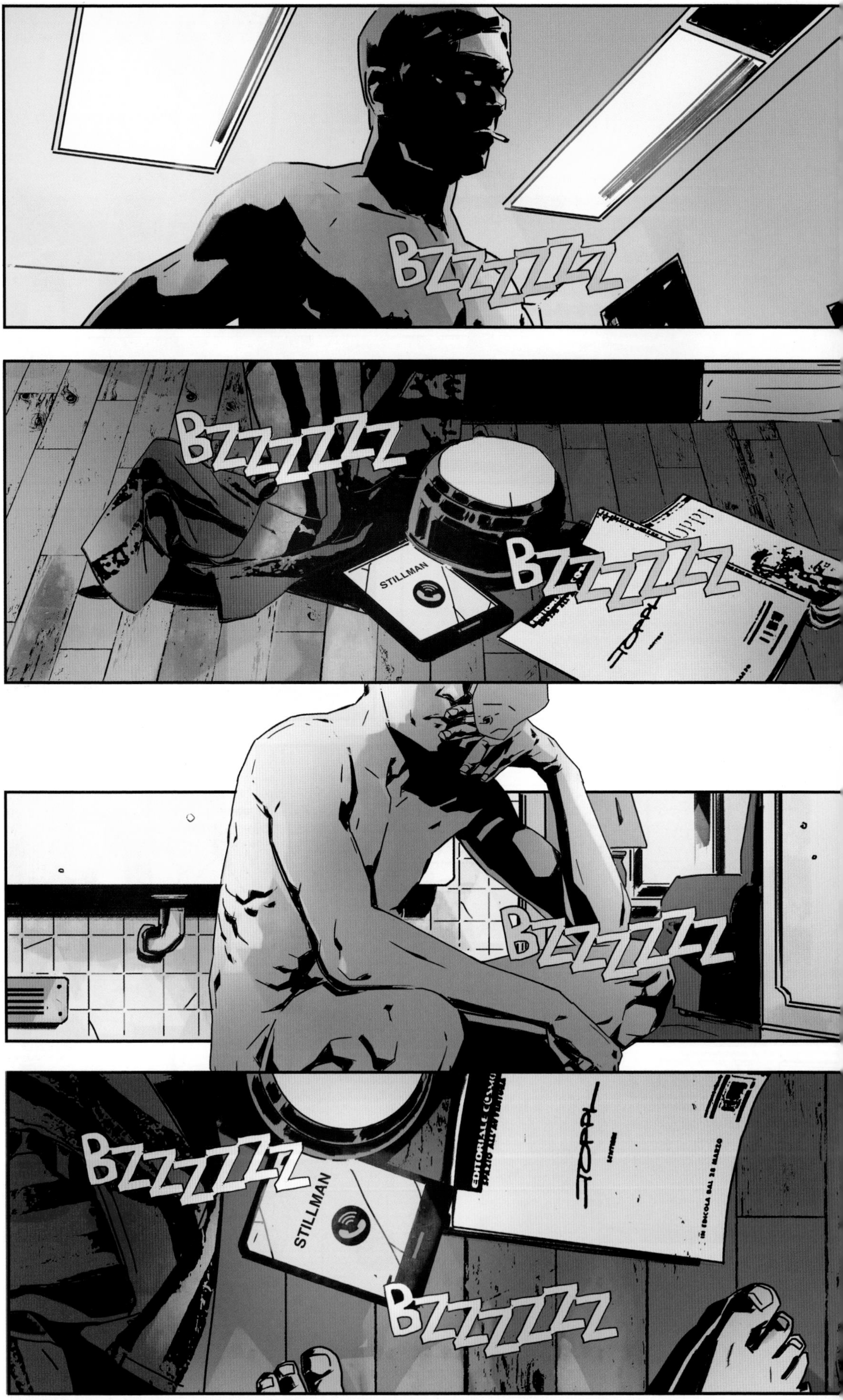
Bzzzzzzz
Bzzzzzzz
STILLMAN
Bzzzzzzz
Bzzzzzzz
Bzzzzzzz
STILLMAN
Bzzzzzzz

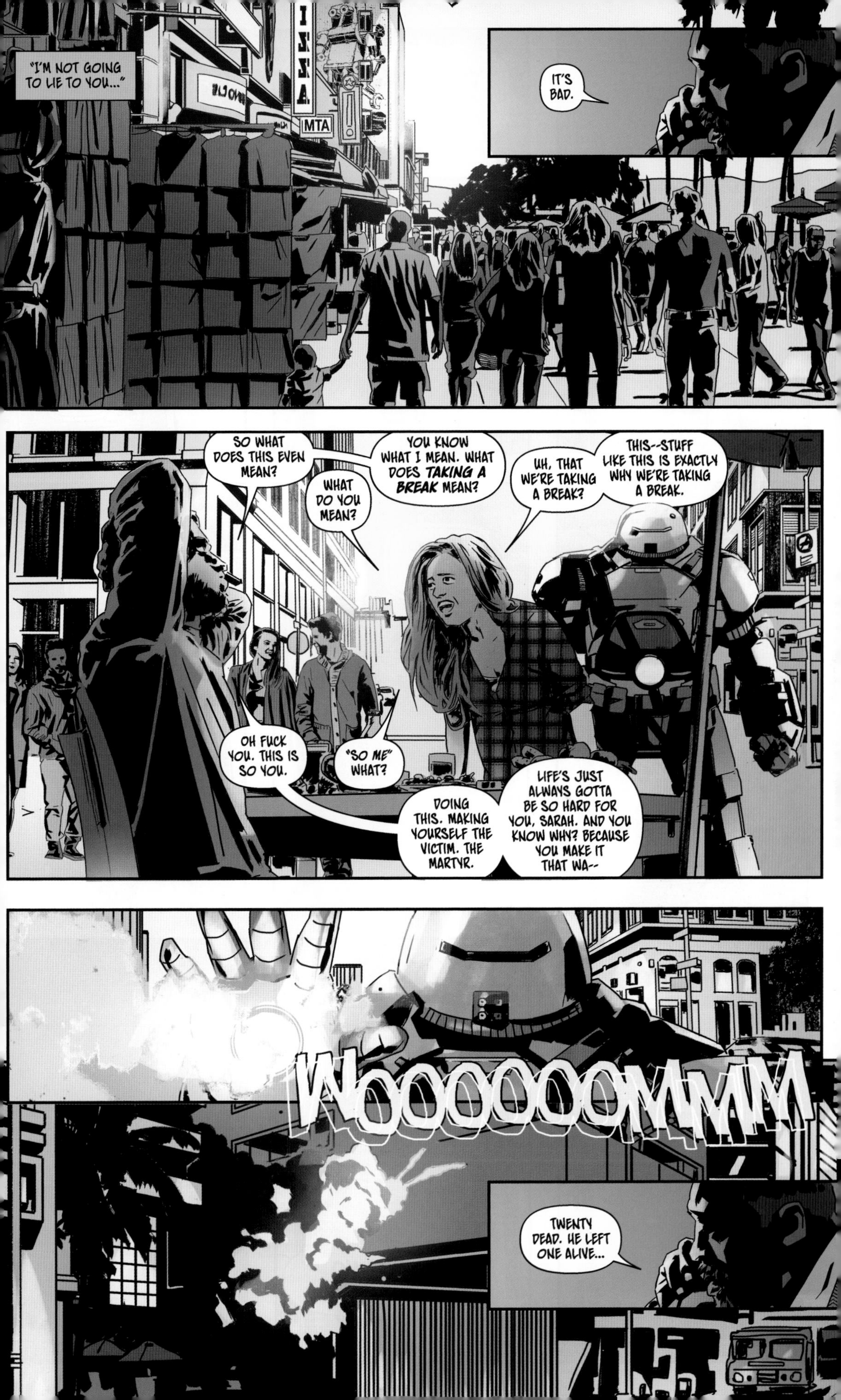
"I'M NOT GOING TO LIE TO YOU..."
IT'S BAD.
MTA
SO WHAT DOES THIS EVEN MEAN?
WHAT DO YOU MEAN?
YOU KNOW WHAT I MEAN. WHAT DOES TAKING A BREAK MEAN?
UH, THAT WE'RE TAKING A BREAK?
THIS--STUFF LIKE THIS IS EXACTLY WHY WE'RE TAKING A BREAK.
OH FUCK YOU. THIS IS SO YOU.
"SO ME" WHAT?
DOING THIS. MAKING YOURSELF THE VICTIM. THE MARTYR.
LIFE'S JUST ALWAYS GOTTA BE SO HARD FOR YOU, SARAH. AND YOU KNOW WHY? BECAUSE YOU MAKE IT THAT WA--
WOOOOOOOMMMM
TWENTY DEAD. HE LEFT ONE ALIVE...

"TO RELAY A MESSAGE."

PLEASE. PLEASE DON'T KILL ME.

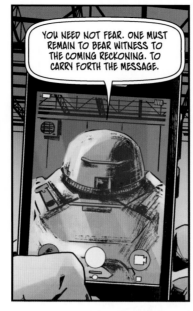

YOU NEED NOT FEAR. ONE MUST REMAIN TO BEAR WITNESS TO THE COMING RECKONING. TO CARRY FORTH THE MESSAGE.

YOU DO WHAT I SAY AND YOU WILL NOT BE HARMED. DO YOU UNDERSTAND?

YES--OH GOD-- I UNDERSTAND.

GOOD.

WYRD.

I WANT TO SPEAK TO PITOR WYRD.

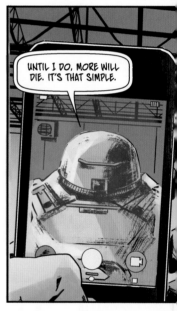

UNTIL I DO, MORE WILL DIE. IT'S THAT SIMPLE.

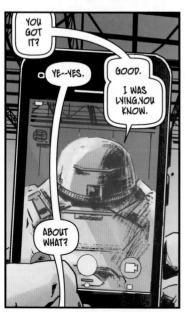

YOU GOT IT?

YE--YES.

GOOD.

I WAS LYING, YOU KNOW.

ABOUT WHAT?

ABOUT NEEDING YOU ALIVE. I JUST NEED THEM TO FIND THE PHONE.

NO--NO PLEASSSSEE...

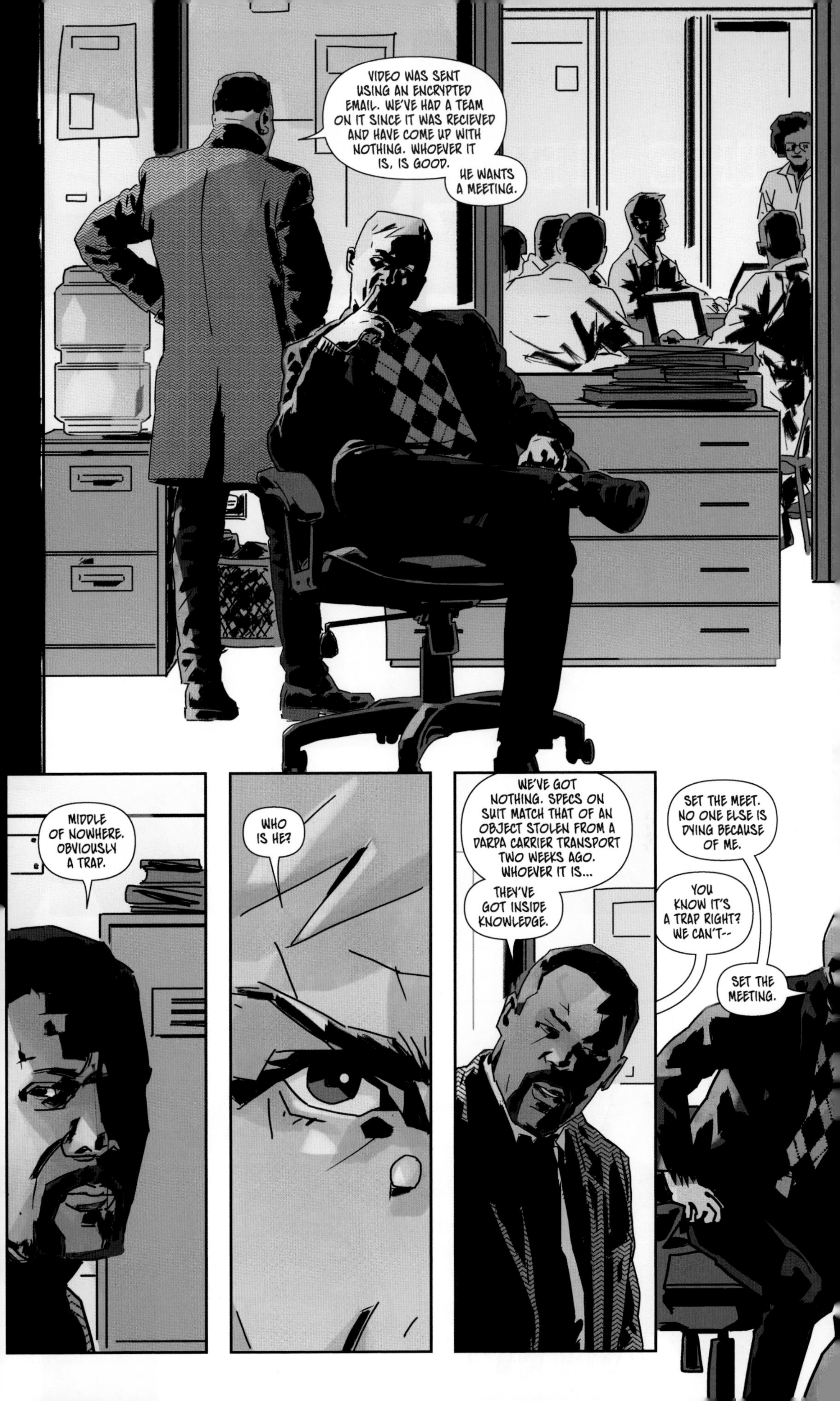
VIDEO WAS SENT USING AN ENCRYPTED EMAIL. WE'VE HAD A TEAM ON IT SINCE IT WAS RECIEVED AND HAVE COME UP WITH NOTHING. WHOEVER IT IS, IS GOOD.
HE WANTS A MEETING.
MIDDLE OF NOWHERE. OBVIOUSLY A TRAP.
WHO IS HE?
WE'VE GOT NOTHING. SPECS ON SUIT MATCH THAT OF AN OBJECT STOLEN FROM A DARPA CARRIER TRANSPORT TWO WEEKS AGO. WHOEVER IT IS...
THEY'VE GOT INSIDE KNOWLEDGE.
SET THE MEET. NO ONE ELSE IS DYING BECAUSE OF ME.
YOU KNOW IT'S A TRAP RIGHT? WE CAN'T--
SET THE MEETING.

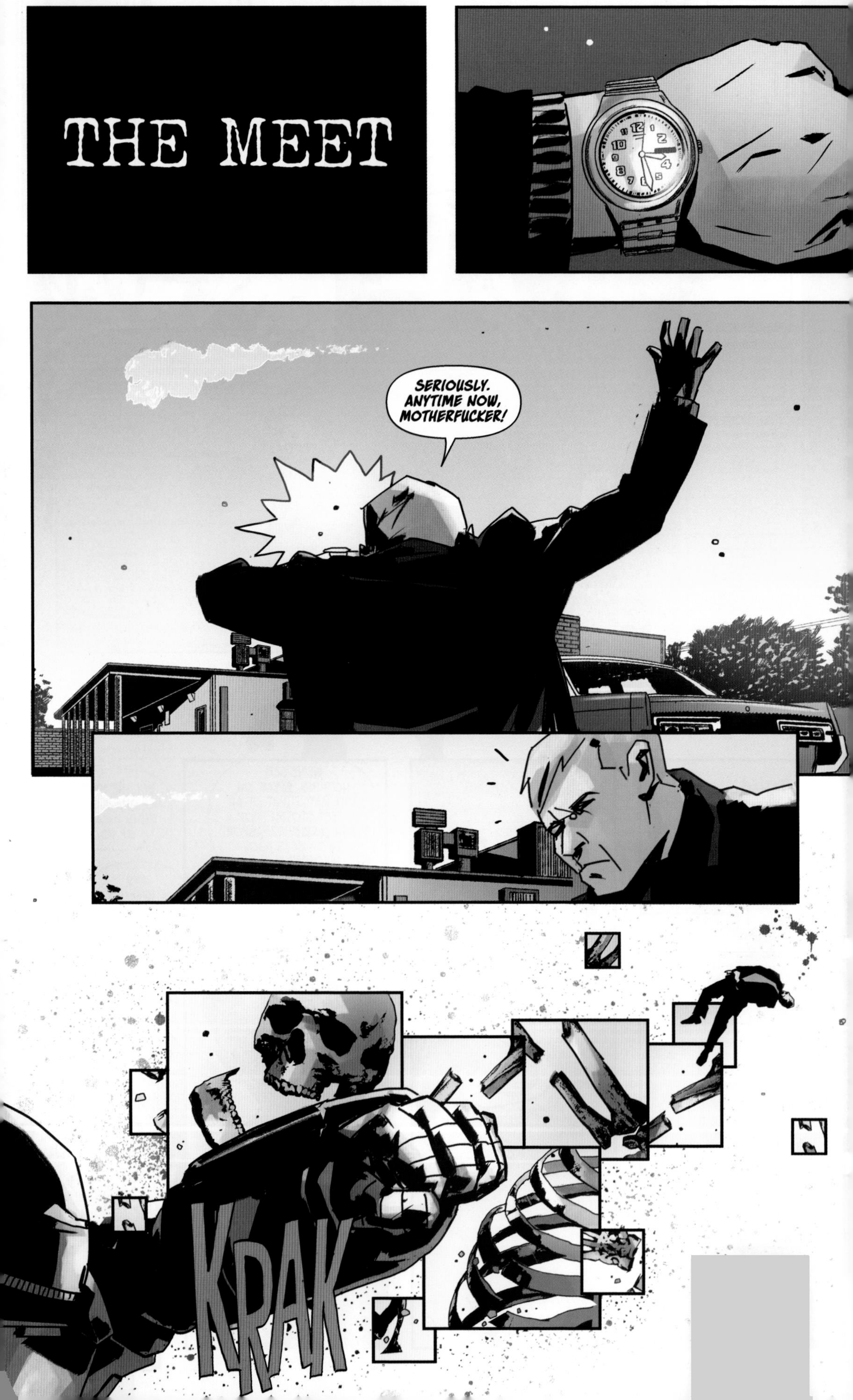
THE MEET
SERIOUSLY. ANYTIME NOW, MOTHERFUCKER!
KRAK

THE MEET. FOR REAL.

OH GOOD, YOU'RE UP.

SORRY ABOUT THE ROPE. SURELY A MERE FORMALITY FOR SOMEONE AS GIFTED AS YOURSELF.

YOU KNOW, IF YOU WANTED TO ENGAGE IN A LITTLE LIGHT BDSM YOU COULD HAVE JUST RESPONDED TO MY BACKPAGE POST.

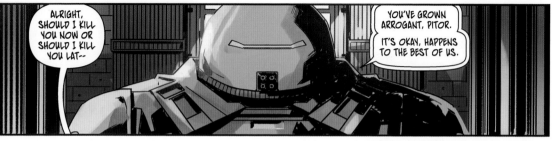

ALRIGHT, SHOULD I KILL YOU NOW OR SHOULD I KILL YOU LAT--

YOU'VE GROWN ARROGANT, PITOR.

IT'S OKAY, HAPPENS TO THE BEST OF US.

I AM NOT SOME PIGFUCKING POLITICIAN NOR AM I SOME MENTALLY DERANGED SOLDIER, WITHERED BY TOO MUCH TIME IN A TEST TUBE.

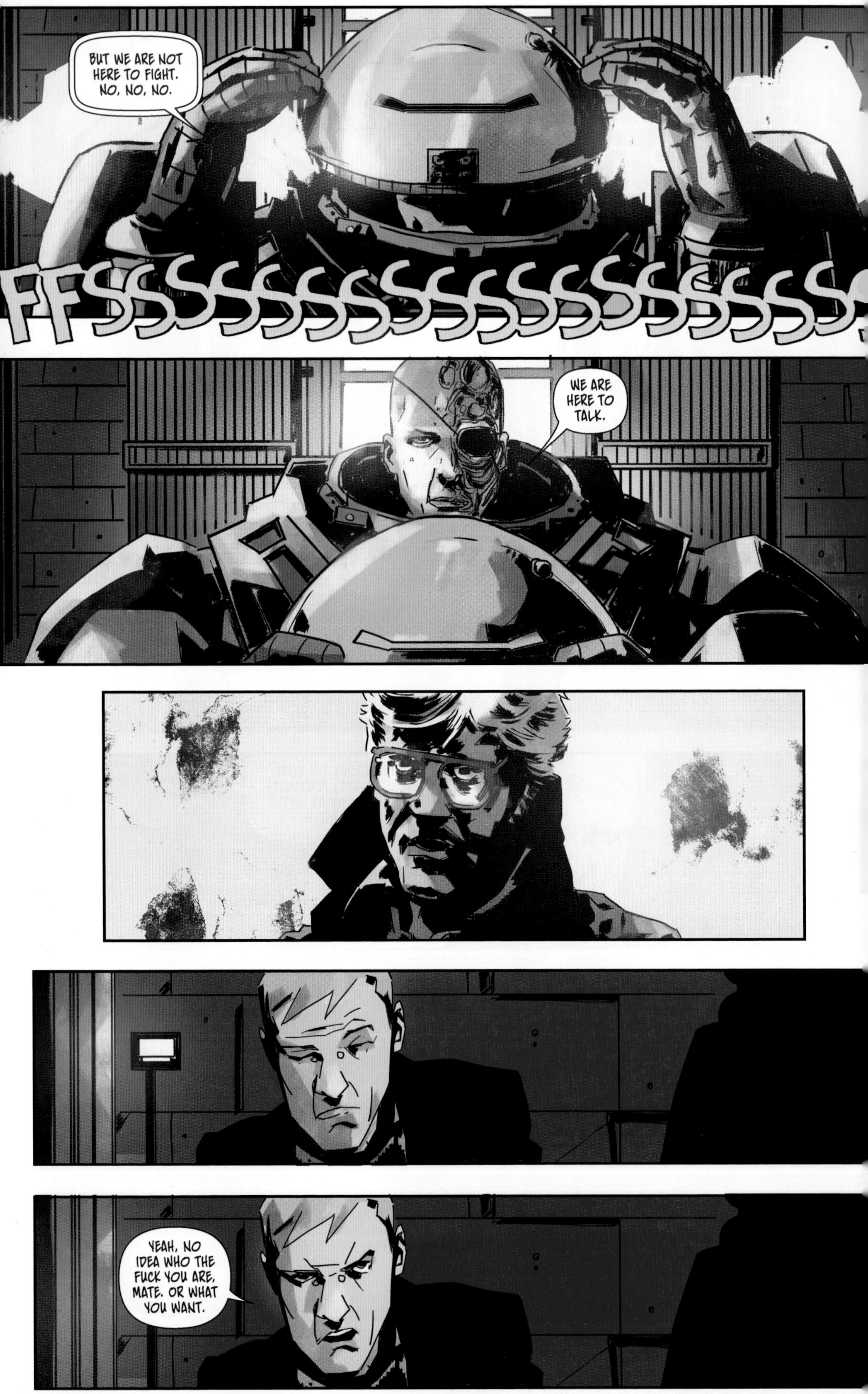
BUT WE ARE NOT HERE TO FIGHT. NO, NO, NO.
FFSSSSSSSSSSSSSSSSSSSS
WE ARE HERE TO TALK.
YEAH, NO IDEA WHO THE FUCK YOU ARE, MATE. OR WHAT YOU WANT.

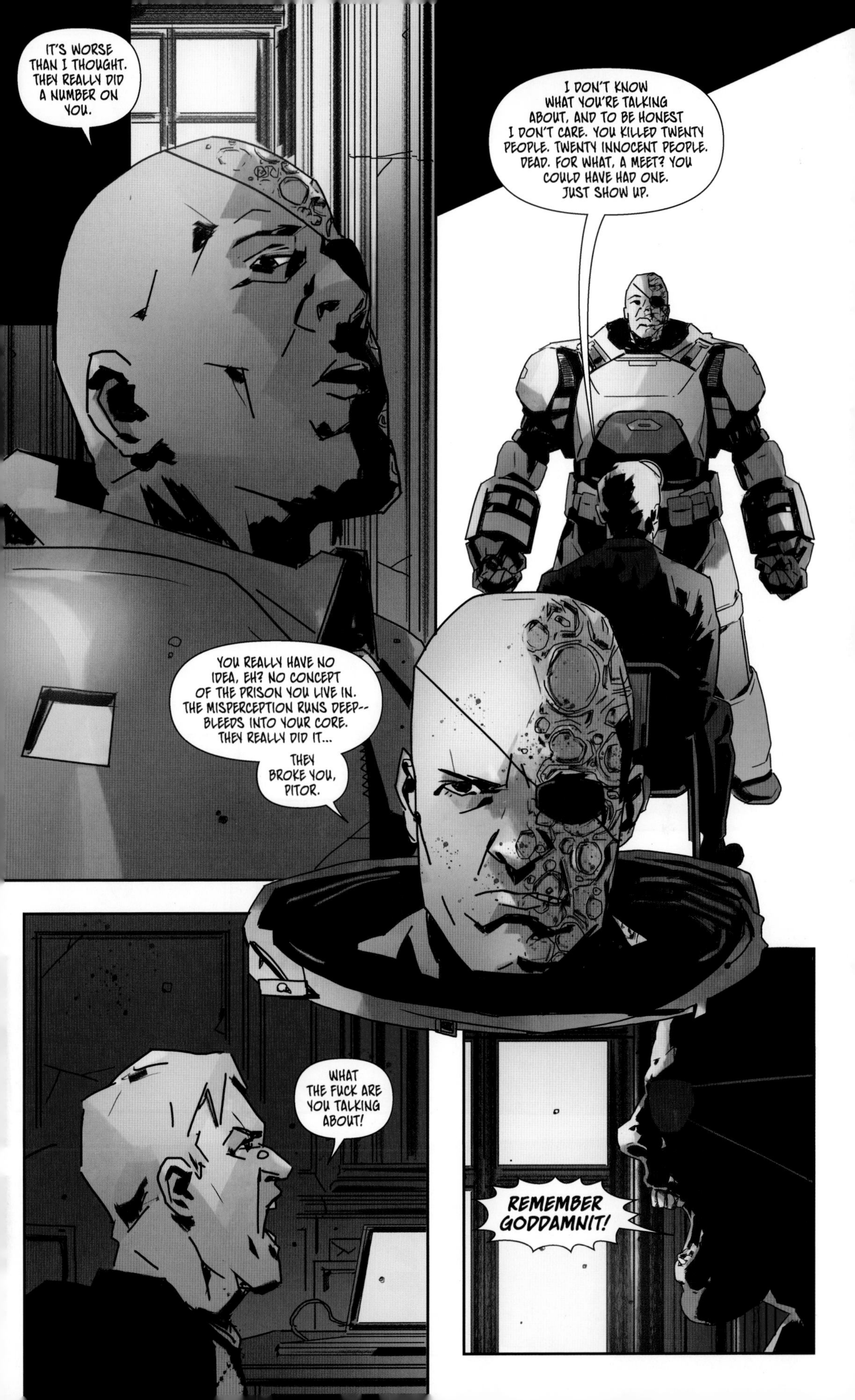
IT'S WORSE THAN I THOUGHT. THEY REALLY DID A NUMBER ON YOU.
I DON'T KNOW WHAT YOU'RE TALKING ABOUT, AND TO BE HONEST I DON'T CARE. YOU KILLED TWENTY PEOPLE. TWENTY INNOCENT PEOPLE. DEAD. FOR WHAT, A MEET? YOU COULD HAVE HAD ONE. JUST SHOW UP.
YOU REALLY HAVE NO IDEA, EH? NO CONCEPT OF THE PRISON YOU LIVE IN. THE MISPERCEPTION RUNS DEEP-- BLEEDS INTO YOUR CORE. THEY REALLY DID IT...
THEY BROKE YOU, PITOR.
WHAT THE FUCK ARE YOU TALKING ABOUT!
REMEMBER GODDAMNIT!

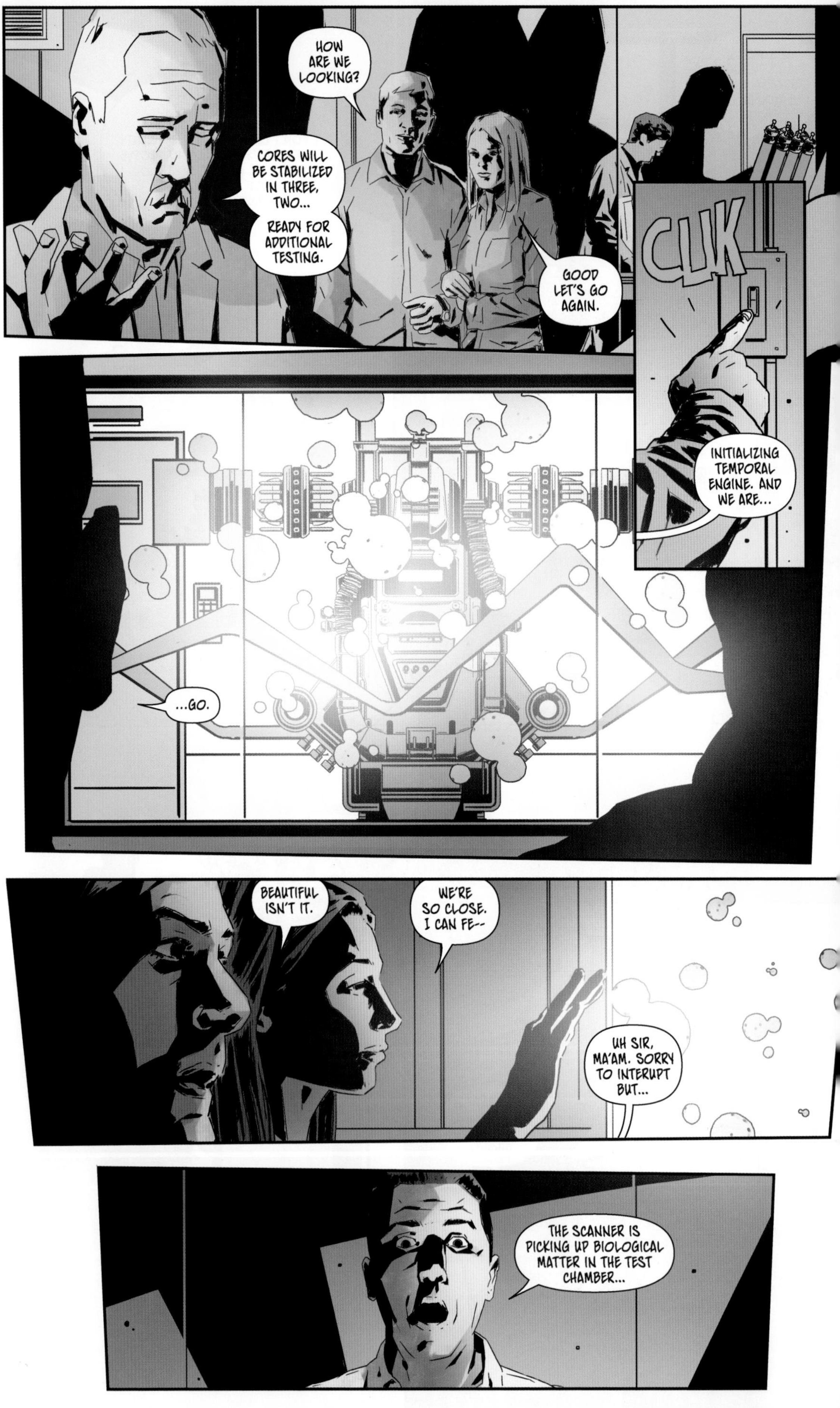
HOW ARE WE LOOKING?
CORES WILL BE STABILIZED IN THREE, TWO...
READY FOR ADDITIONAL TESTING.
GOOD LET'S GO AGAIN.
CLIK
INITIALIZING TEMPORAL ENGINE. AND WE ARE...
...GO.
BEAUTIFUL ISN'T IT.
WE'RE SO CLOSE. I CAN FE--
UH SIR, MA'AM. SORRY TO INTERUPT BUT...
THE SCANNER IS PICKING UP BIOLOGICAL MATTER IN THE TEST CHAMBER...

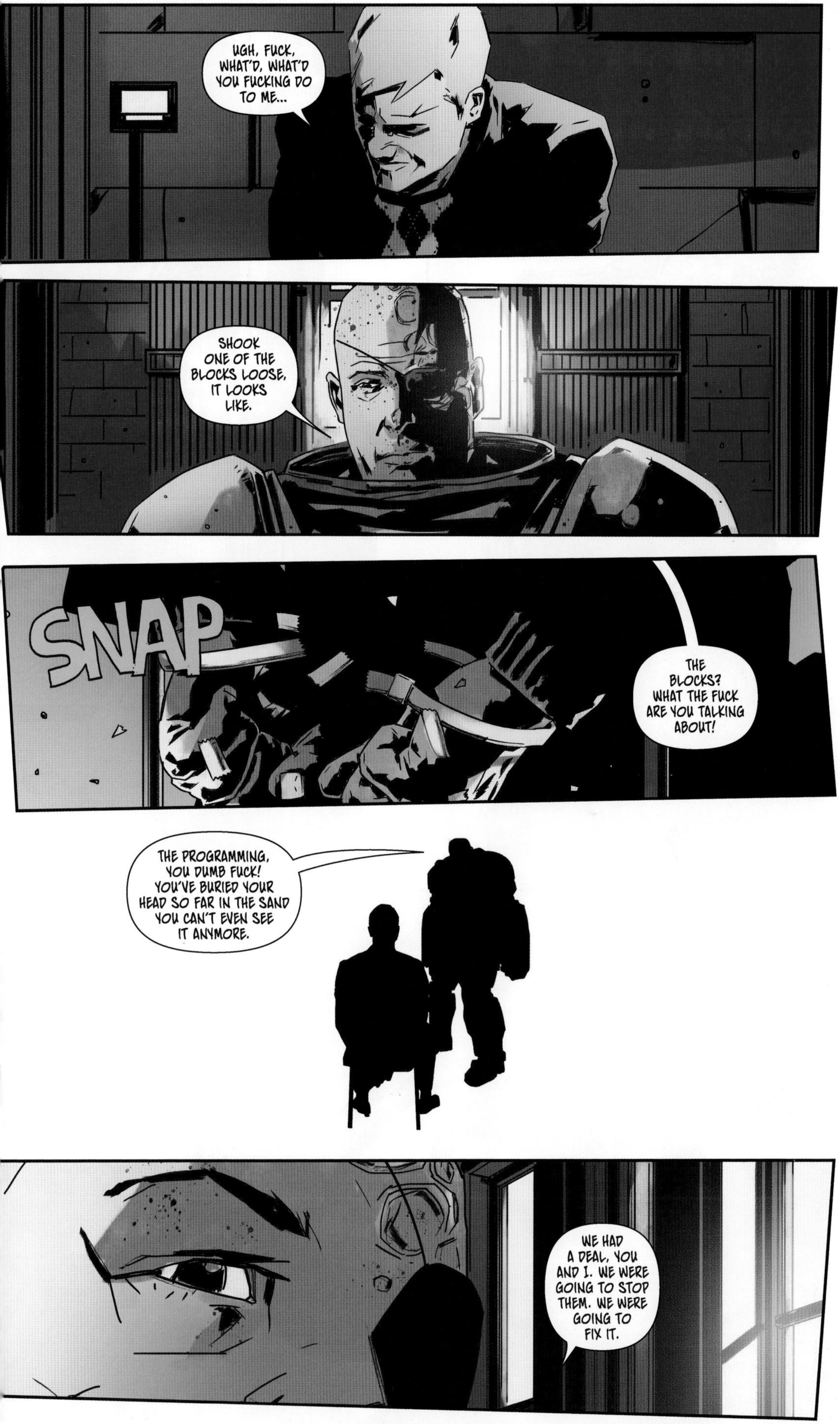
UGH, FUCK, WHAT'D, WHAT'D YOU FUCKING DO TO ME...
SHOOK ONE OF THE BLOCKS LOOSE, IT LOOKS LIKE.
SNAP
THE BLOCKS? WHAT THE FUCK ARE YOU TALKING ABOUT!
THE PROGRAMMING, YOU DUMB FUCK! YOU'VE BURIED YOUR HEAD SO FAR IN THE SAND YOU CAN'T EVEN SEE IT ANYMORE.
WE HAD A DEAL, YOU AND I. WE WERE GOING TO STOP THEM. WE WERE GOING TO FIX IT.

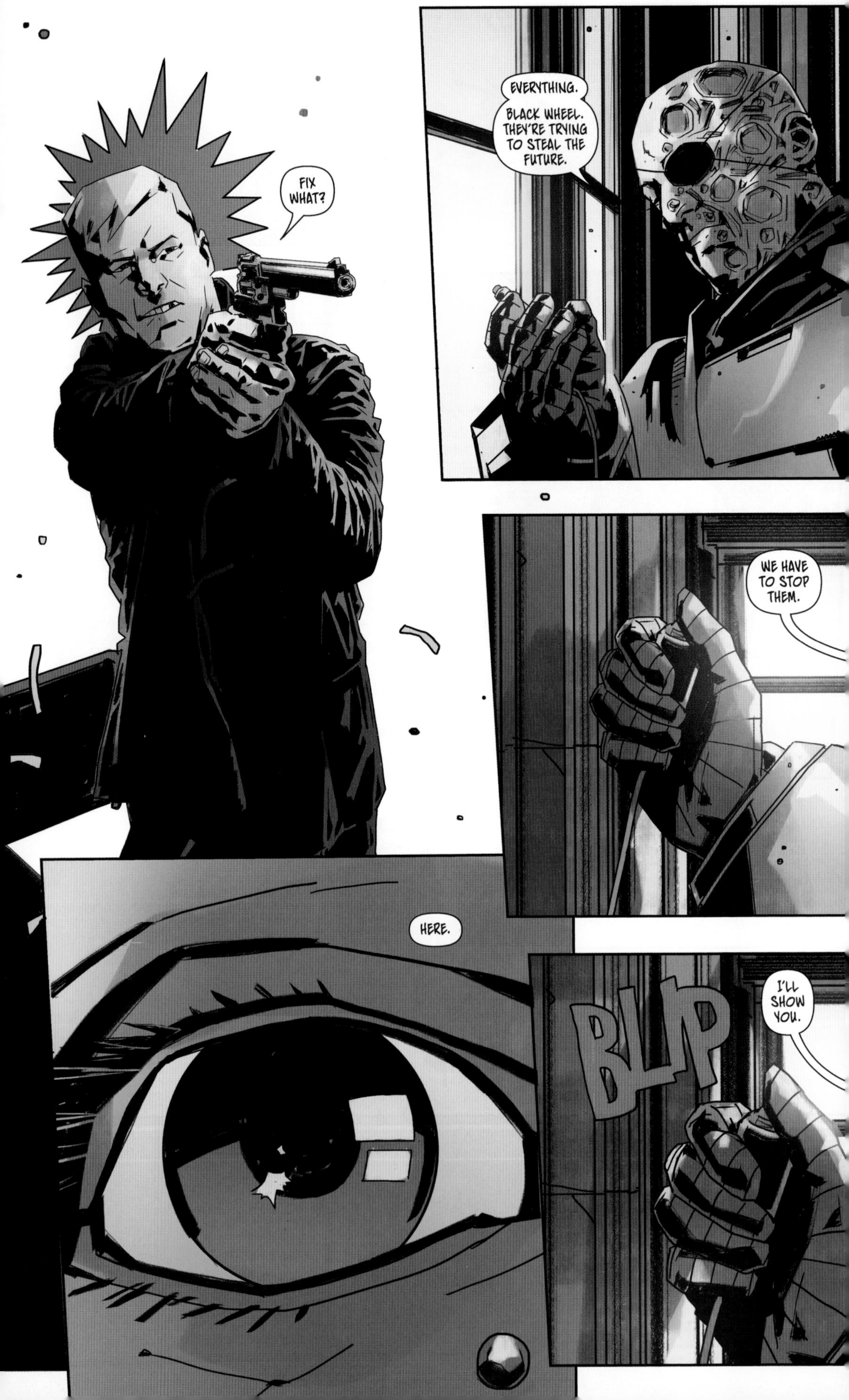
FIX WHAT?
EVERYTHING.
BLACK WHEEL. THEY'RE TRYING TO STEAL THE FUTURE.
WE HAVE TO STOP THEM.
HERE.
BLIP
I'LL SHOW YOU.

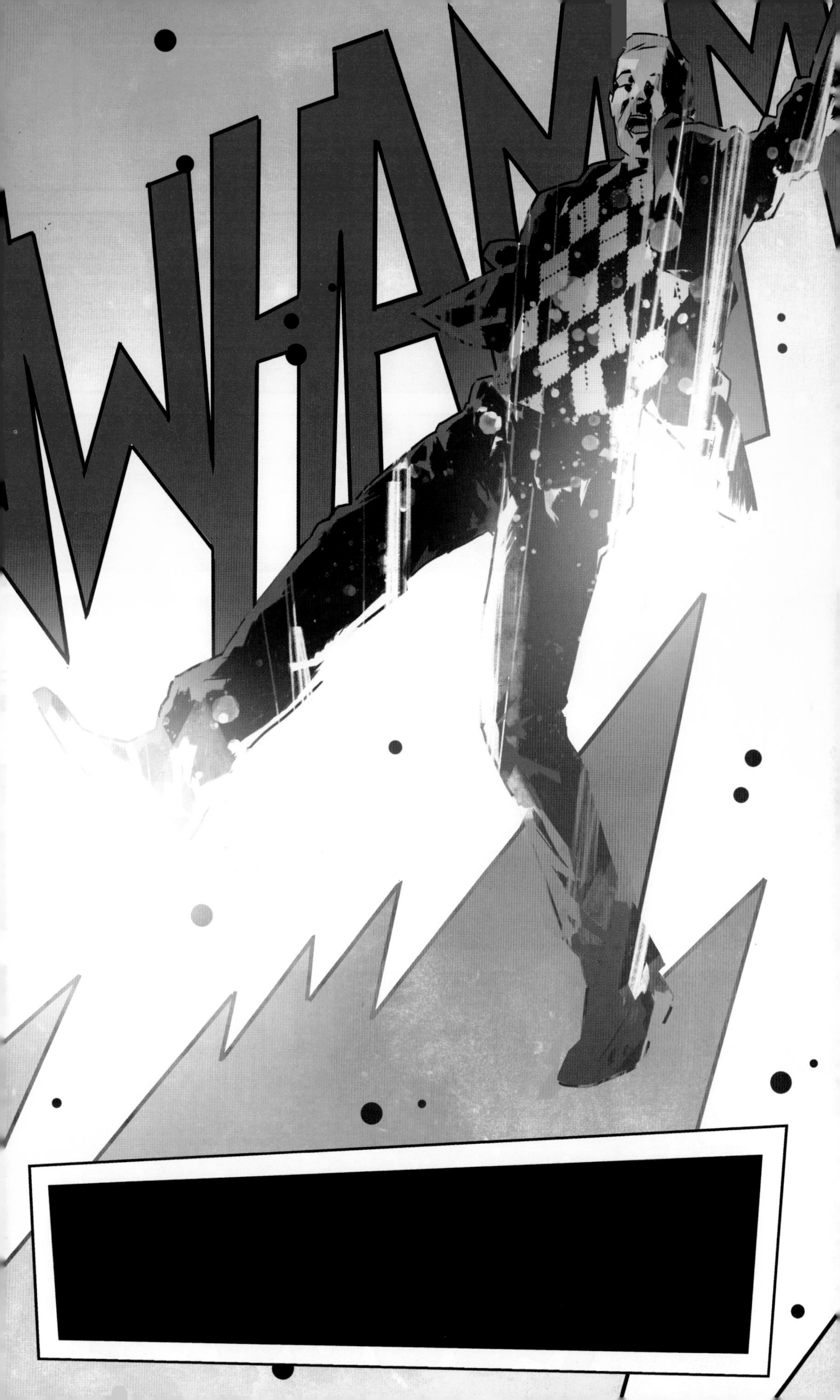
WHAM

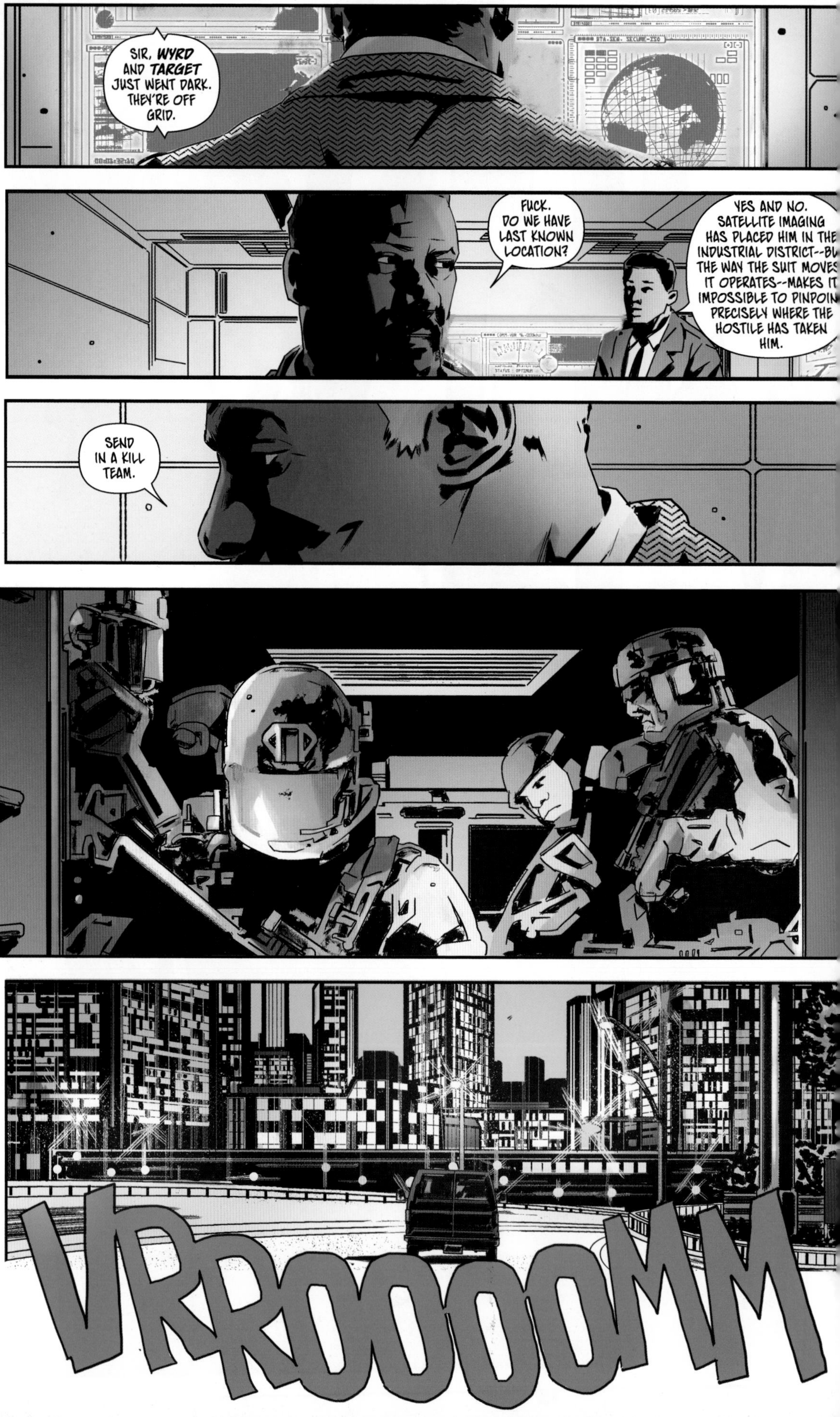

SIR, WYRD AND TARGET JUST WENT DARK. THEY'RE OFF GRID.
FUCK. DO WE HAVE LAST KNOWN LOCATION?
YES AND NO. SATELLITE IMAGING HAS PLACED HIM IN THE INDUSTRIAL DISTRICT--BU THE WAY THE SUIT MOVES IT OPERATES--MAKES IT IMPOSSIBLE TO PINPOIN PRECISELY WHERE THE HOSTILE HAS TAKEN HIM.
SEND IN A KILL TEAM.
VRROOOOMM

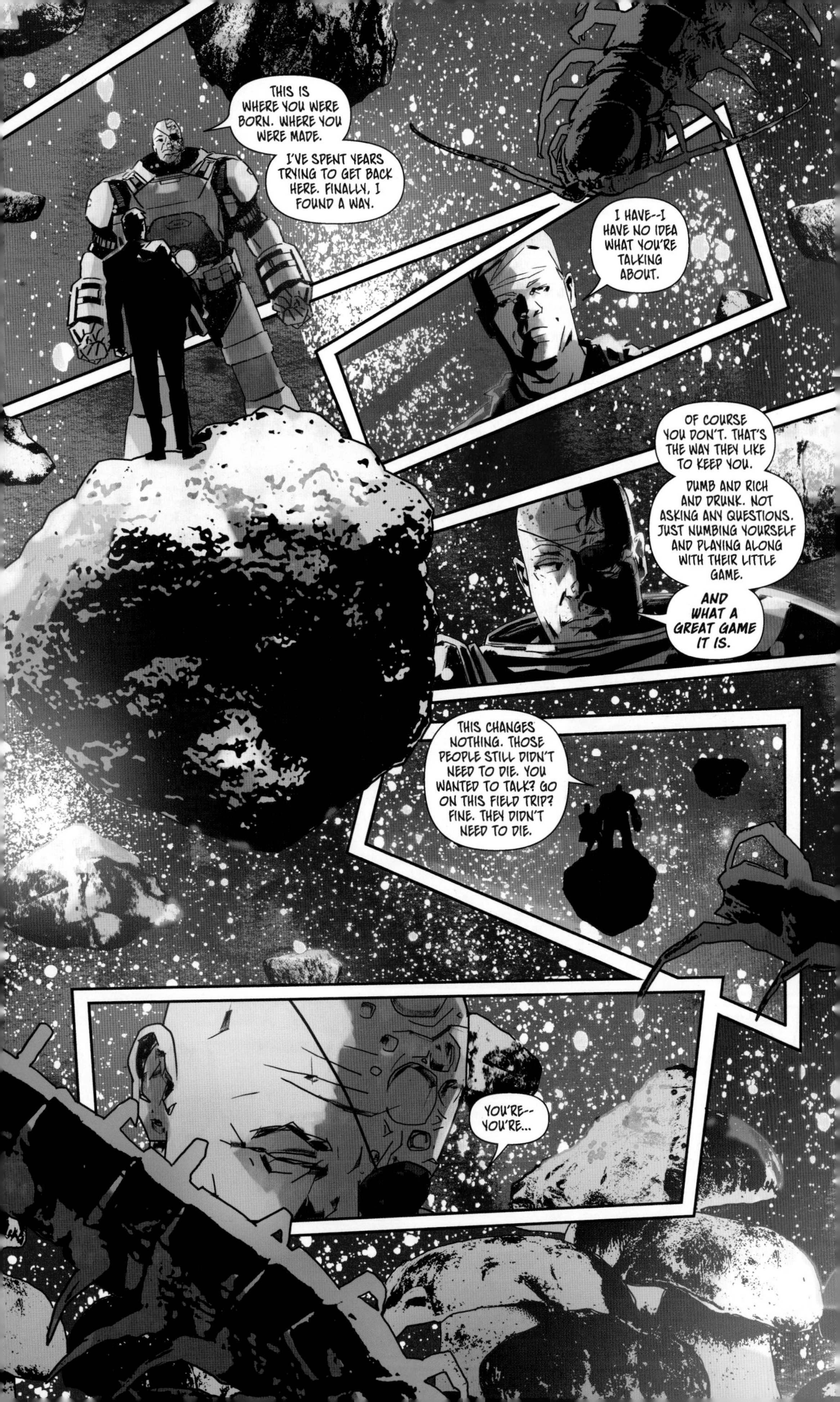
THIS IS WHERE YOU WERE BORN. WHERE YOU WERE MADE.
I'VE SPENT YEARS TRYING TO GET BACK HERE. FINALLY, I FOUND A WAY.
I HAVE--I HAVE NO IDEA WHAT YOU'RE TALKING ABOUT.
OF COURSE YOU DON'T. THAT'S THE WAY THEY LIKE TO KEEP YOU.
DUMB AND RICH AND DRUNK. NOT ASKING ANY QUESTIONS. JUST NUMBING YOURSELF AND PLAYING ALONG WITH THEIR LITTLE GAME.
AND WHAT A GREAT GAME IT IS.
THIS CHANGES NOTHING. THOSE PEOPLE STILL DIDN'T NEED TO DIE. YOU WANTED TO TALK? GO ON THIS FIELD TRIP? FINE. THEY DIDN'T NEED TO DIE.
YOU'RE-- YOU'RE...

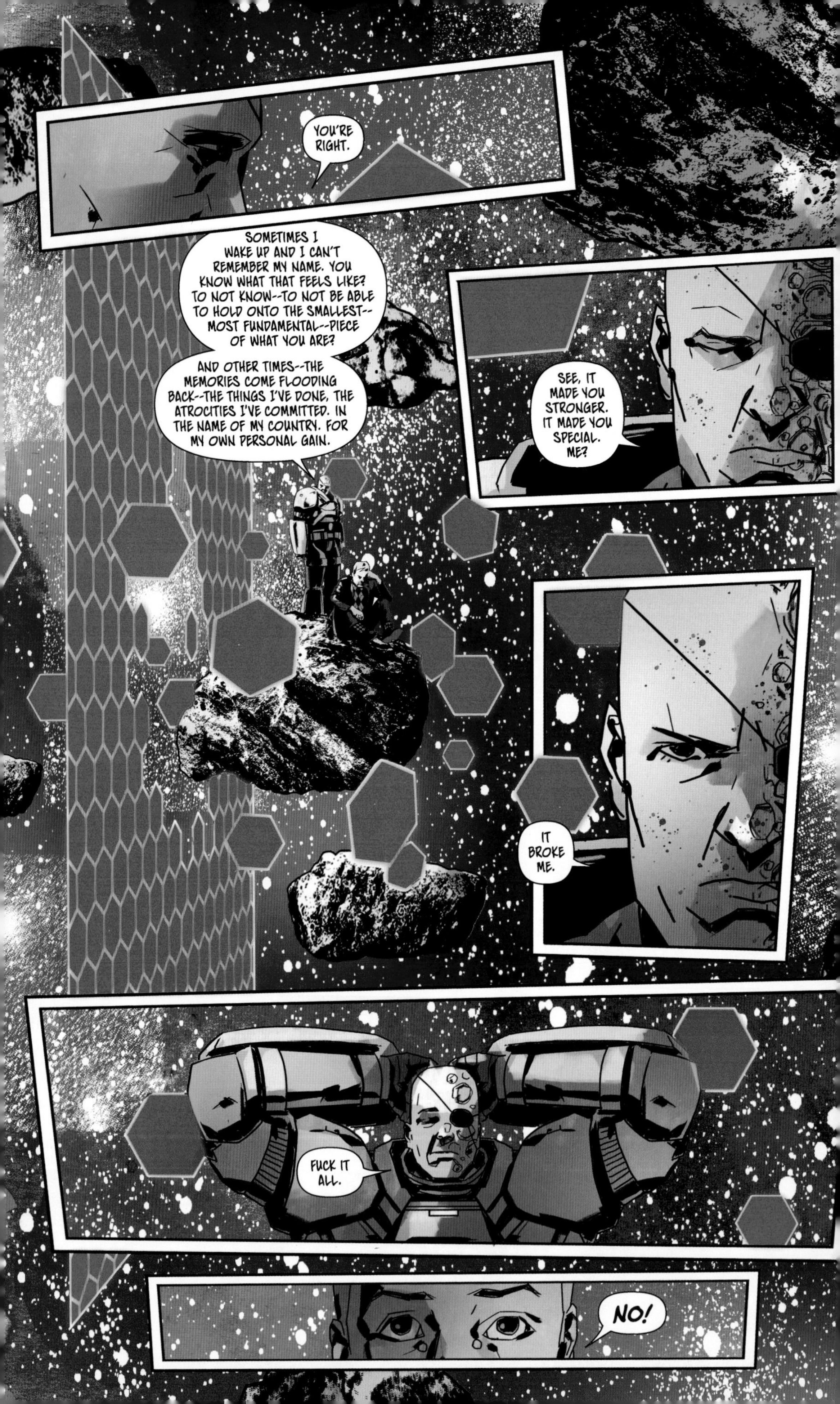
YOU'RE RIGHT.
SOMETIMES I WAKE UP AND I CAN'T REMEMBER MY NAME. YOU KNOW WHAT THAT FEELS LIKE? TO NOT KNOW--TO NOT BE ABLE TO HOLD ONTO THE SMALLEST--MOST FUNDAMENTAL--PIECE OF WHAT YOU ARE?
AND OTHER TIMES--THE MEMORIES COME FLOODING BACK--THE THINGS I'VE DONE, THE ATROCITIES I'VE COMMITTED. IN THE NAME OF MY COUNTRY. FOR MY OWN PERSONAL GAIN.
SEE, IT MADE YOU STRONGER. IT MADE YOU SPECIAL. ME?
IT BROKE ME.
FUCK IT ALL.
NO!

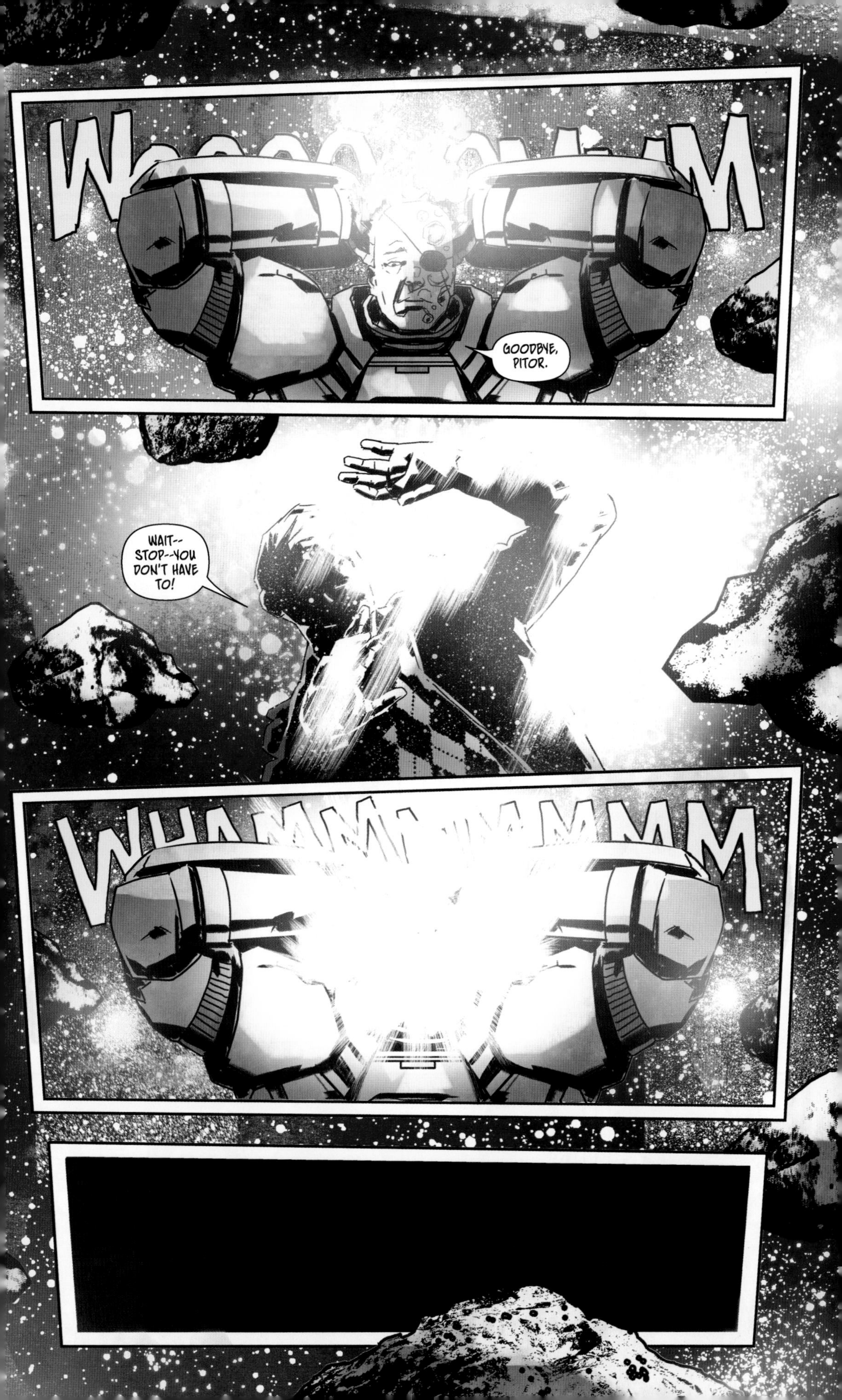
GOODBYE, PITOR.
WAIT-- STOP--YOU DON'T HAVE TO!

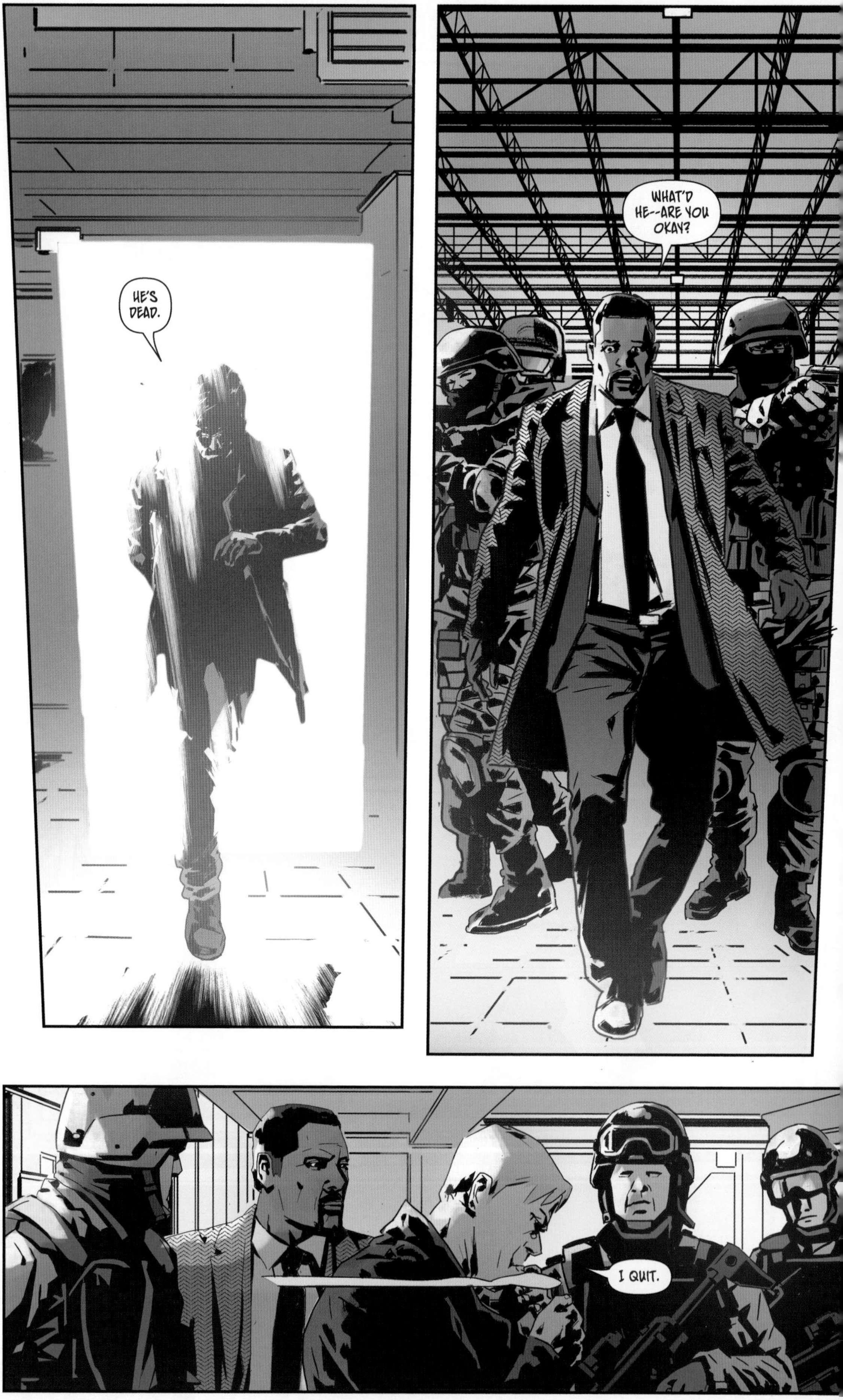
HE'S DEAD.
WHAT'D HE--ARE YOU OKAY?
I QUIT.

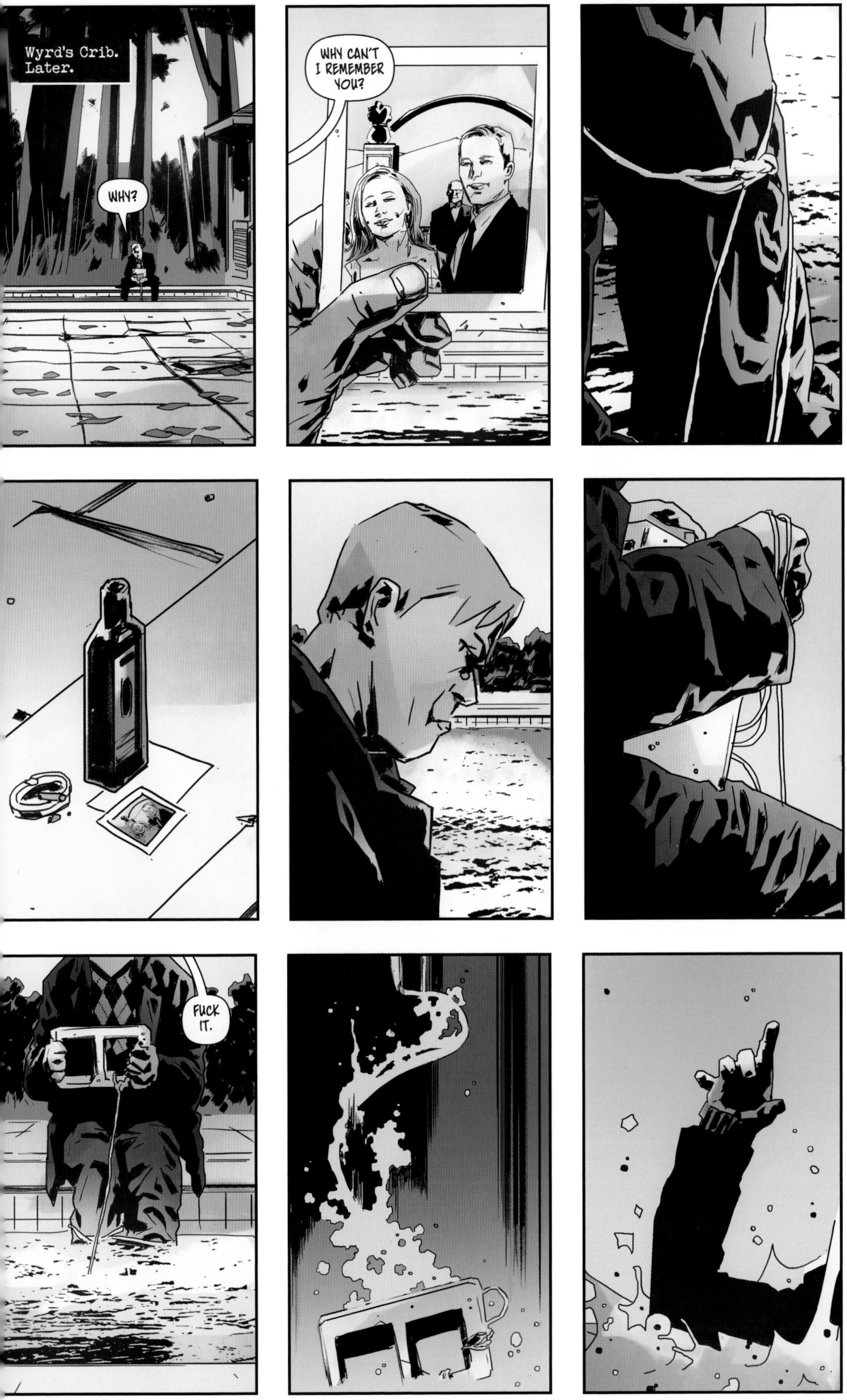
Wyrd's Crib.
Later.
WHY?
WHY CAN'T I REMEMBER YOU?
FUCK IT.

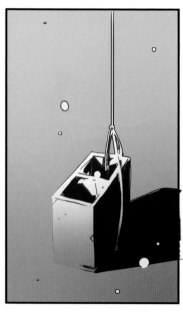
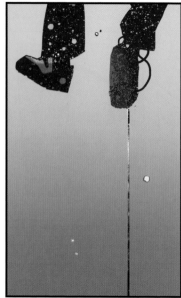
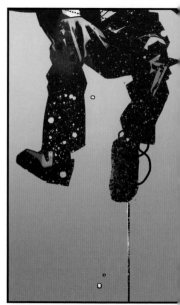

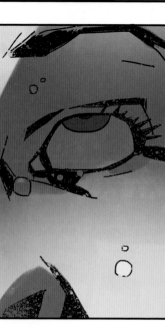

"To unpathed waters,
undreamed shores."

-William
Shakespeare

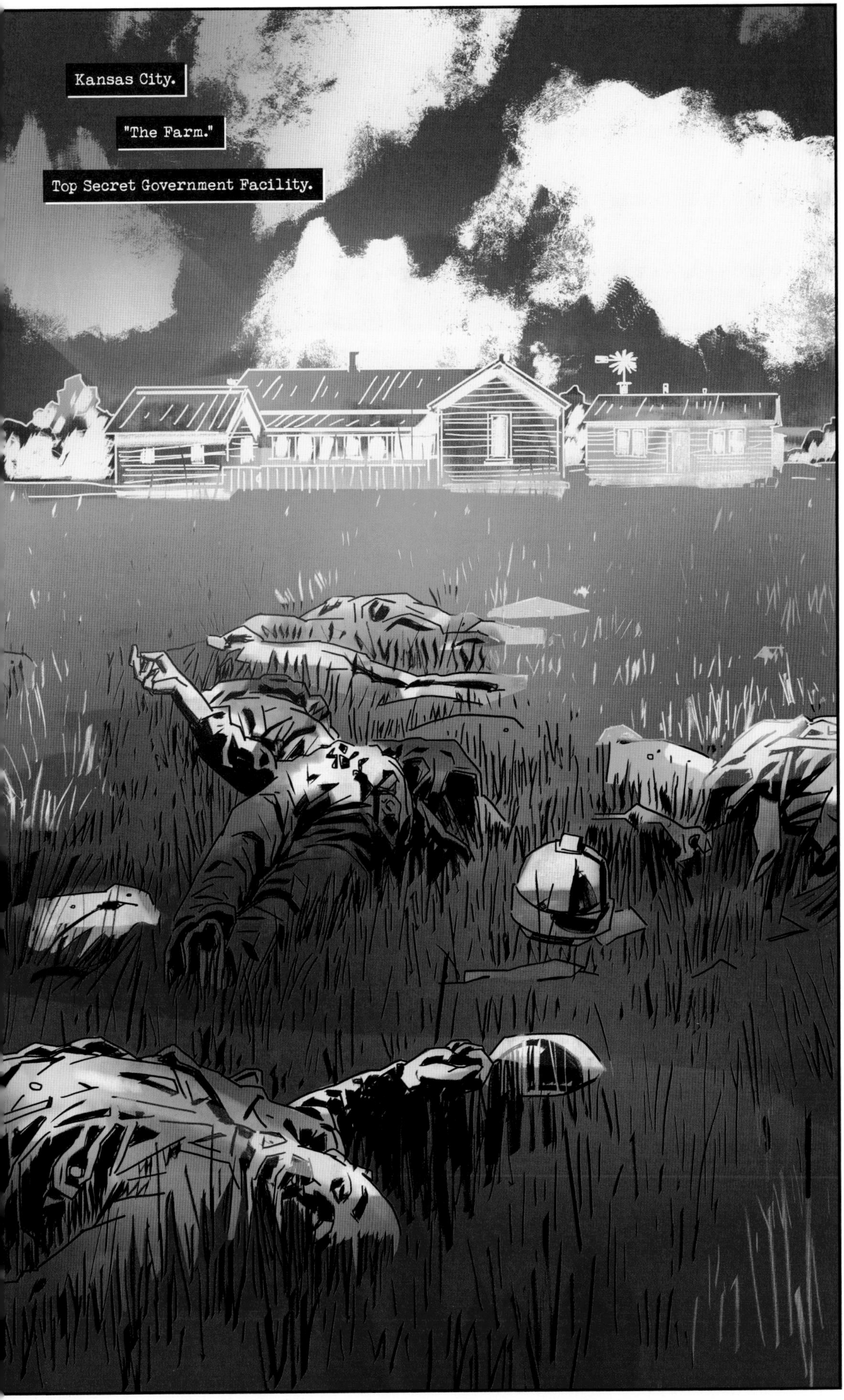
Kansas City.
"The Farm."
Top Secret Government Facility.

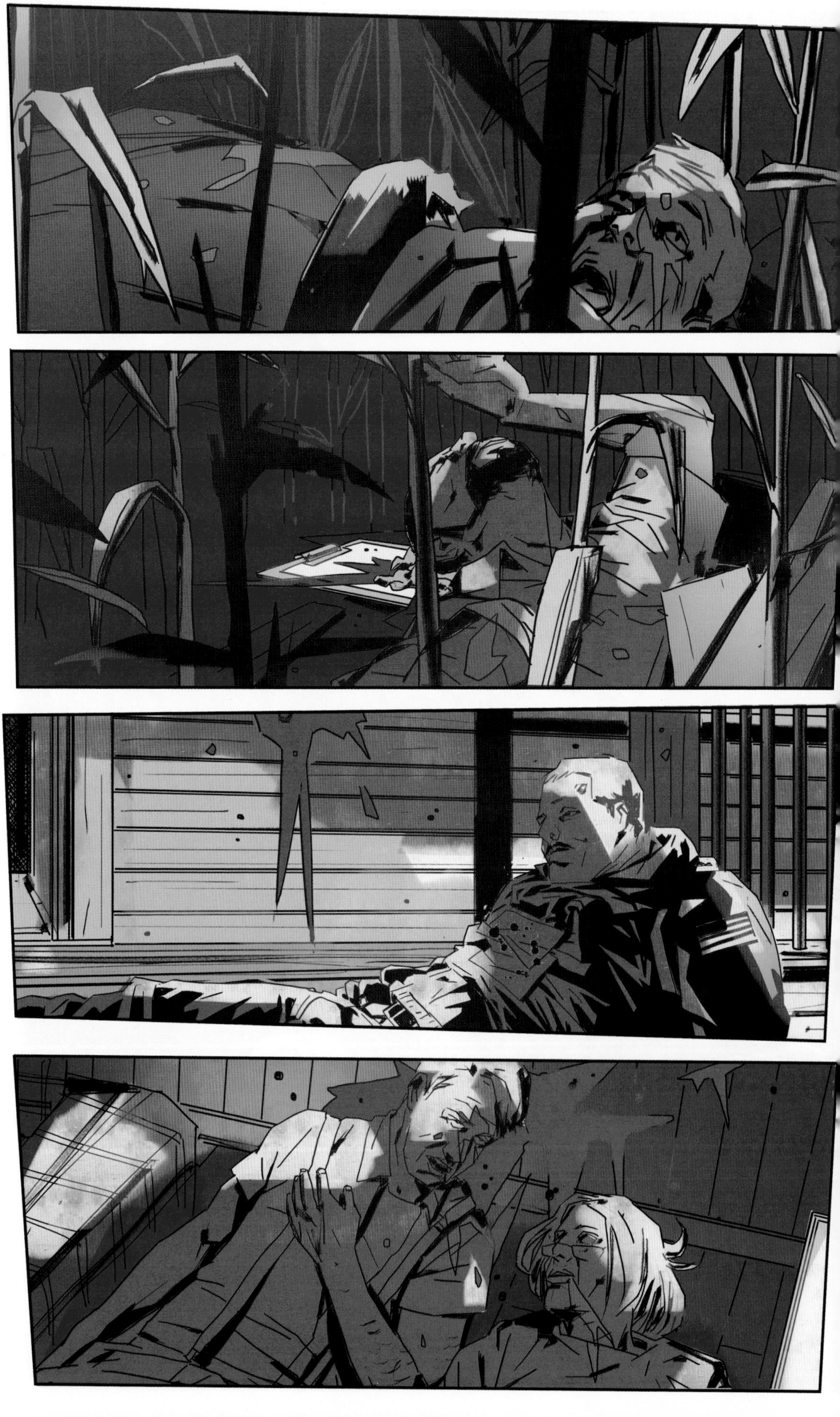

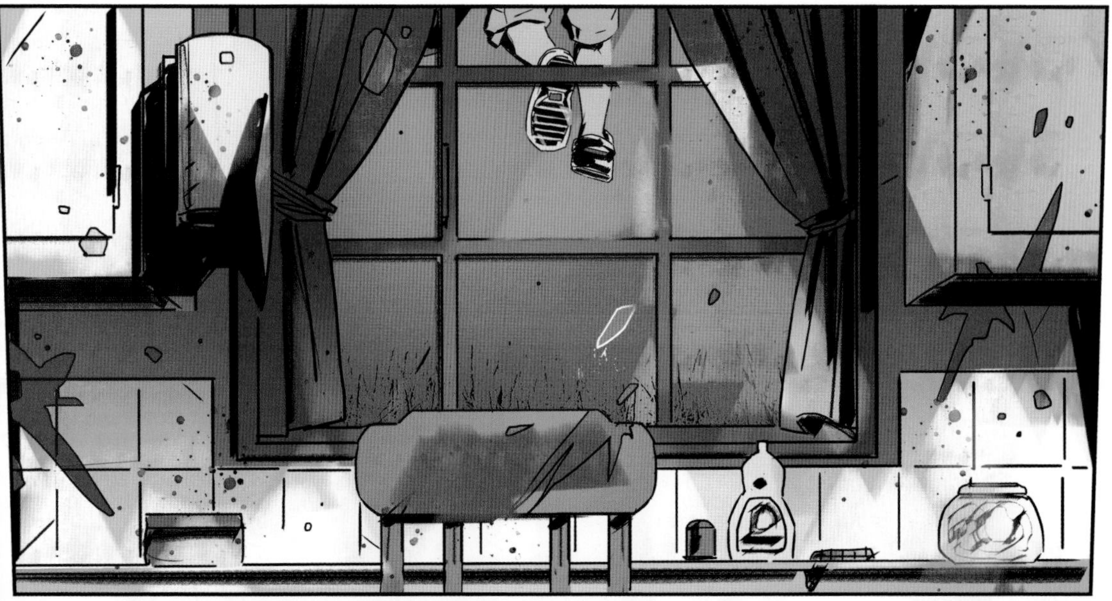
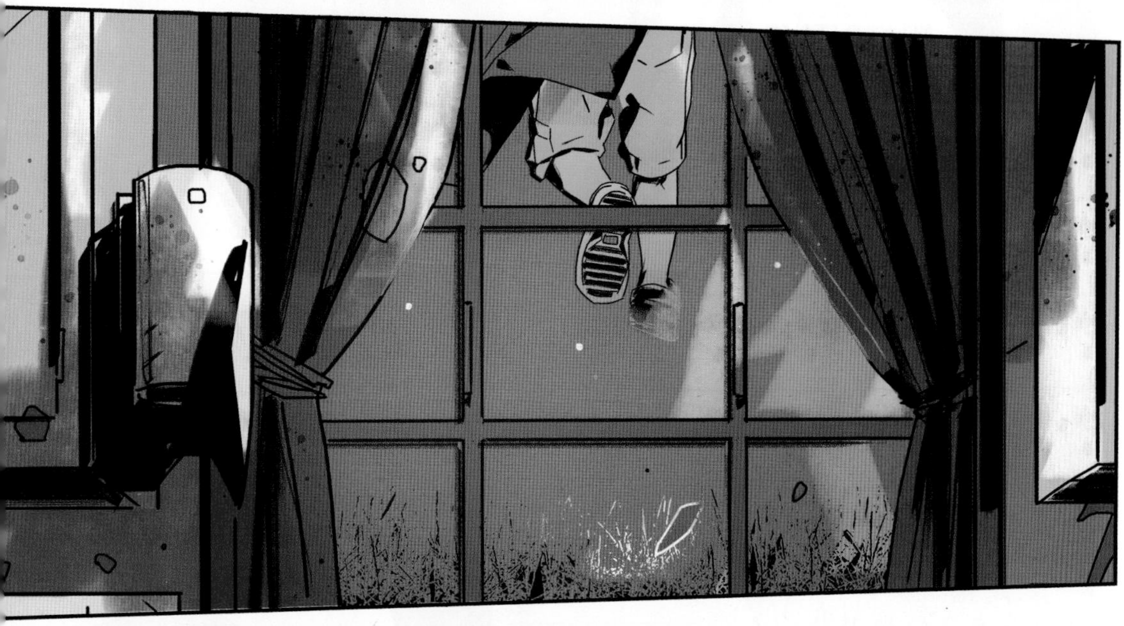
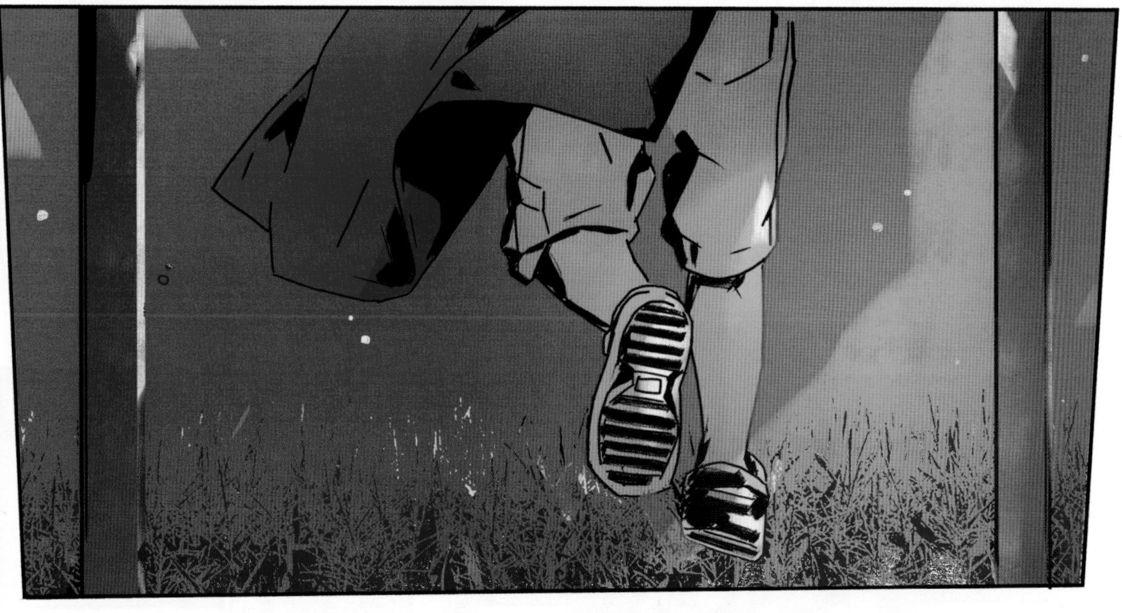

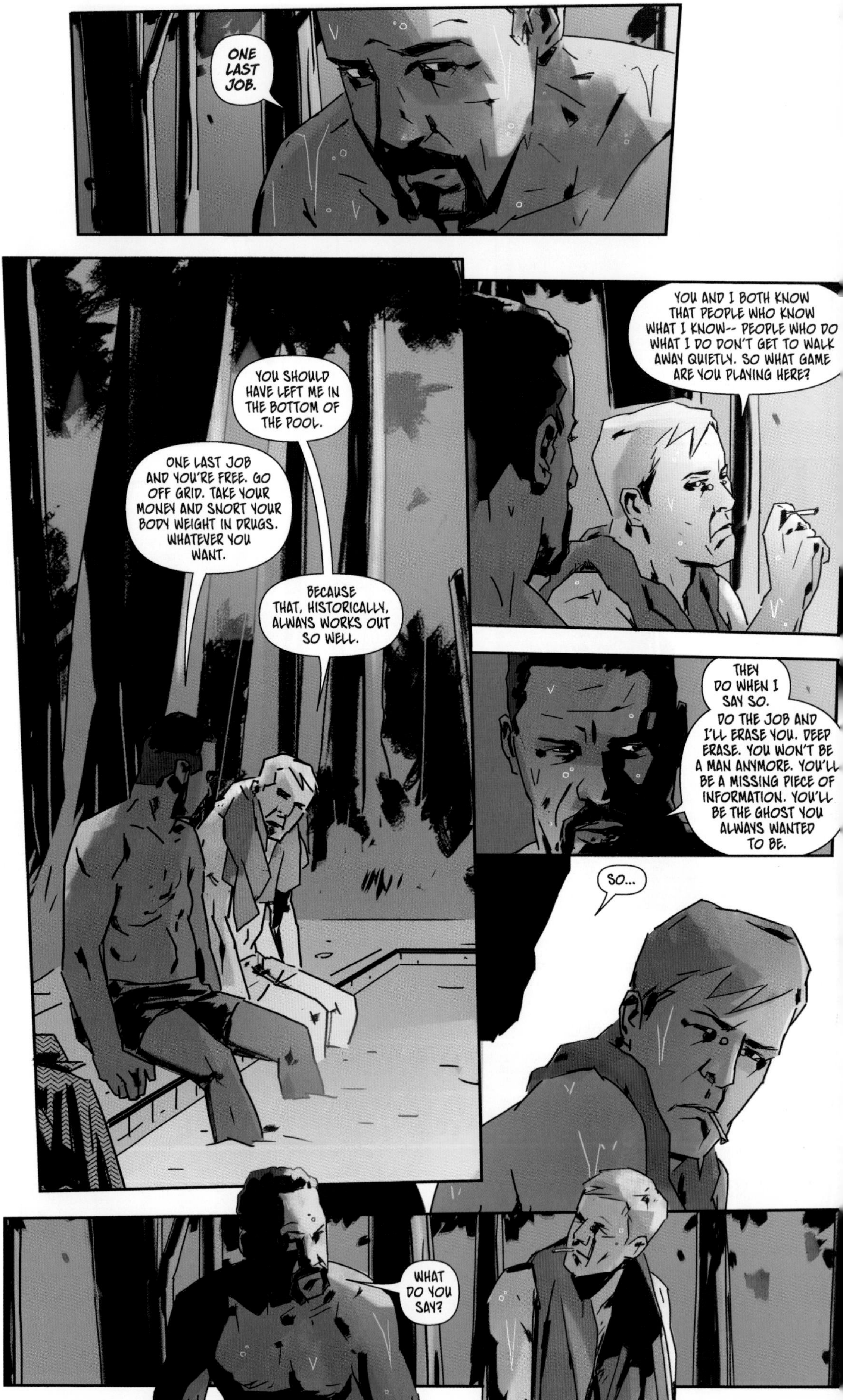
ONE LAST JOB.
YOU SHOULD HAVE LEFT ME IN THE BOTTOM OF THE POOL.
ONE LAST JOB AND YOU'RE FREE. GO OFF GRID. TAKE YOUR MONEY AND SNORT YOUR BODY WEIGHT IN DRUGS. WHATEVER YOU WANT.
BECAUSE THAT, HISTORICALLY, ALWAYS WORKS OUT SO WELL.
YOU AND I BOTH KNOW THAT PEOPLE WHO KNOW WHAT I KNOW-- PEOPLE WHO DO WHAT I DO DON'T GET TO WALK AWAY QUIETLY. SO WHAT GAME ARE YOU PLAYING HERE?
THEY DO WHEN I SAY SO.
DO THE JOB AND I'LL ERASE YOU. DEEP ERASE. YOU WON'T BE A MAN ANYMORE. YOU'LL BE A MISSING PIECE OF INFORMATION. YOU'LL BE THE GHOST YOU ALWAYS WANTED TO BE.
SO...
WHAT DO YOU SAY?

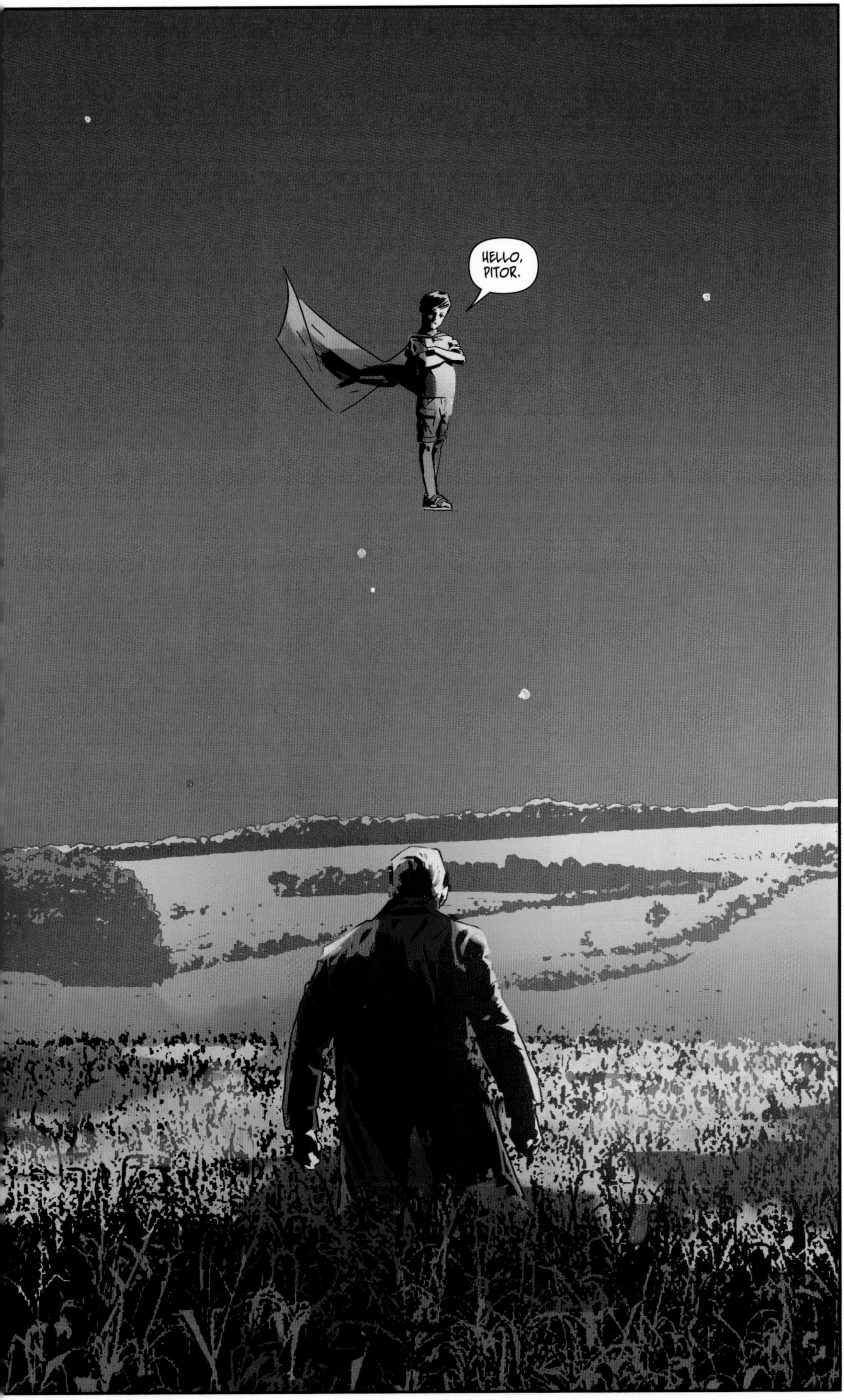
HELLO, PITOR.

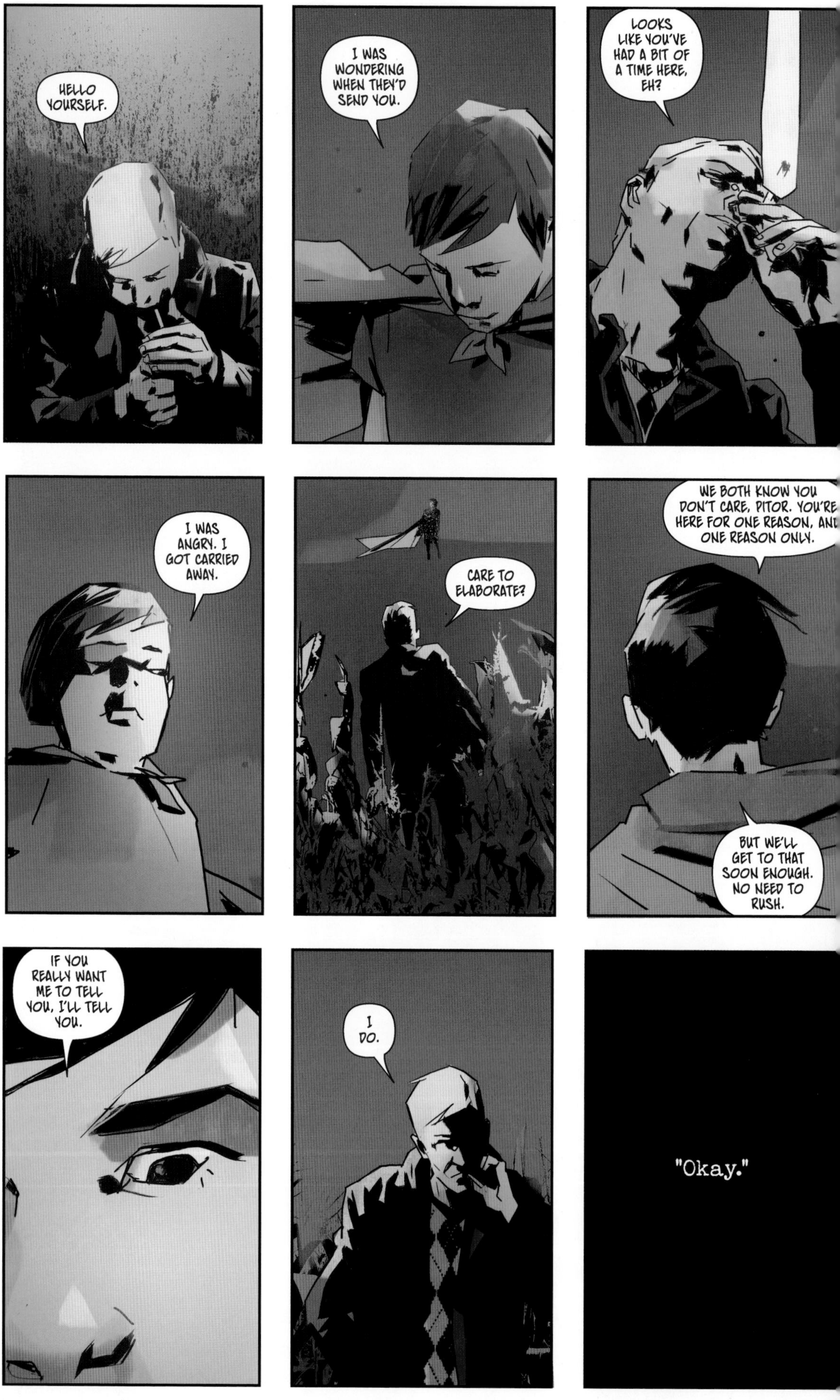
HELLO YOURSELF.
I WAS WONDERING WHEN THEY'D SEND YOU.
LOOKS LIKE YOU'VE HAD A BIT OF A TIME HERE, EH?
I WAS ANGRY. I GOT CARRIED AWAY.
CARE TO ELABORATE?
WE BOTH KNOW YOU DON'T CARE, PITOR. YOU'RE HERE FOR ONE REASON, AND ONE REASON ONLY.
BUT WE'LL GET TO THAT SOON ENOUGH. NO NEED TO RUSH.
IF YOU REALLY WANT ME TO TELL YOU, I'LL TELL YOU.
I DO.
"Okay."

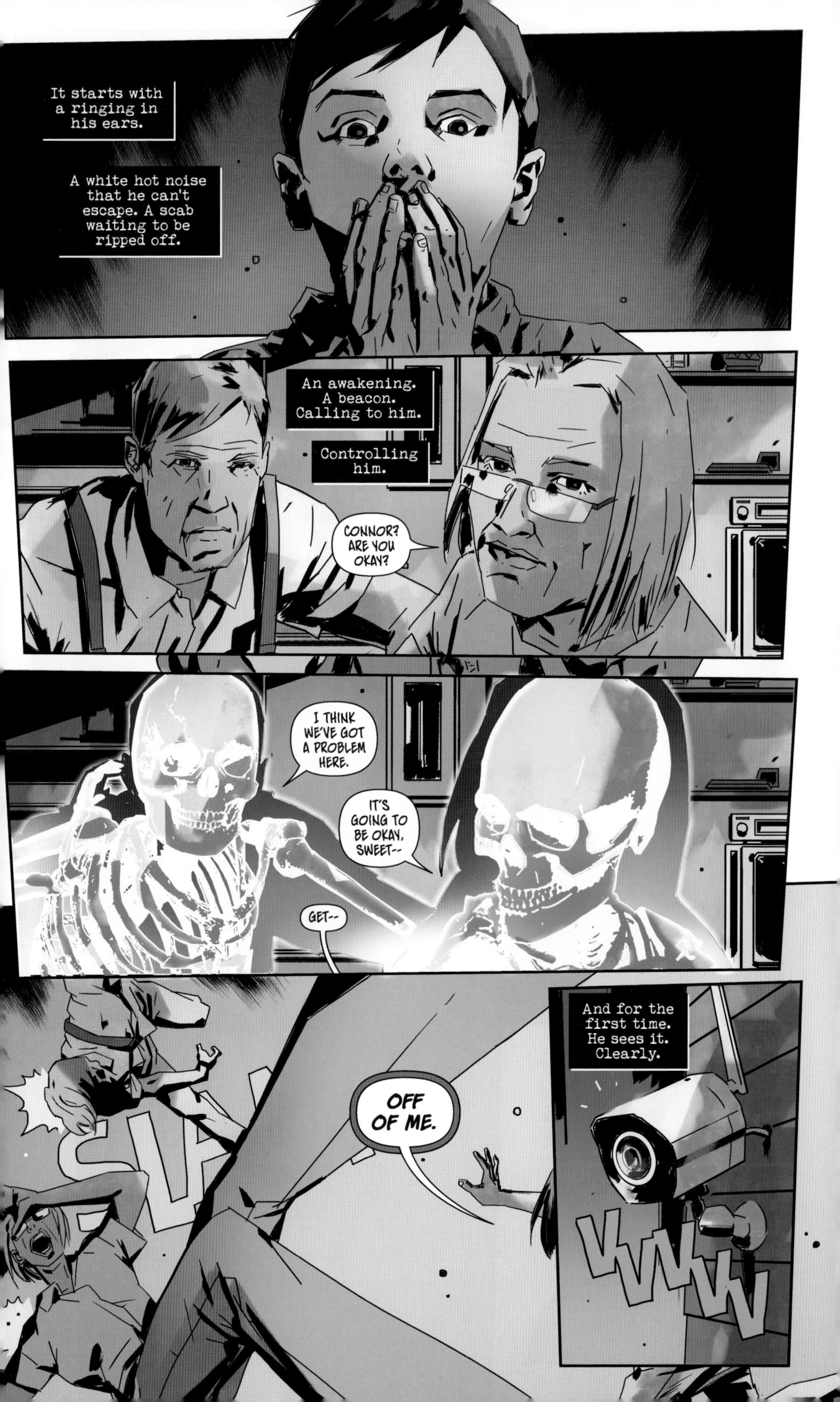
It starts with a ringing in his ears.
A white hot noise that he can't escape. A scab waiting to be ripped off.
An awakening. A beacon. Calling to him.
Controlling him.
CONNOR? ARE YOU OKAY?
I THINK WE'VE GOT A PROBLEM HERE.
IT'S GOING TO BE OKAY, SWEET--
GET--
OFF OF ME.
And for the first time. He sees it. Clearly.
VVVVV

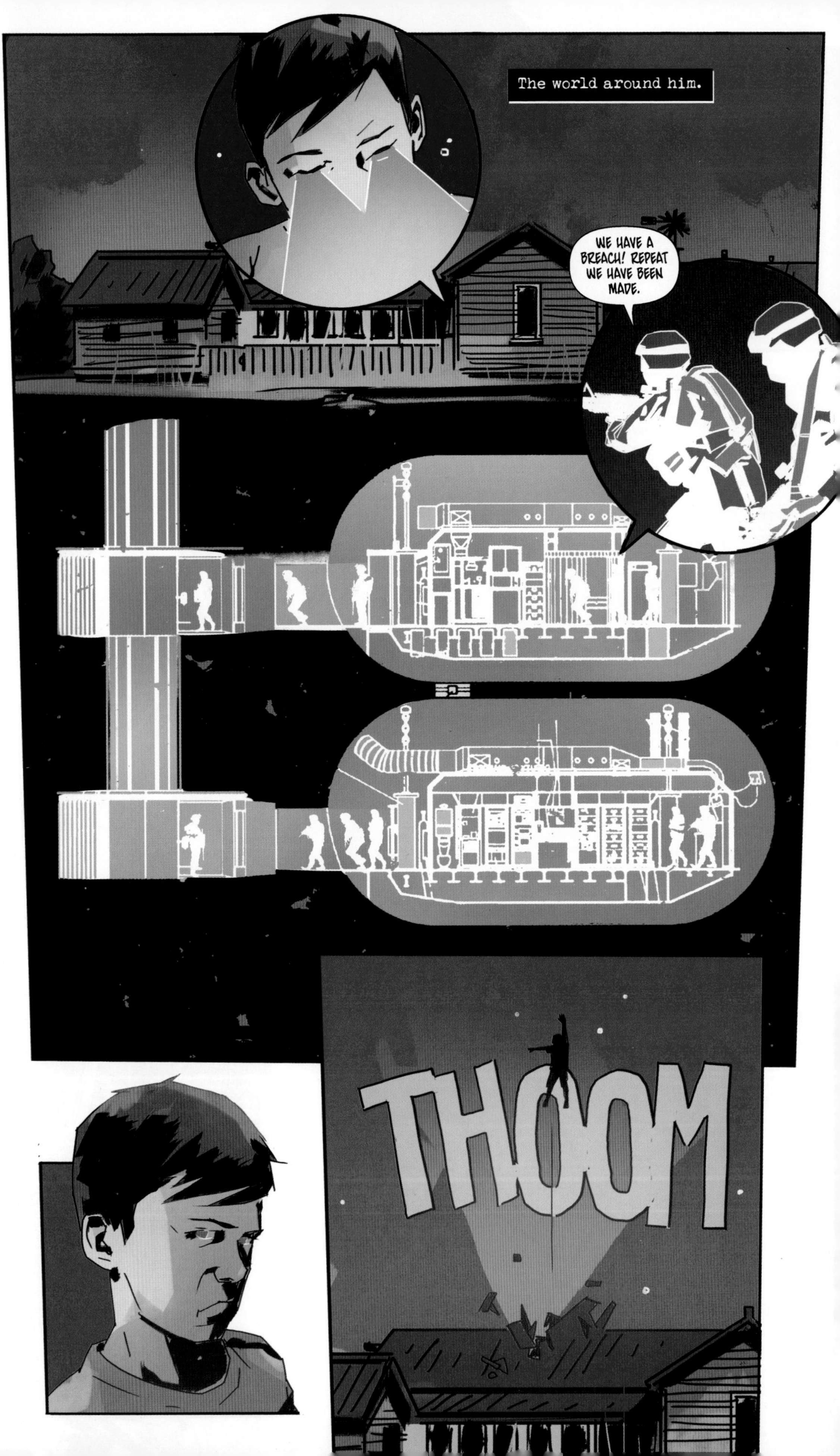

The world around him.
WE HAVE A BREACH! REPEAT WE HAVE BEEN MADE.
THOOM

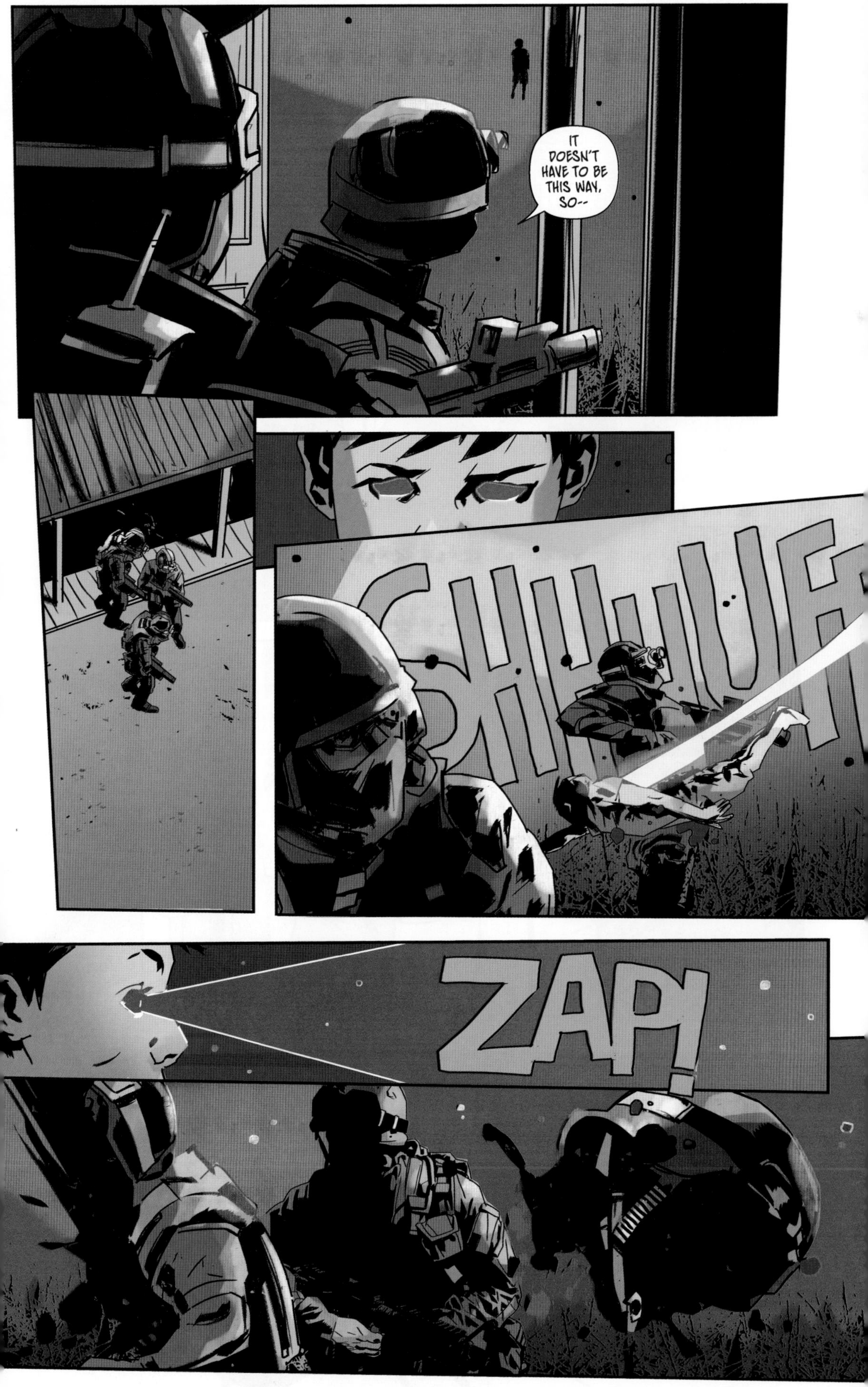
IT DOESN'T HAVE TO BE THIS WAY, SO--
CHHHUFF
ZAP!

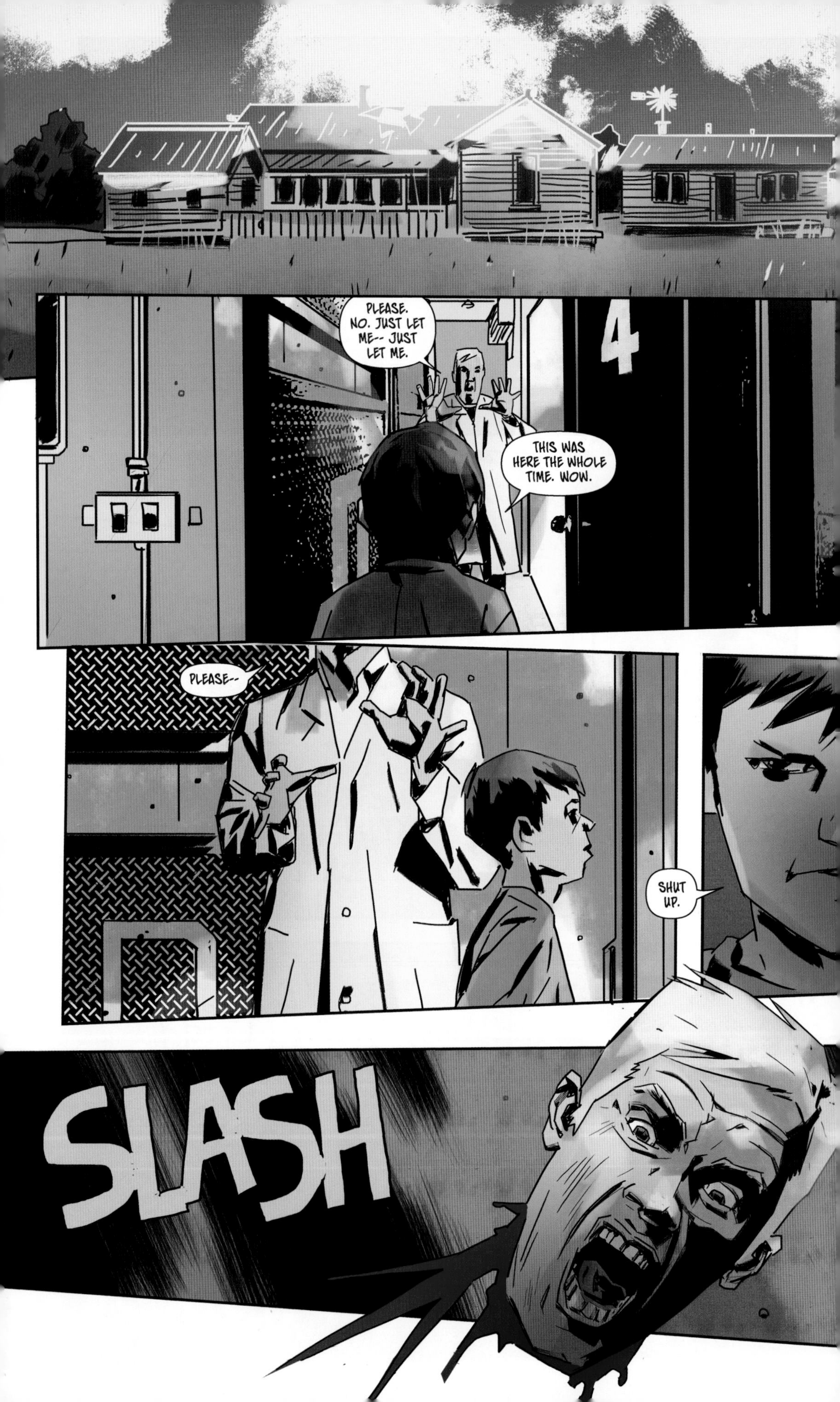
4
PLEASE. NO. JUST LET ME-- JUST LET ME.
THIS WAS HERE THE WHOLE TIME. WOW.
PLEASE--
SHUT UP.
SLASH

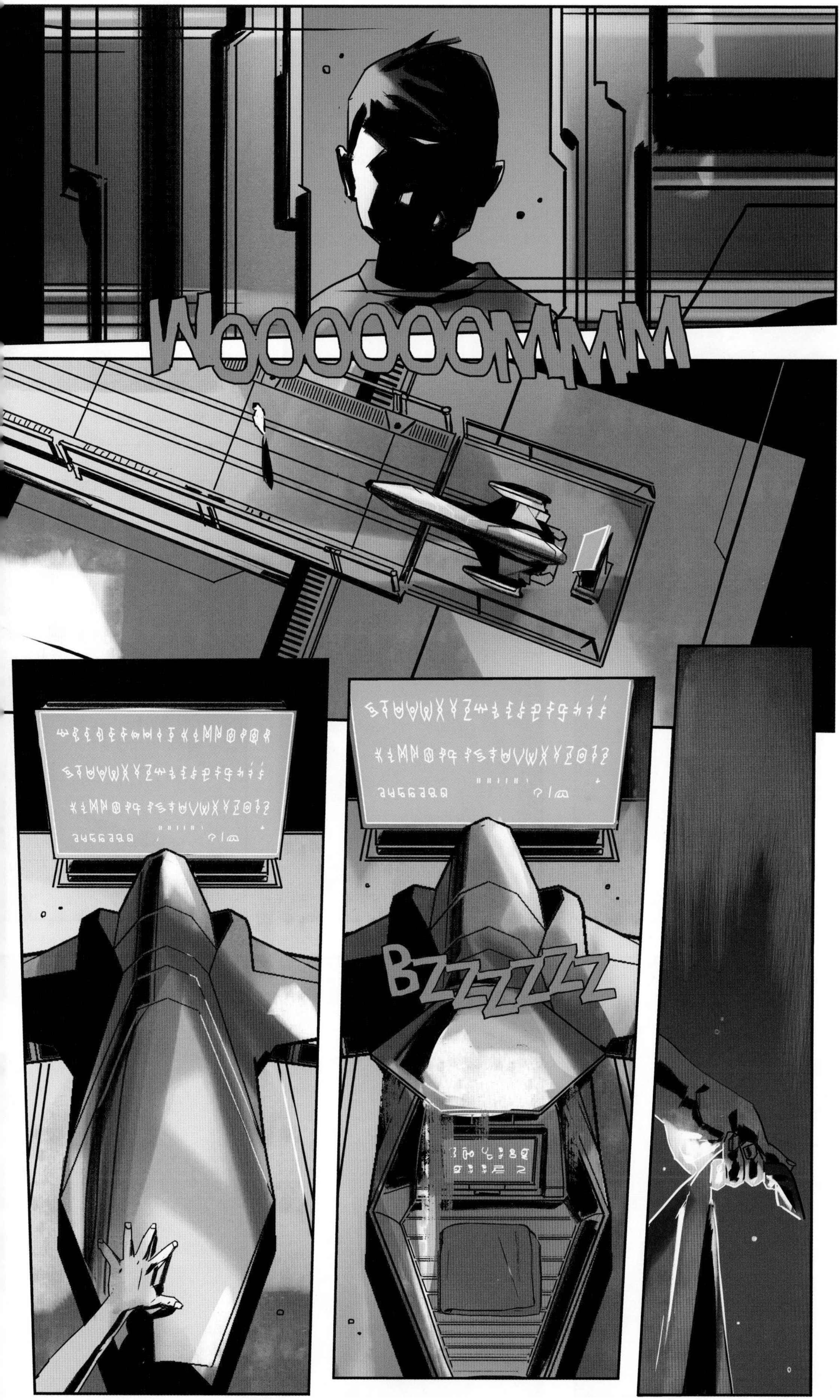
WOOOOOOMMMM
BZZZZZZ

WHEN I TOUCHED IT, IT CHANGED ME. I UNDERSTAND WHAT I AM NOW.

WHAT'S THAT, A KID IN A CAPE?

I'D SUGGEST YOU WATCH YOUR TONE, PITOR.

THIS ISN'T A CAPE. THIS IS A *LIVING, BREATHING* PIECE OF TECHNOLOGY. THIS IS THE SMARTEST BIOLOGICAL ORGANISM ON THIS *LITTLE PEBBLE* YOU A CALL A PLANET.

OH. I THINK I'M STARTING TO LIKE YOU. YOU KNOW THAT?

I BITE. WHAT DID IT SHOW YOU?

IT SHOWED ME EVERYTHING. THE FUTURE. THE PAST. EVERYTHING IN BETWEEN.

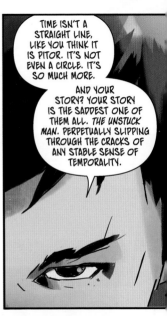

TIME ISN'T A STRAIGHT LINE, LIKE YOU THINK IT IS PITOR. IT'S NOT EVEN A CIRCLE. IT'S SO MUCH MORE.

AND YOUR STORY? YOUR STORY IS THE SADDEST ONE OF THEM ALL. *THE UNSTUCK MAN.* PERPETUALLY SLIPPING THROUGH THE CRACKS OF ANY STABLE SENSE OF TEMPORALITY.

ENOUGH. LET'S GET THIS OVER WITH.

OH, PITOR, YOU STILL THINK YOU WERE SENT HERE TO KILL ME?

YOU WEREN'T.

YOU WERE SENT TO DIE.

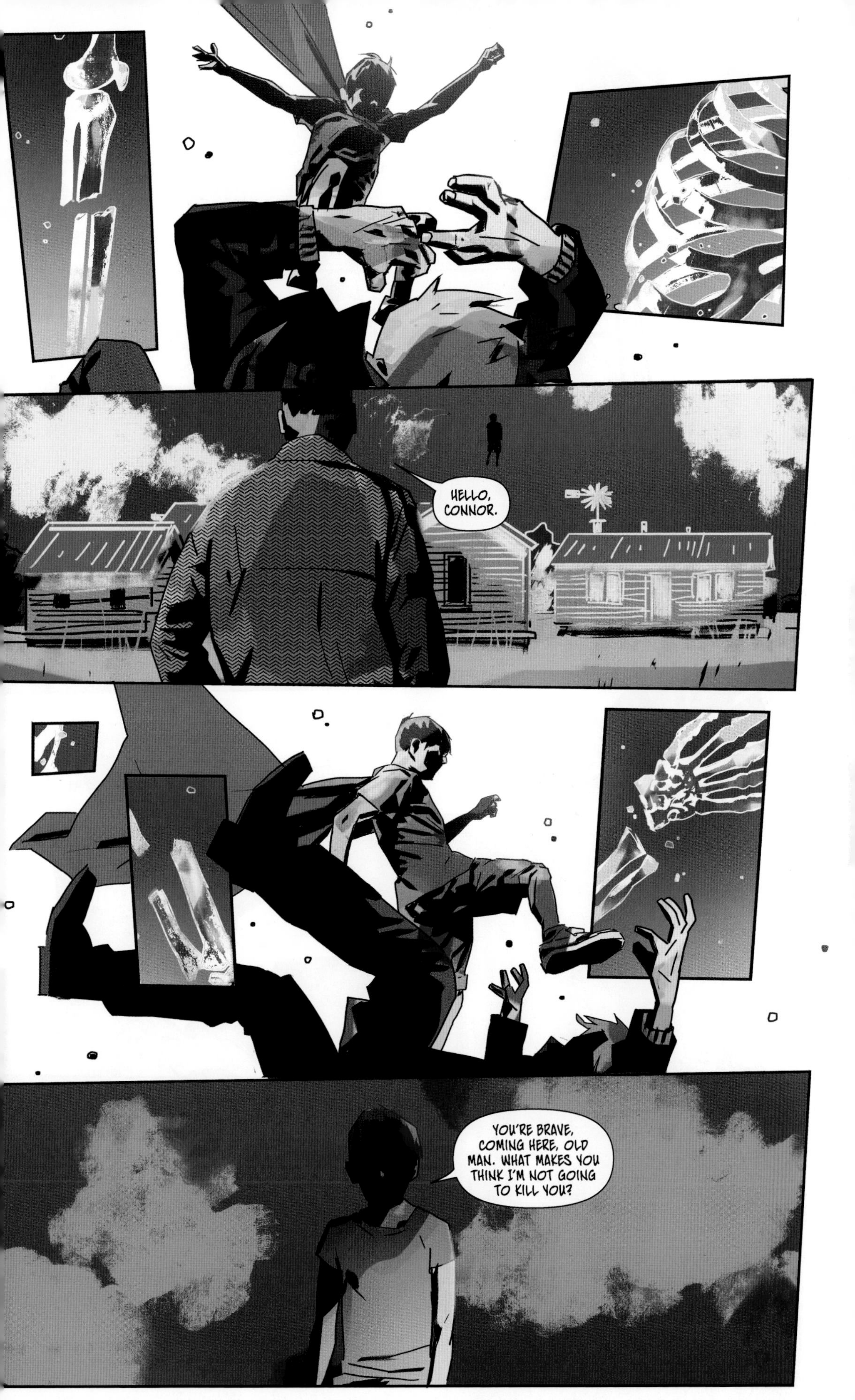
HELLO, CONNOR.
YOU'RE BRAVE, COMING HERE, OLD MAN. WHAT MAKES YOU THINK I'M NOT GOING TO KILL YOU?

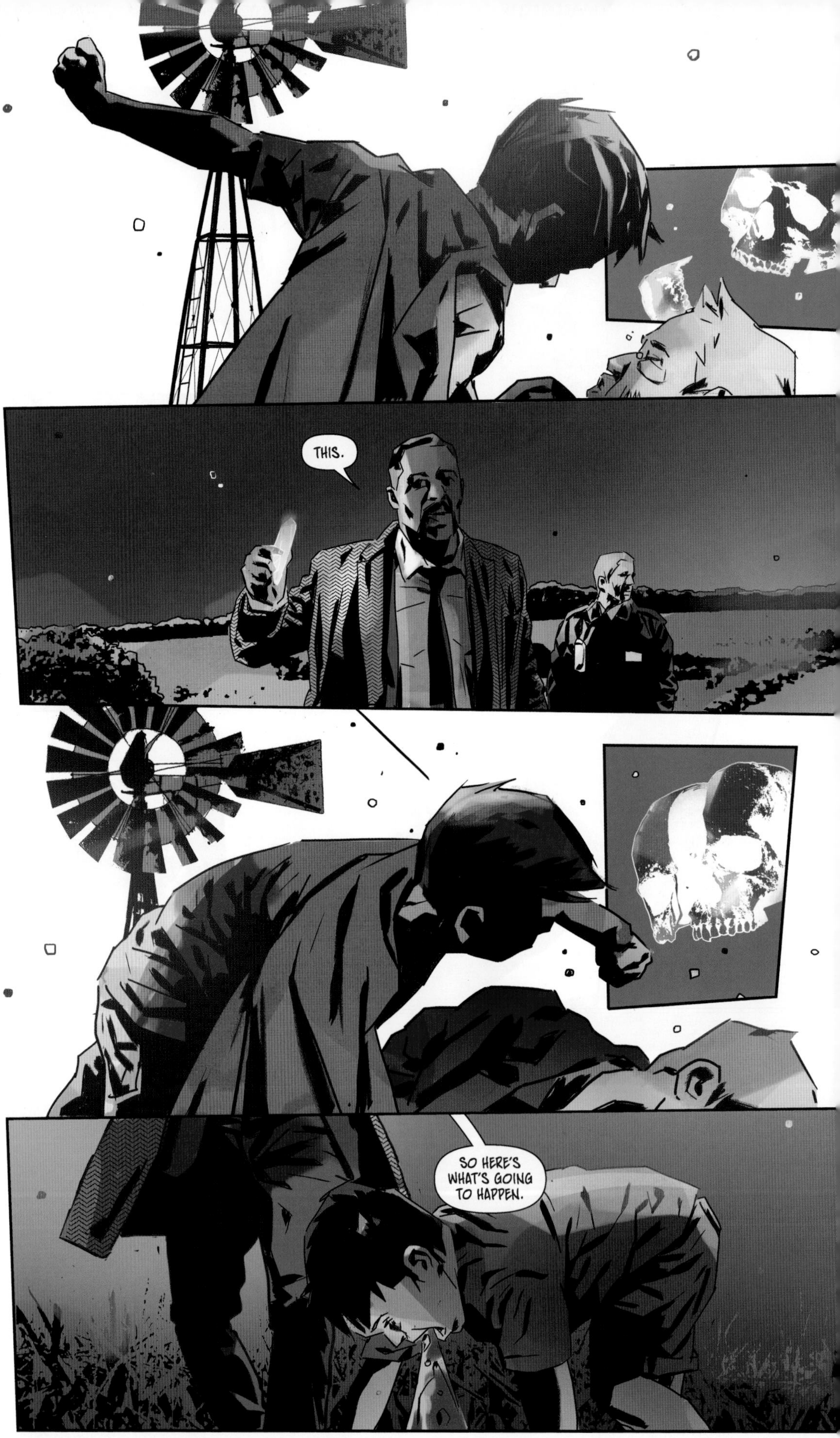
THIS.
SO HERE'S WHAT'S GOING TO HAPPEN.

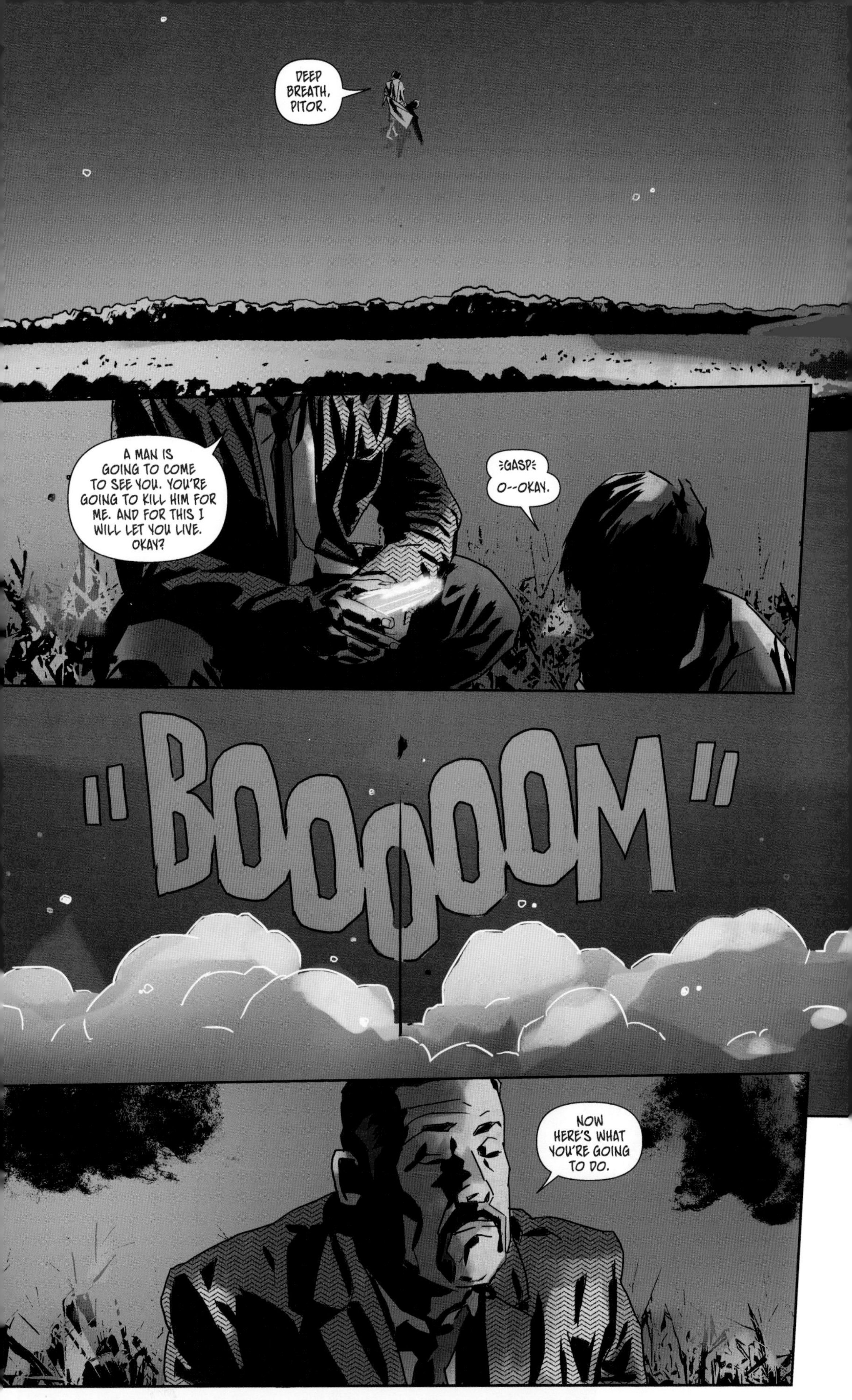

DEEP BREATH, PITOR.
A MAN IS GOING TO COME TO SEE YOU. YOU'RE GOING TO KILL HIM FOR ME. AND FOR THIS I WILL LET YOU LIVE. OKAY?
GASP
O--OKAY.
"BOOOOOM"
NOW HERE'S WHAT YOU'RE GOING TO DO.

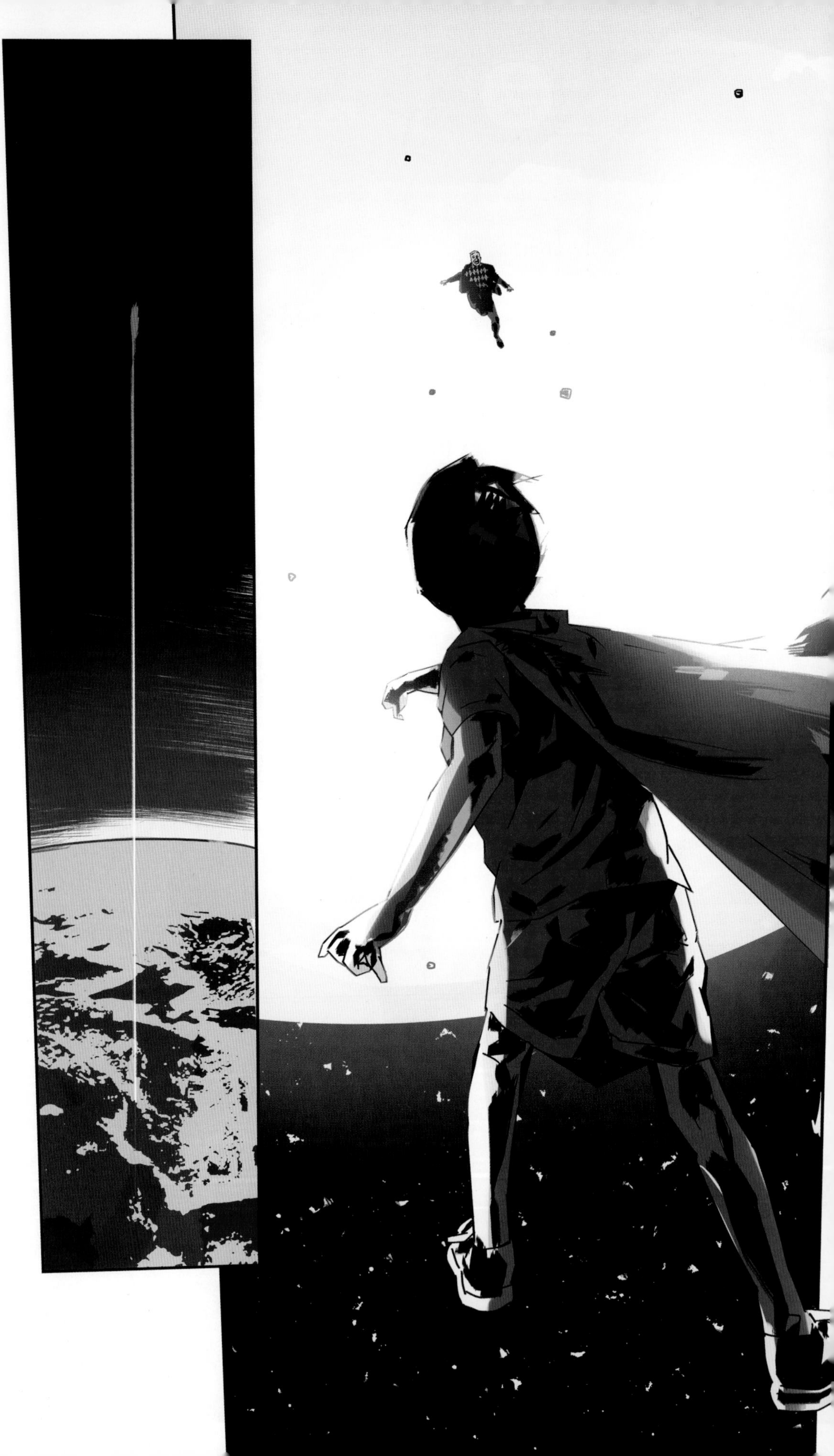

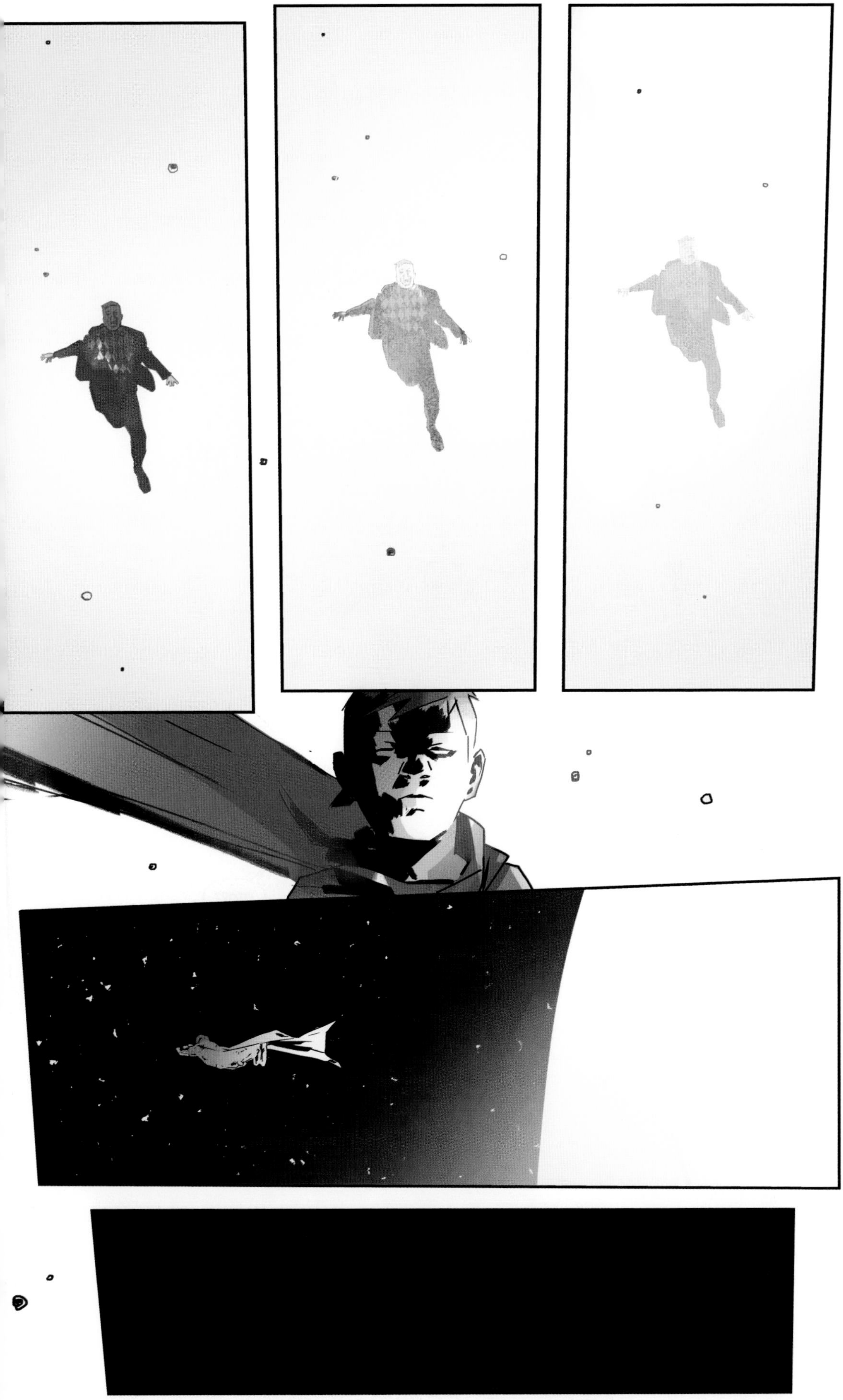

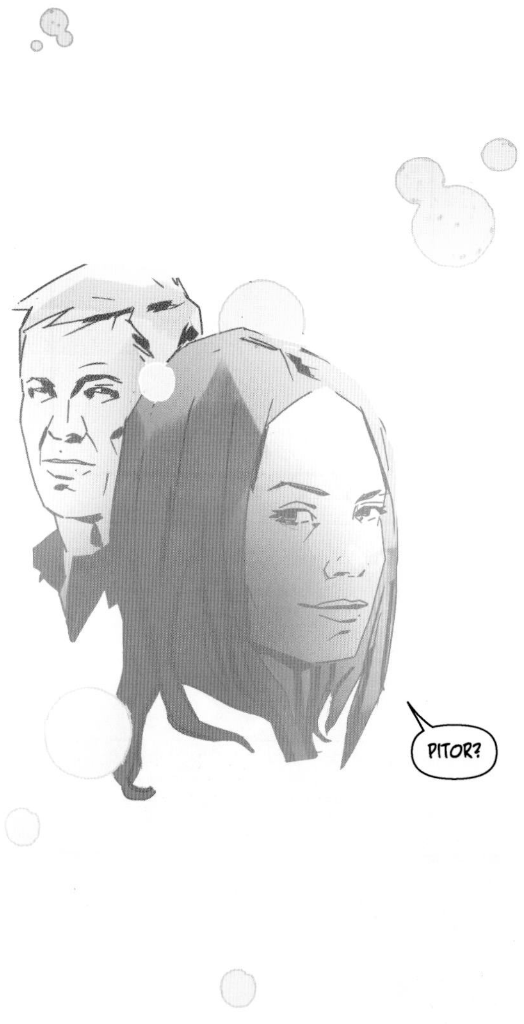
PITOR?

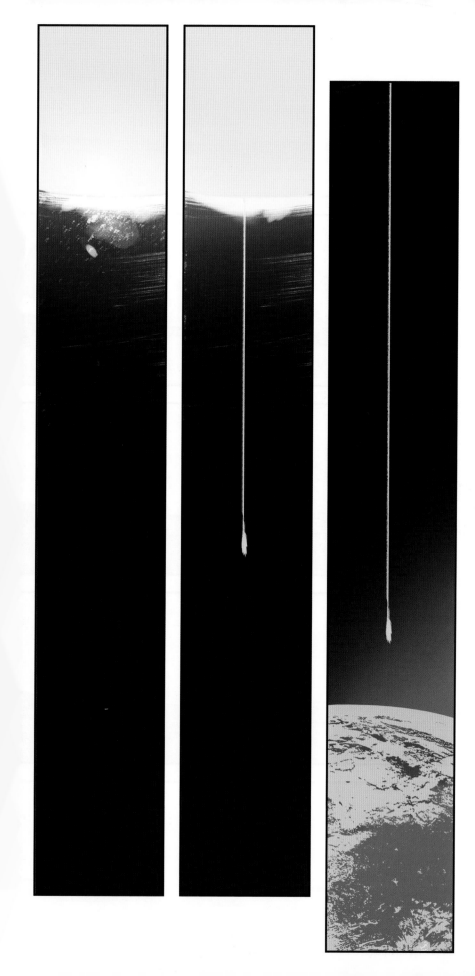

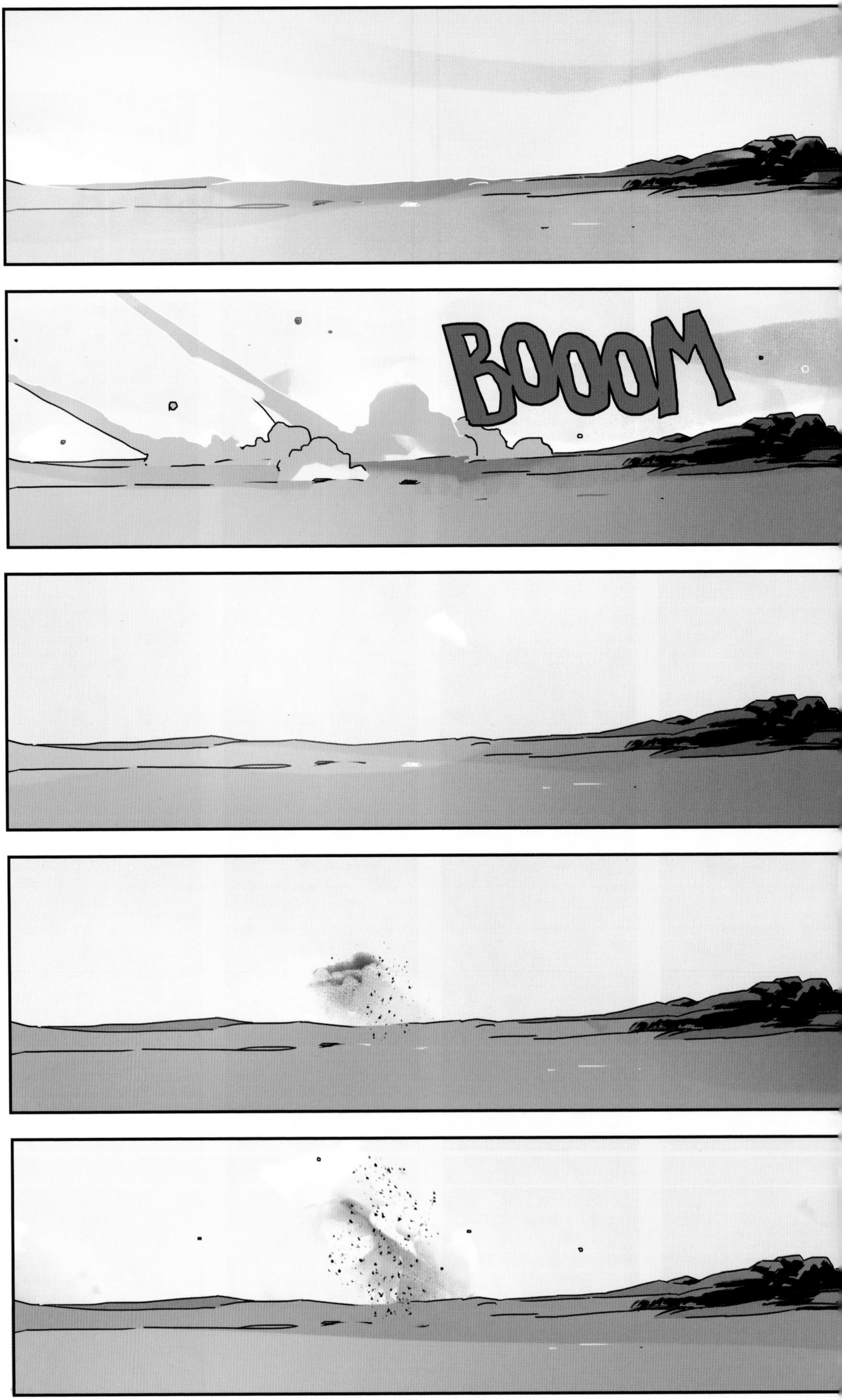
BOOOM

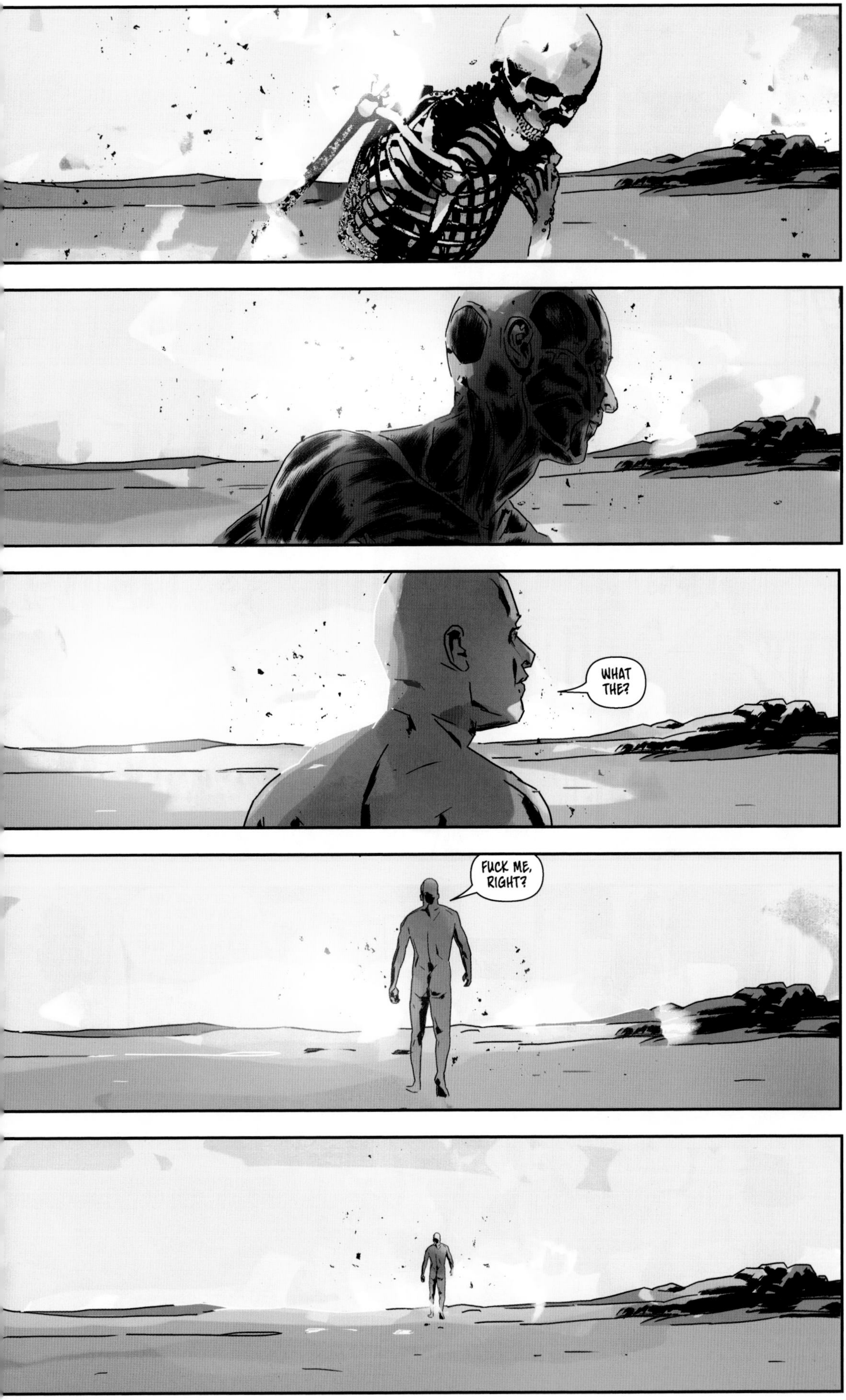
WHAT THE?
FUCK ME, RIGHT?

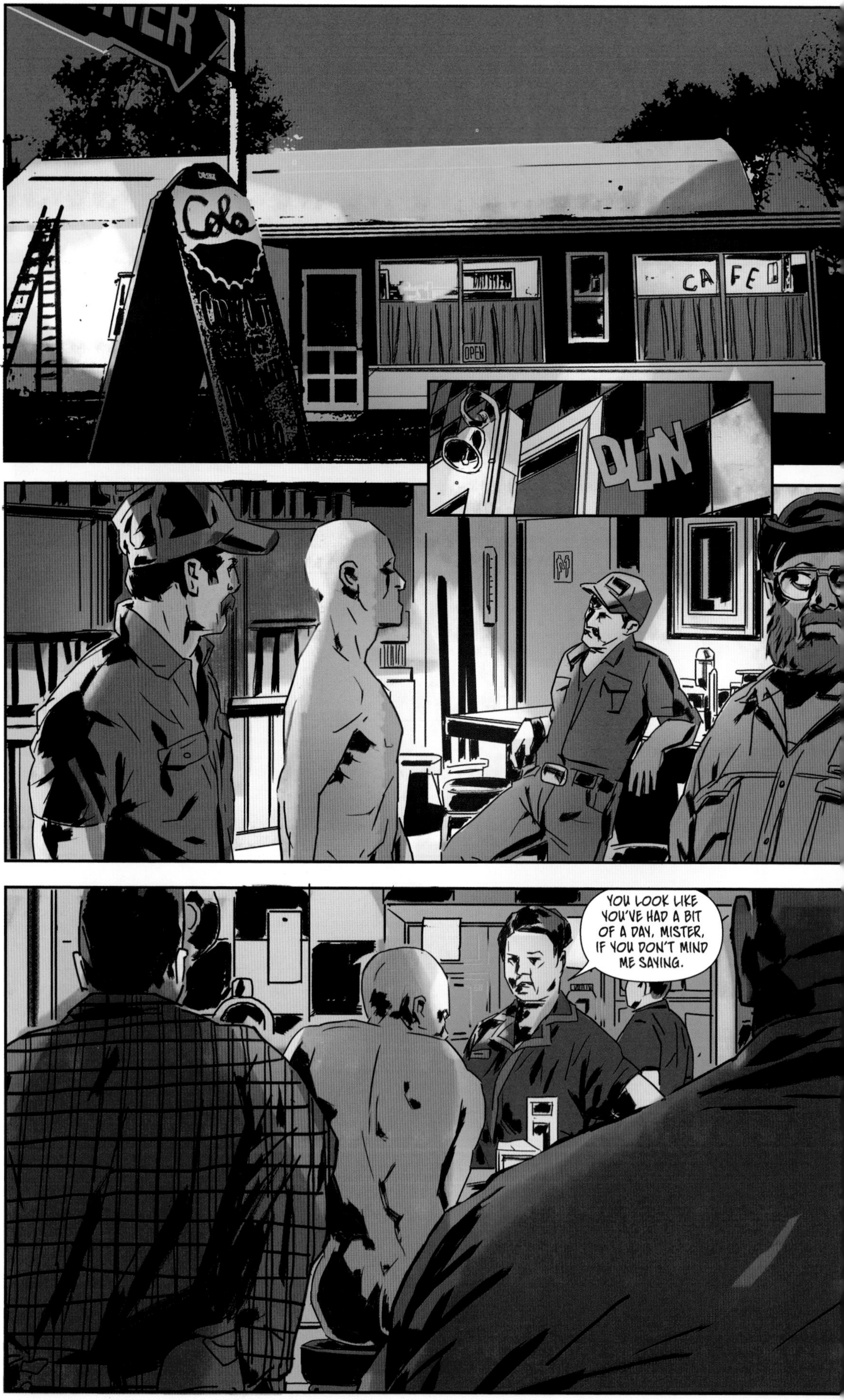

NER
Cola
CAFE
OPEN
DUN
YOU LOOK LIKE YOU'VE HAD A BIT OF A DAY, MISTER, IF YOU DON'T MIND ME SAYING.

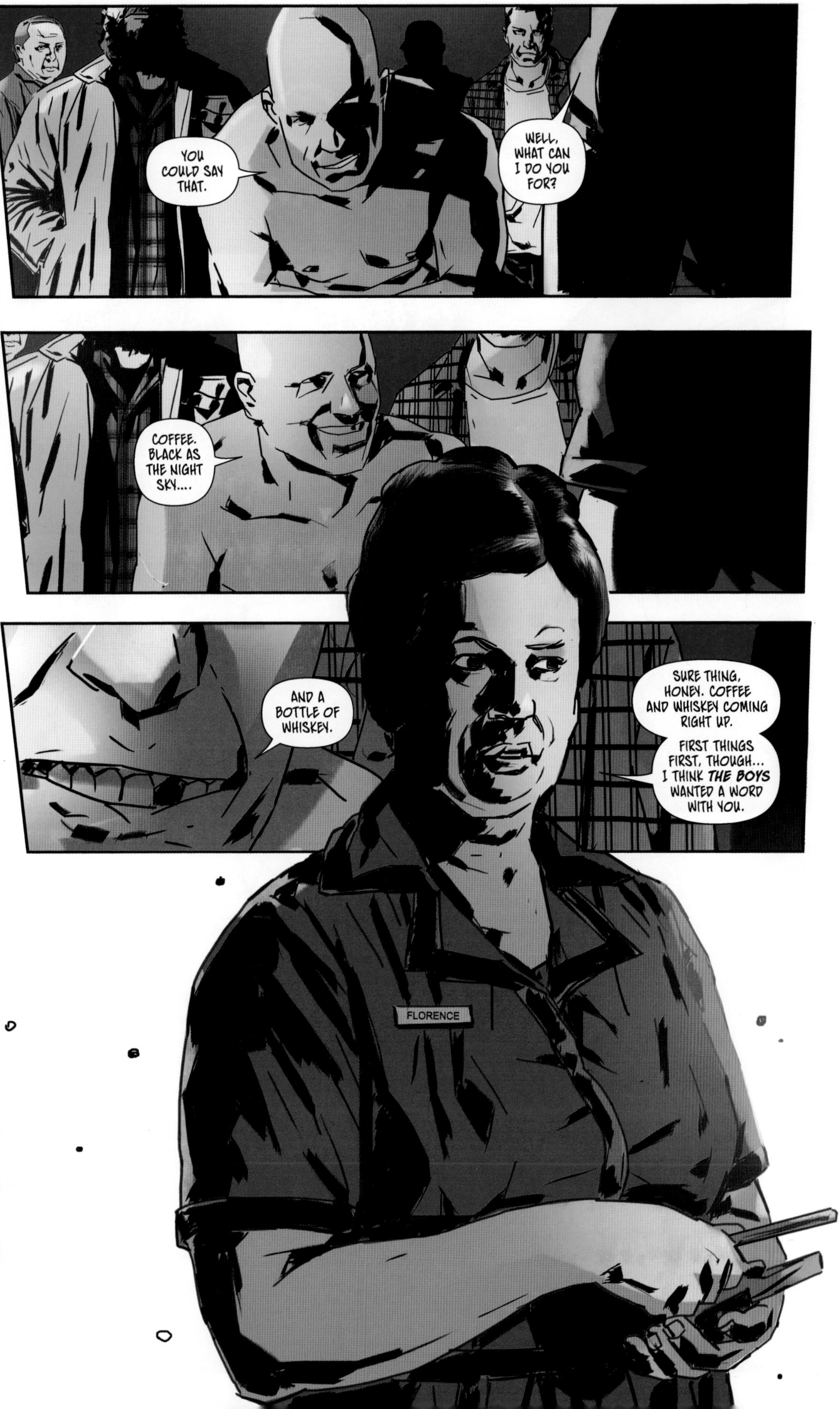
YOU COULD SAY THAT.
WELL, WHAT CAN I DO YOU FOR?
COFFEE. BLACK AS THE NIGHT SKY....
AND A BOTTLE OF WHISKEY.
SURE THING, HONEY. COFFEE AND WHISKEY COMING RIGHT UP.
FIRST THINGS FIRST, THOUGH... I THINK *THE BOYS* WANTED A WORD WITH YOU.
FLORENCE

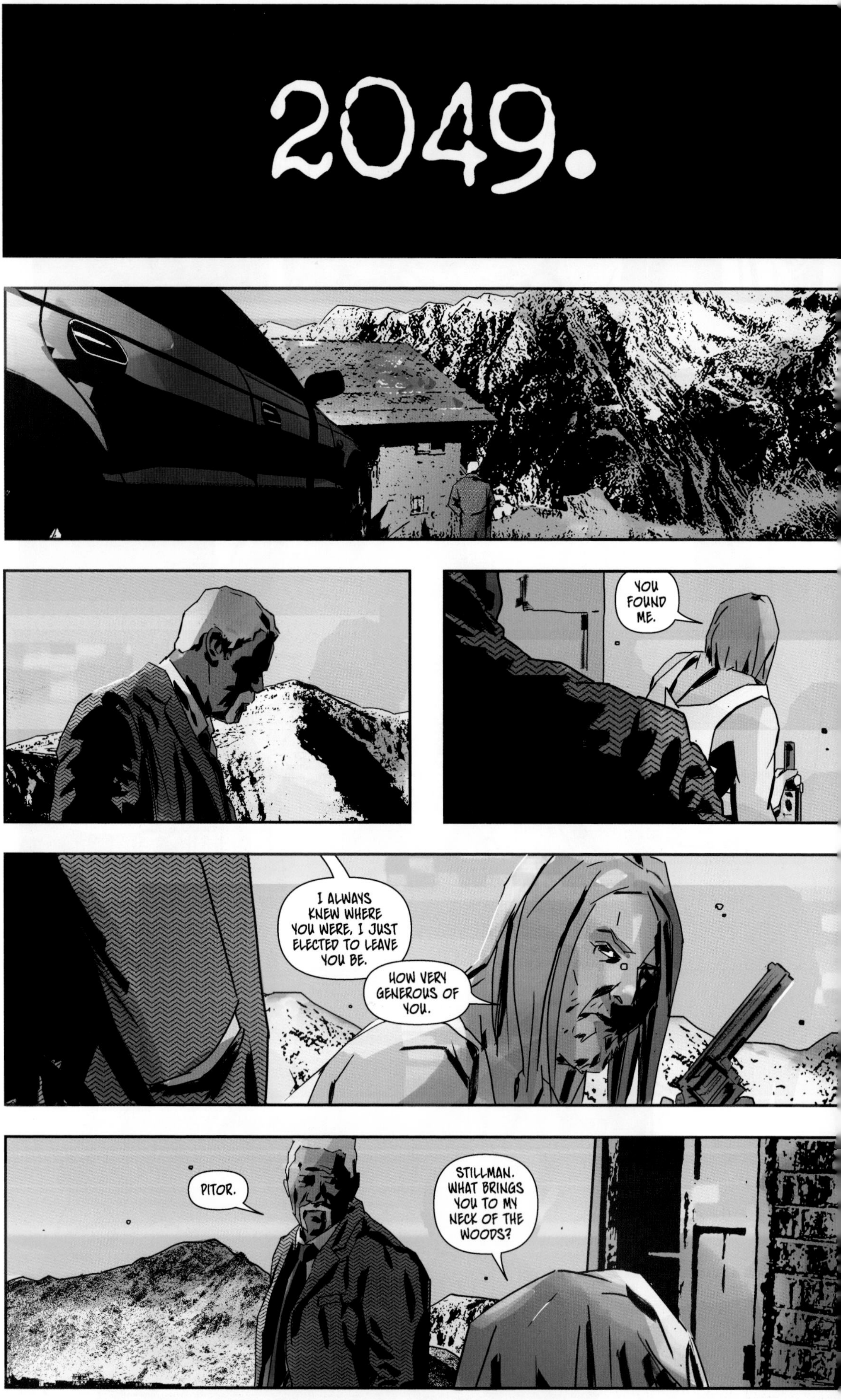
2049.
YOU FOUND ME.
I ALWAYS KNEW WHERE YOU WERE, I JUST ELECTED TO LEAVE YOU BE.
HOW VERY GENEROUS OF YOU.
PITOR.
STILLMAN. WHAT BRINGS YOU TO MY NECK OF THE WOODS?

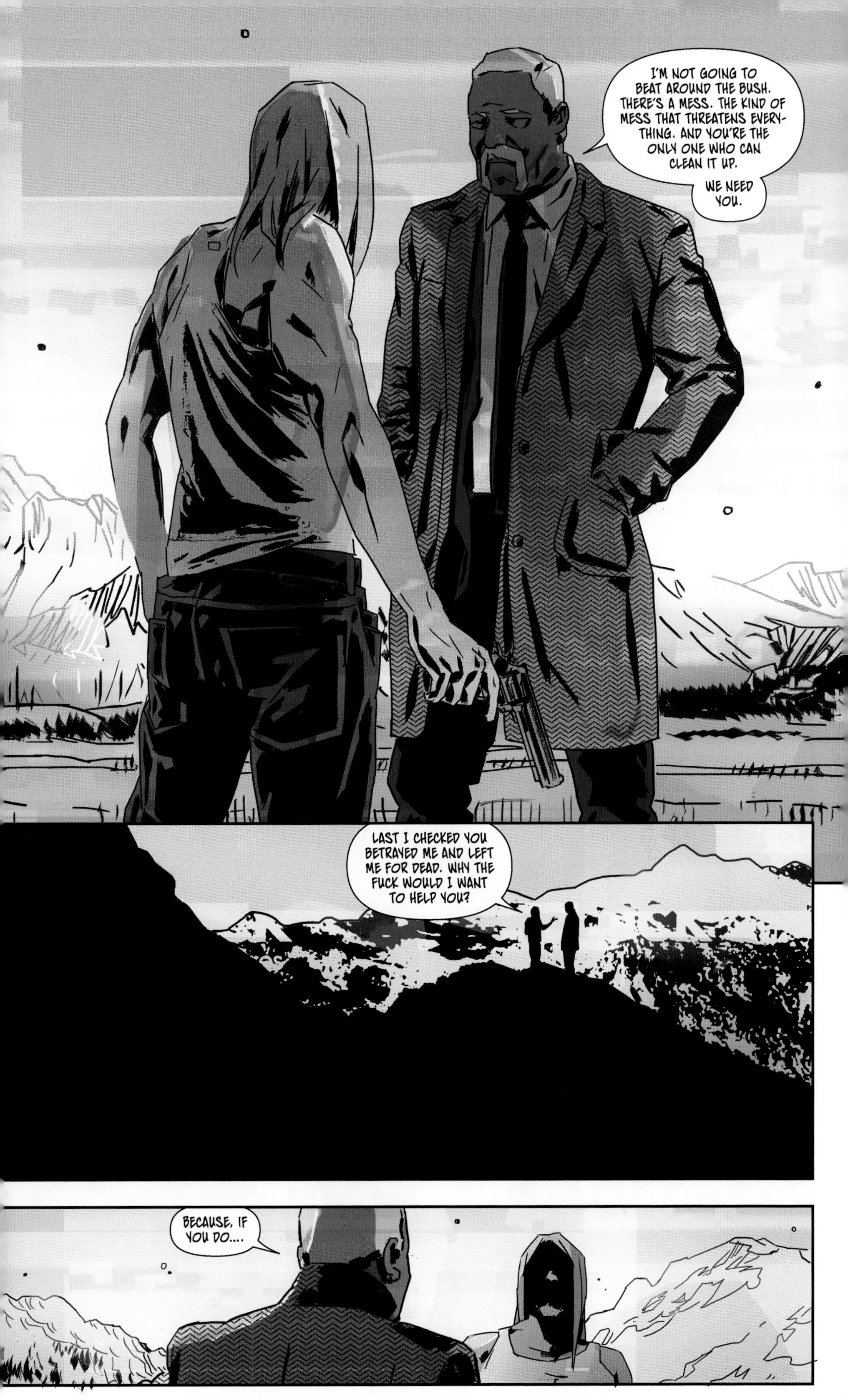
I'M NOT GOING TO BEAT AROUND THE BUSH. THERE'S A MESS. THE KIND OF MESS THAT THREATENS EVERYTHING. AND YOU'RE THE ONLY ONE WHO CAN CLEAN IT UP.
WE NEED YOU.
LAST I CHECKED YOU BETRAYED ME AND LEFT ME FOR DEAD. WHY THE FUCK WOULD I WANT TO HELP YOU?
BECAUSE, IF YOU DO....

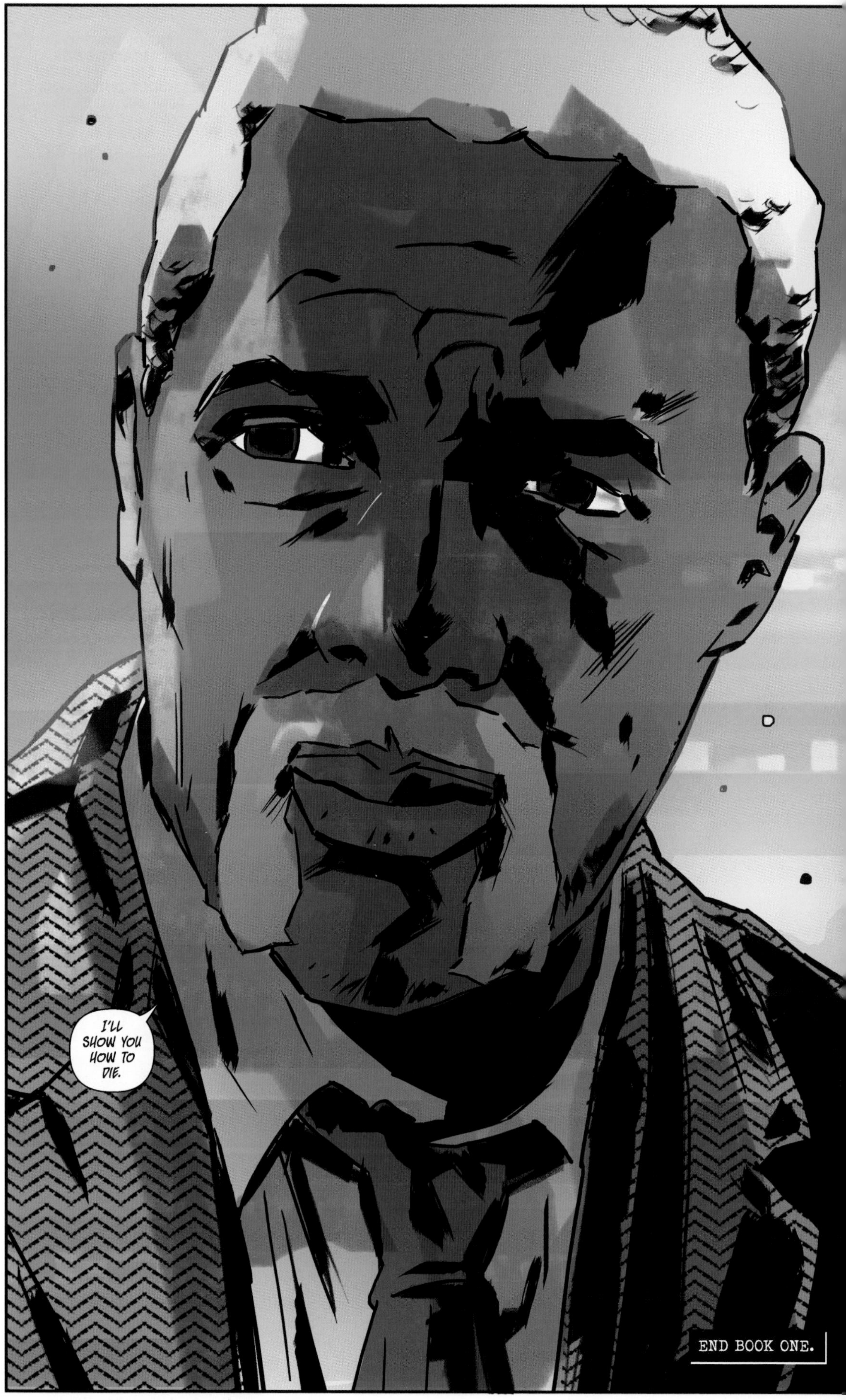
I'LL SHOW YOU HOW TO DIE.
END BOOK ONE.

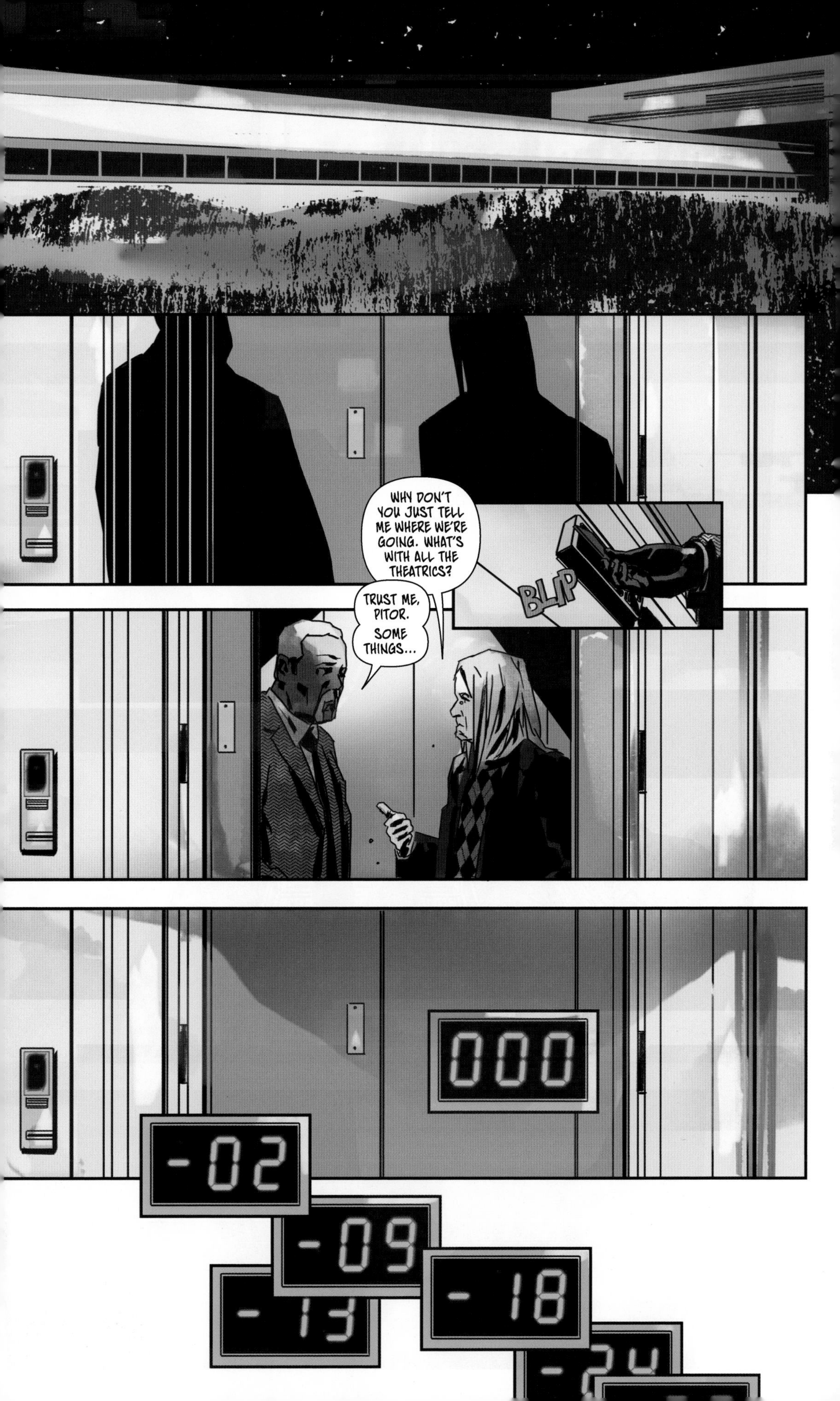

WHY DON'T YOU JUST TELL ME WHERE WE'RE GOING. WHAT'S WITH ALL THE THEATRICS?
BLIP
TRUST ME, PITOR.
SOME THINGS...
000
-02
-09
-13
-18
-24

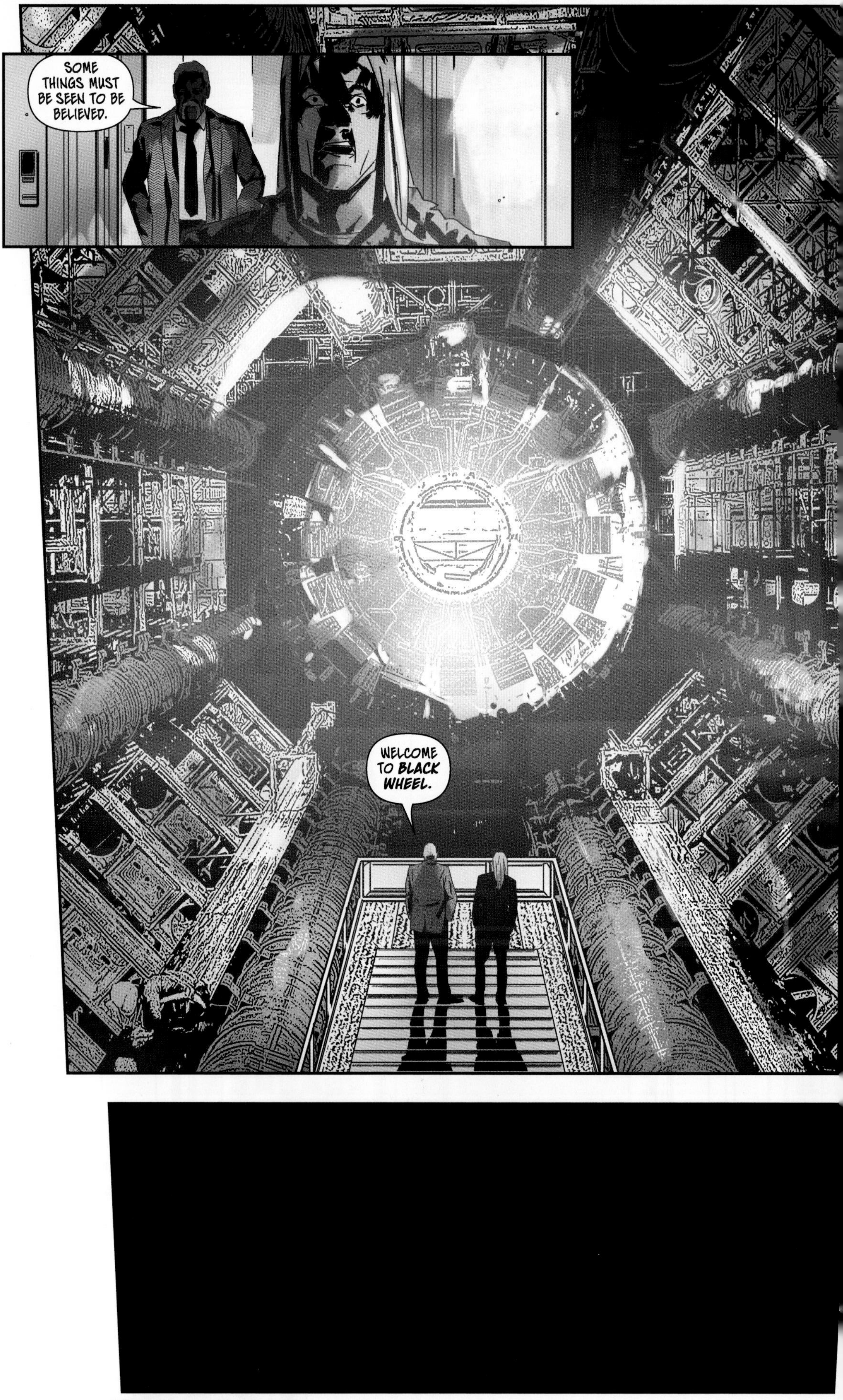
SOME THINGS MUST BE SEEN TO BE BELIEVED.
WELCOME TO BLACK WHEEL.

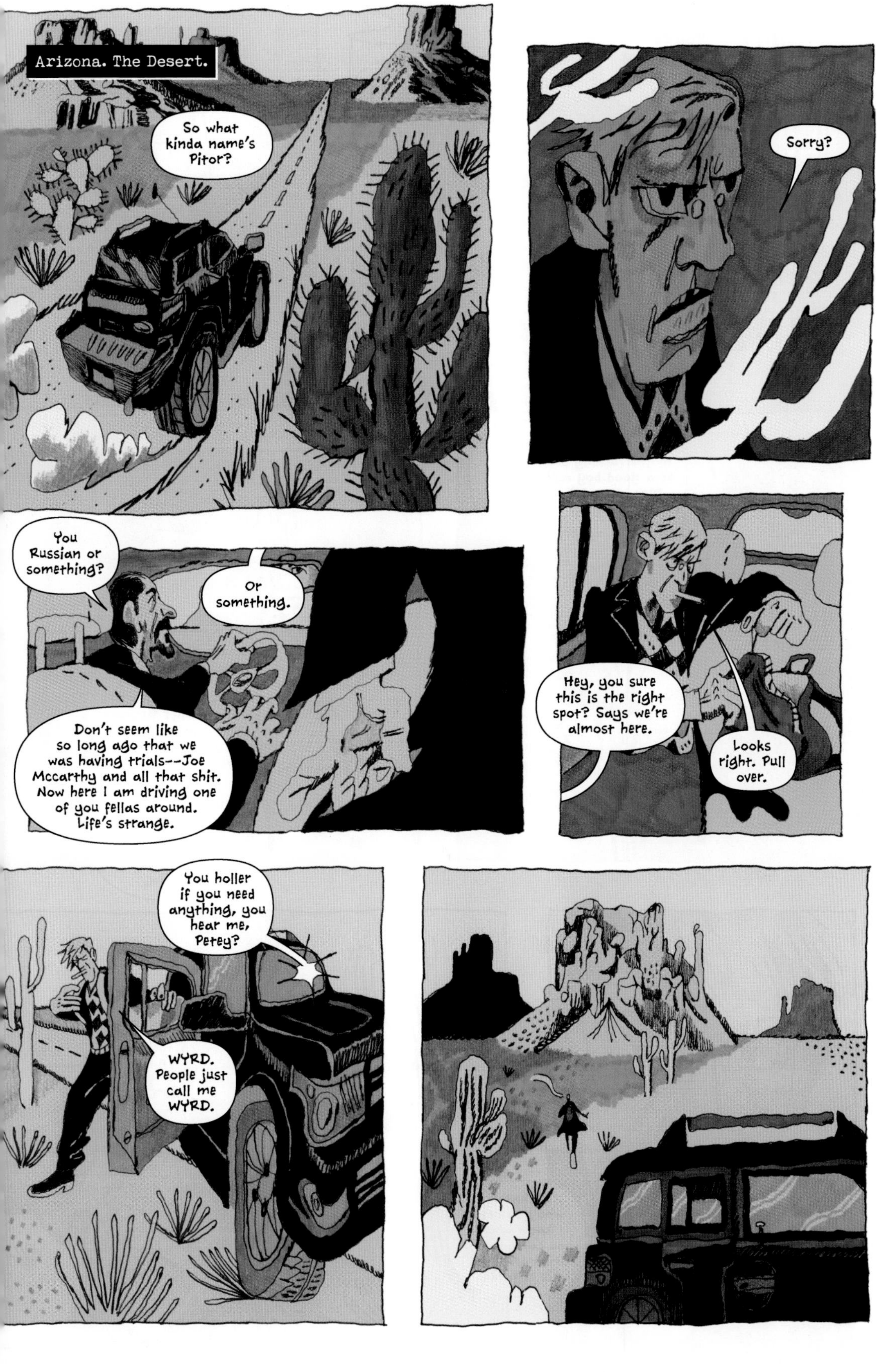
Arizona. The Desert.
So what kinda name's Pitor?
Sorry?
You Russian or something?
Or something.
Don't seem like so long ago that we was having trials--Joe Mccarthy and all that shit. Now here I am driving one of you fellas around. Life's strange.
Hey, you sure this is the right spot? Says we're almost here.
Looks right. Pull over.
You holler if you need anything, you hear me, Petey?
WYRD. People just call me WYRD.

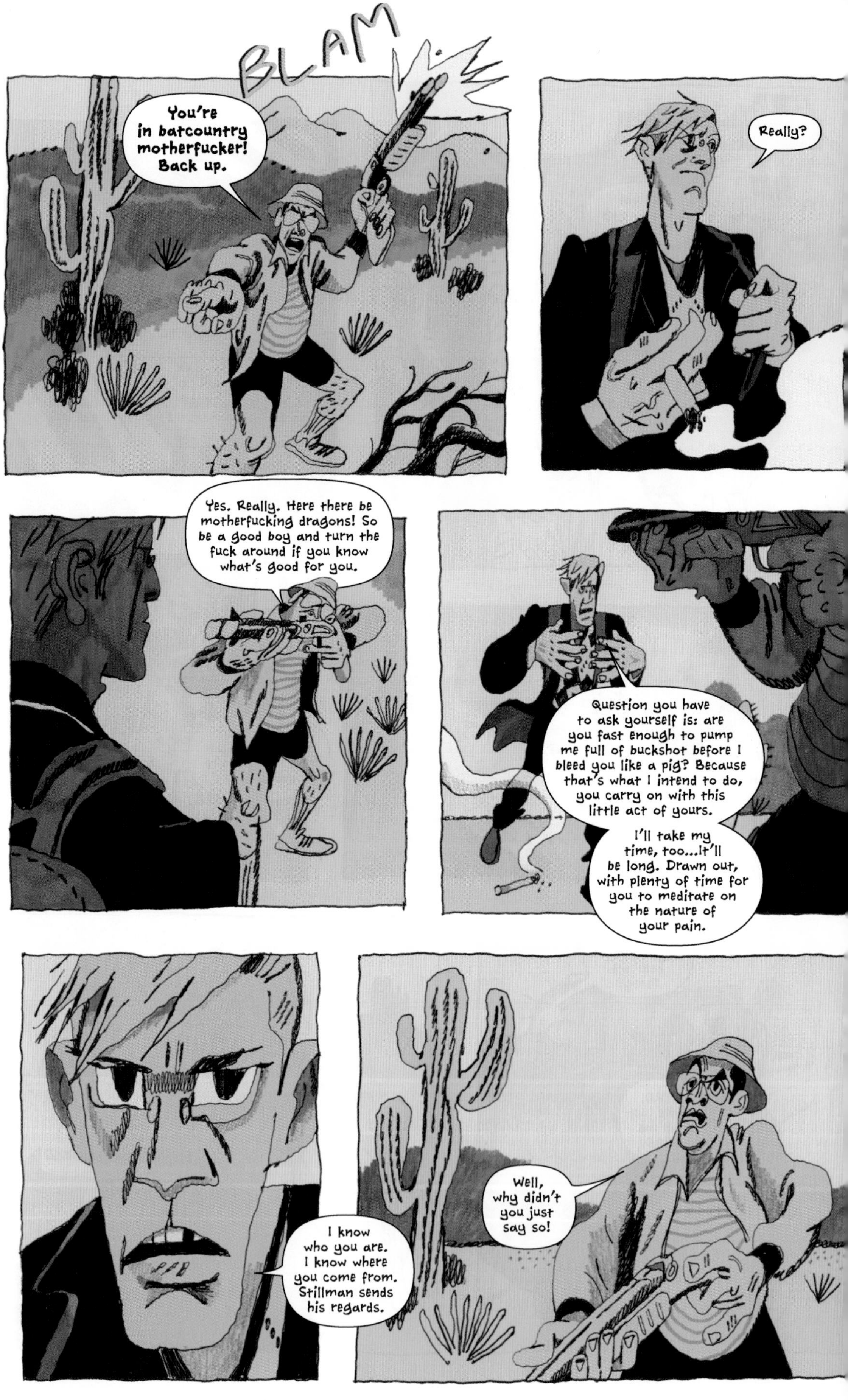
BLAM
You're in batcountry motherfucker! Back up.
Really?
Yes. Really. Here there be motherfucking dragons! So be a good boy and turn the fuck around if you know what's good for you.
Question you have to ask yourself is: are you fast enough to pump me full of buckshot before I bleed you like a pig? Because that's what I intend to do, you carry on with this little act of yours.
I'll take my time, too...It'll be long. Drawn out, with plenty of time for you to meditate on the nature of your pain.
I know who you are. I know where you come from. Stillman sends his regards.
Well, why didn't you just say so!

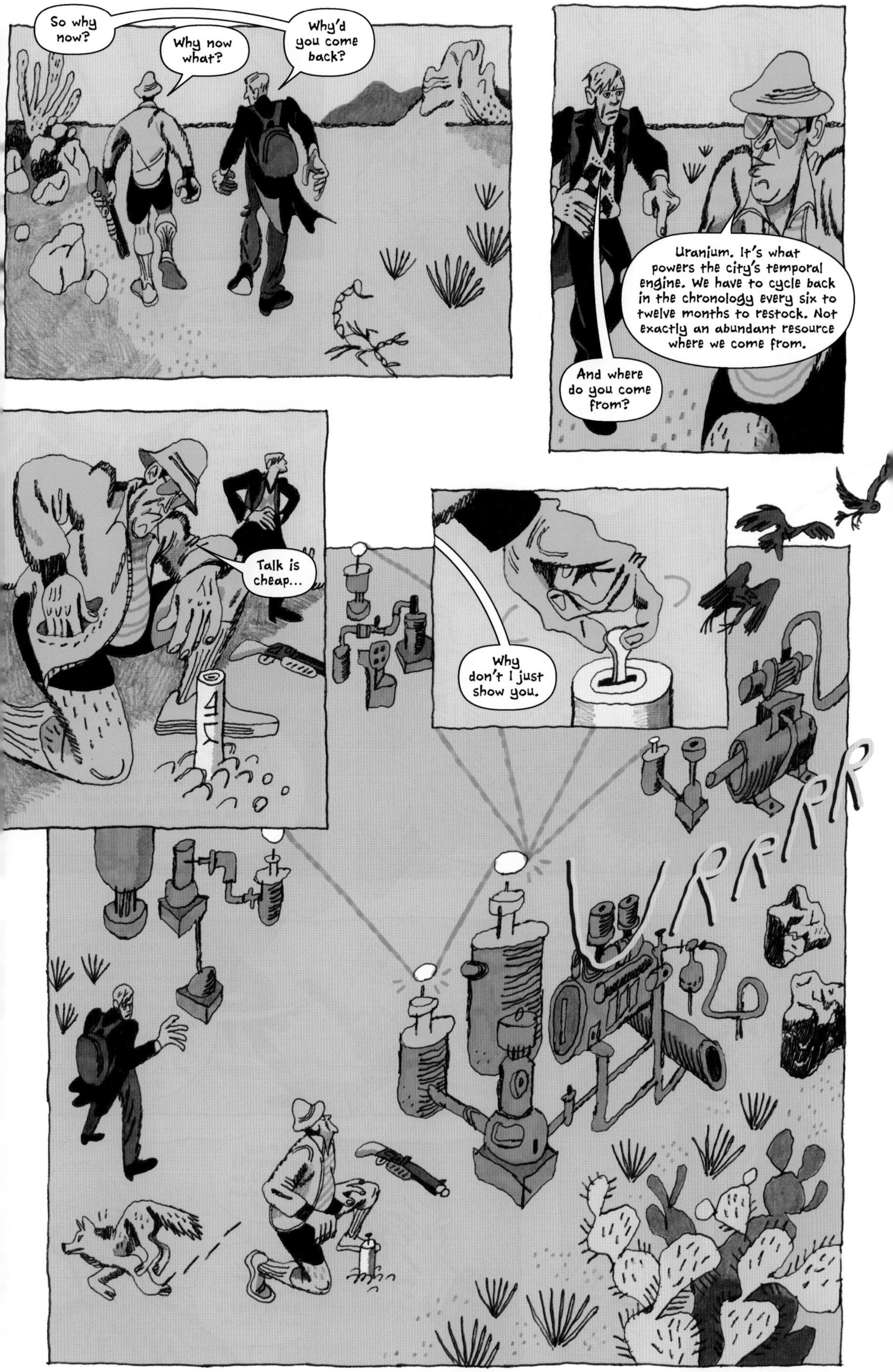
So why now?
Why now what?
Why'd you come back?
Uranium. It's what powers the city's temporal engine. We have to cycle back in the chronology every six to twelve months to restock. Not exactly an abundant resource where we come from.
And where do you come from?
Talk is cheap...
Why don't I just show you.
URRRRRR

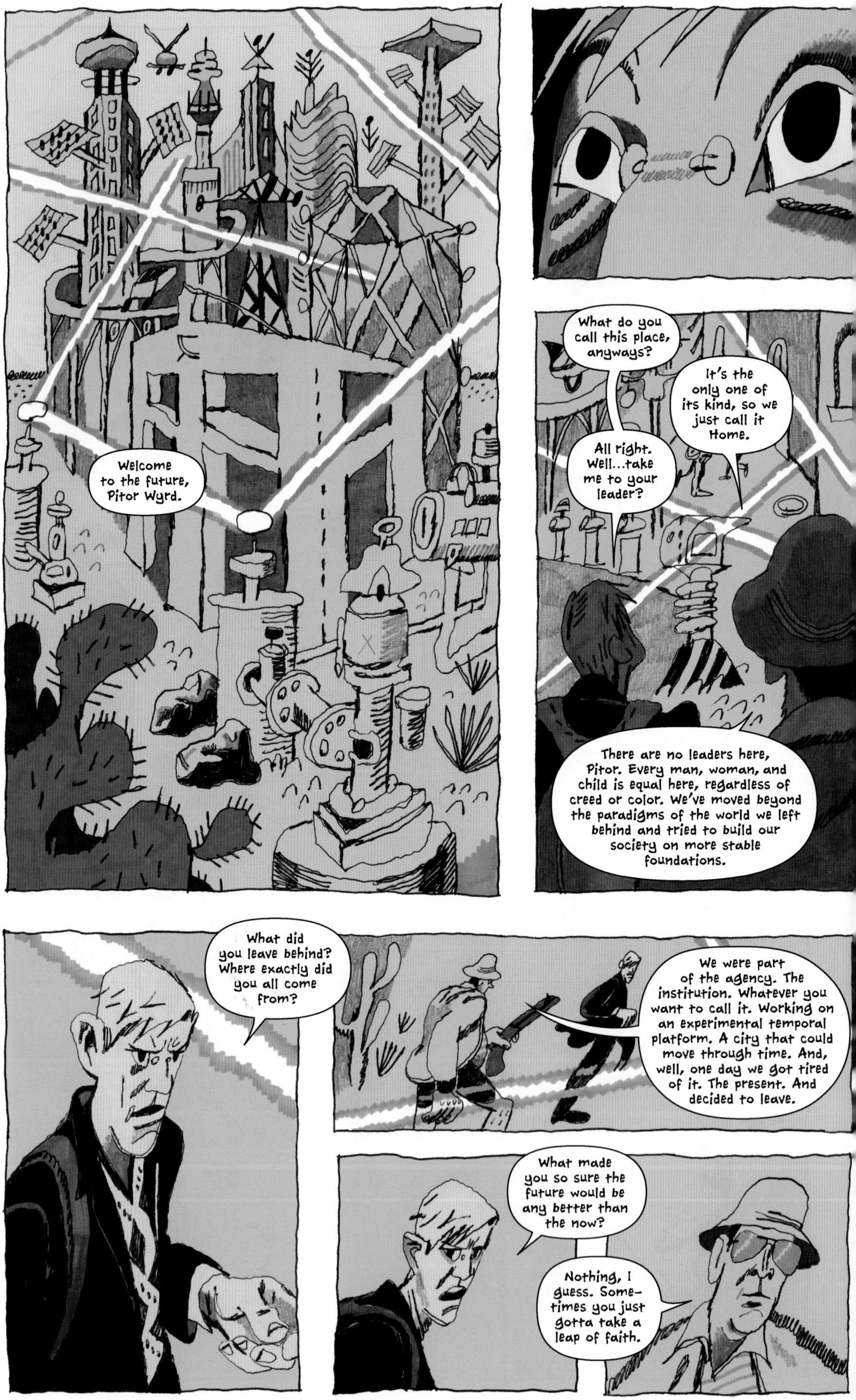
Welcome to the future, Pitor Wyrd.
What do you call this place, anyways?
It's the only one of its kind, so we just call it Home.
All right. Well...take me to your leader?
There are no leaders here, Pitor. Every man, woman, and child is equal here, regardless of creed or color. We've moved beyond the paradigms of the world we left behind and tried to build our society on more stable foundations.
What did you leave behind? Where exactly did you all come from?
We were part of the agency. The institution. Whatever you want to call it. Working on an experimental temporal platform. A city that could move through time. And, well, one day we got tired of it. The present. And decided to leave.
What made you so sure the future would be any better than the now?
Nothing, I guess. Sometimes you just gotta take a leap of faith.

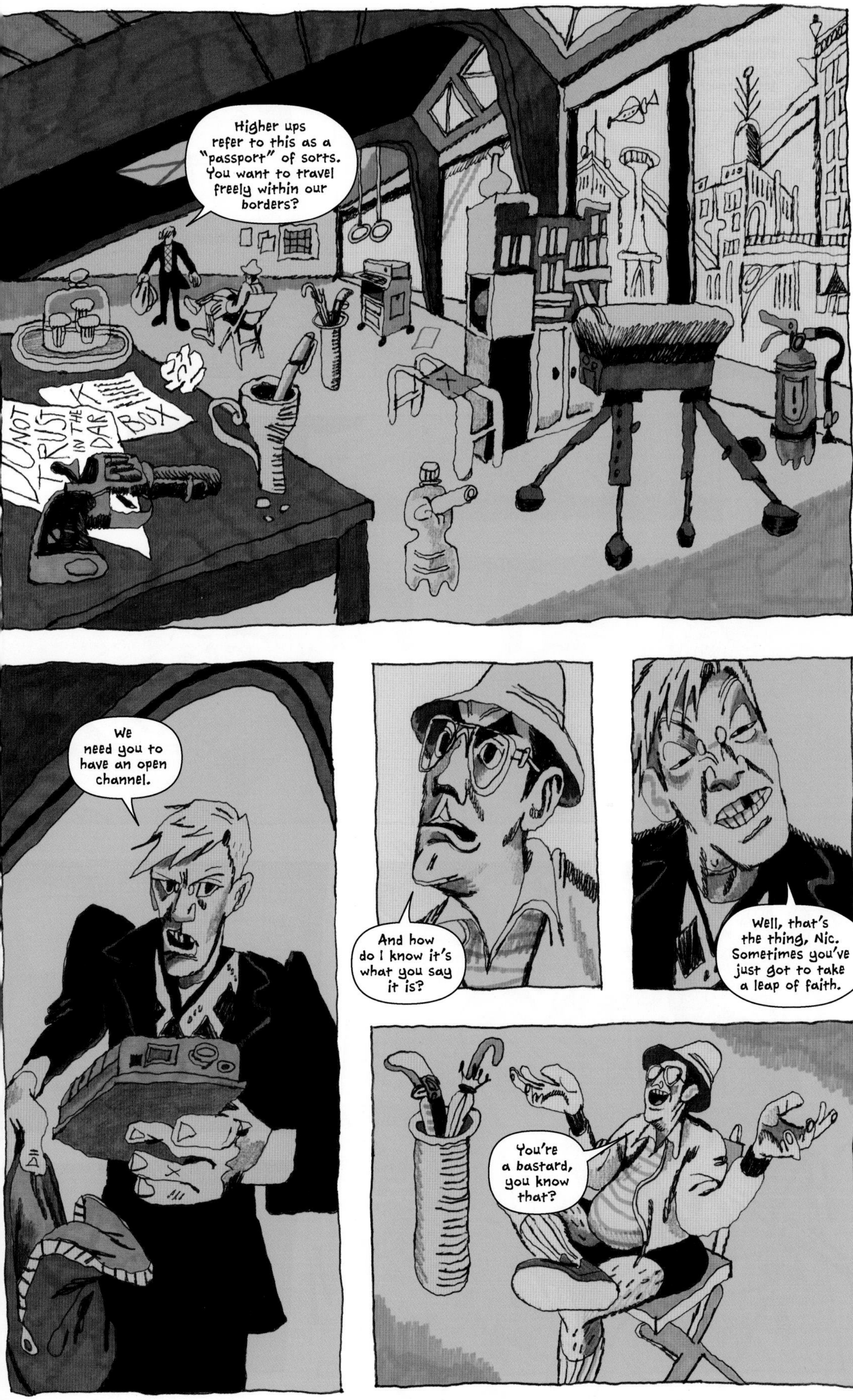
Higher ups refer to this as a "passport" of sorts. You want to travel freely within our borders?
We need you to have an open channel.
And how do I know it's what you say it is?
Well, that's the thing, Nic. Sometimes you've just got to take a leap of faith.
You're a bastard, you know that?

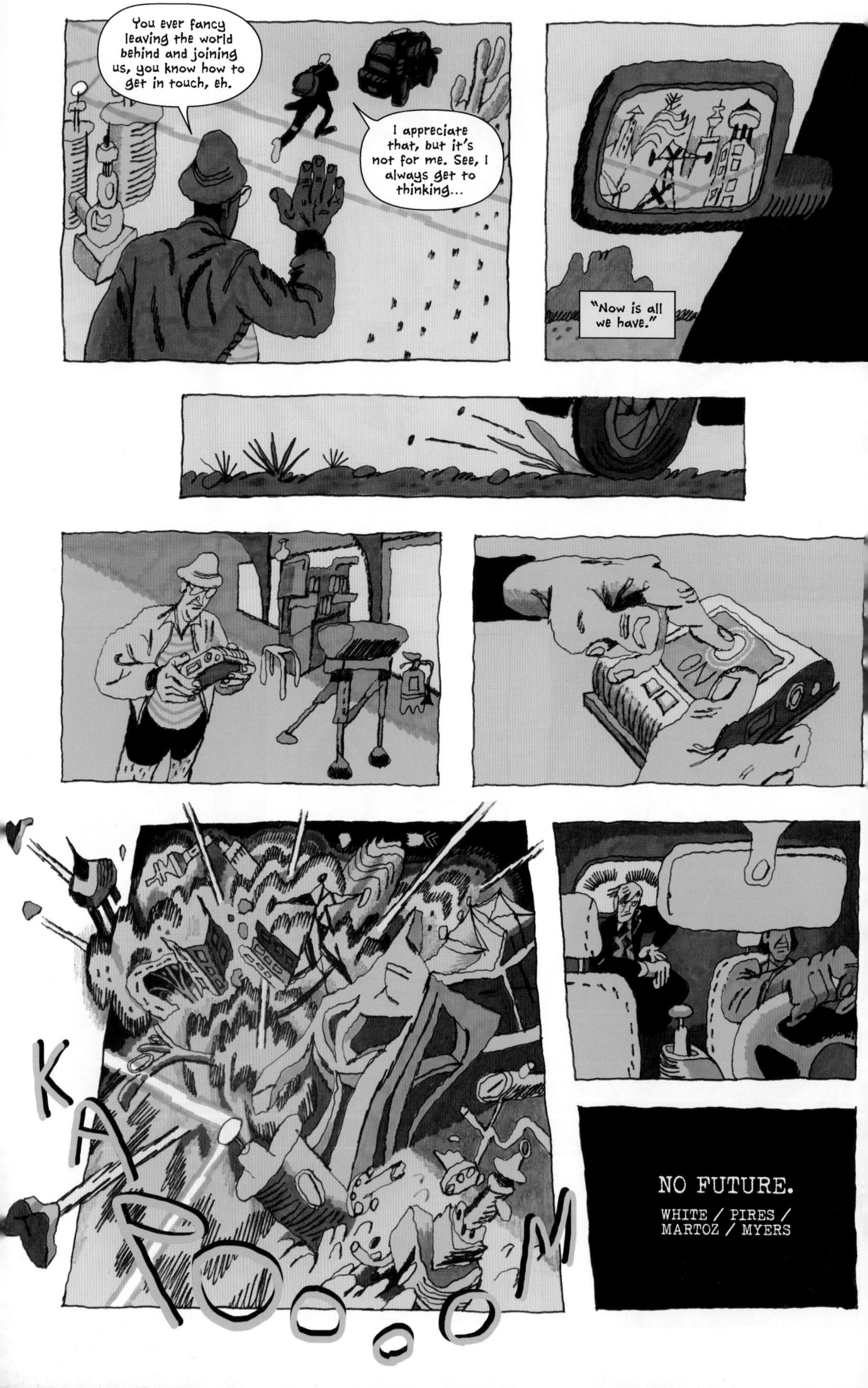
You ever fancy leaving the world behind and joining us, you know how to get in touch, eh.
I appreciate that, but it's not for me. See, I always get to thinking...
"Now is all we have."
KAROOOOOM
NO FUTURE.
WHITE / PIRES / MARTOZ / MYERS

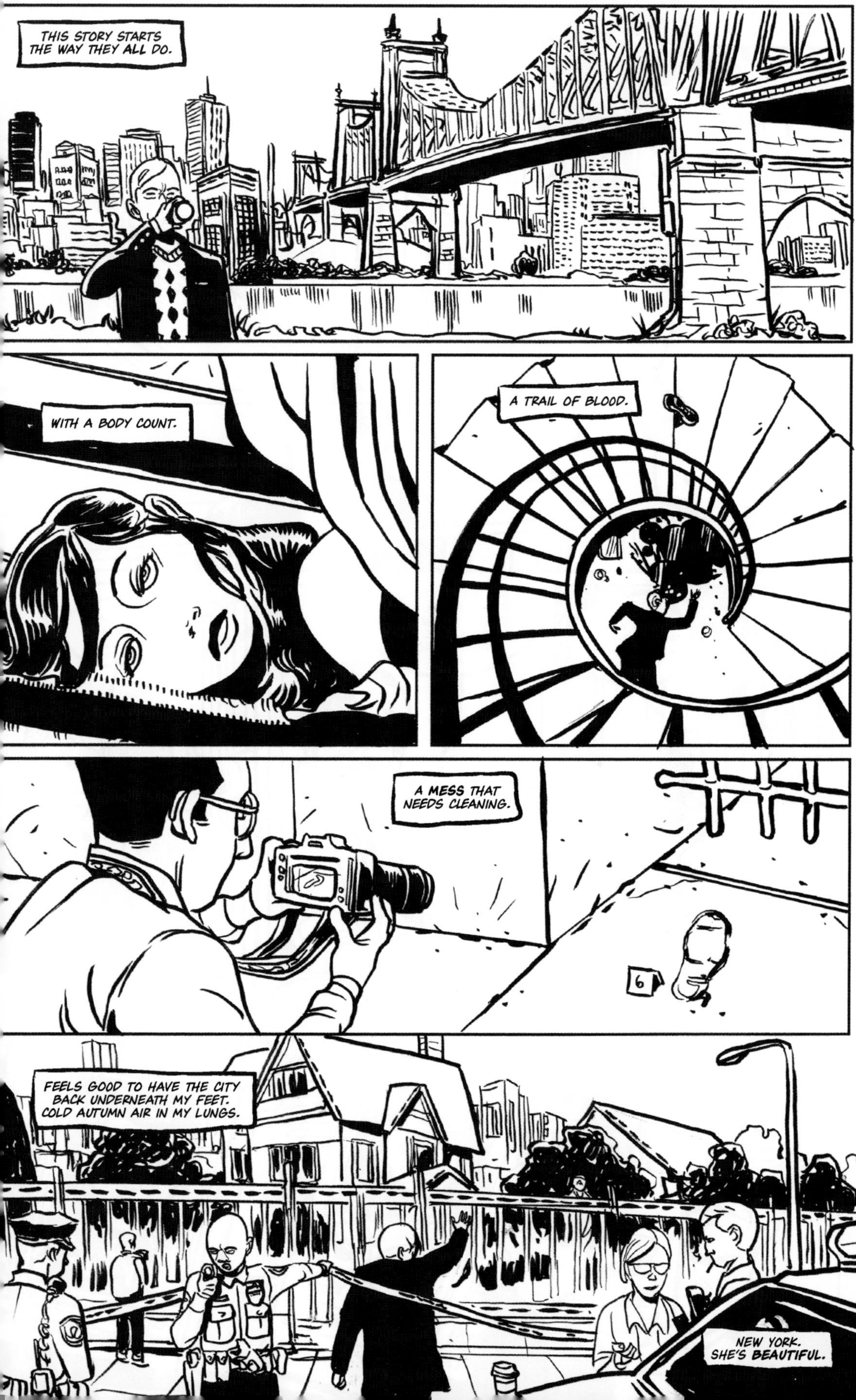
THIS STORY STARTS THE WAY THEY ALL DO.
WITH A BODY COUNT.
A TRAIL OF BLOOD.
A MESS THAT NEEDS CLEANING.
6
FEELS GOOD TO HAVE THE CITY BACK UNDERNEATH MY FEET. COLD AUTUMN AIR IN MY LUNGS.
NEW YORK. SHE'S BEAUTIFUL.

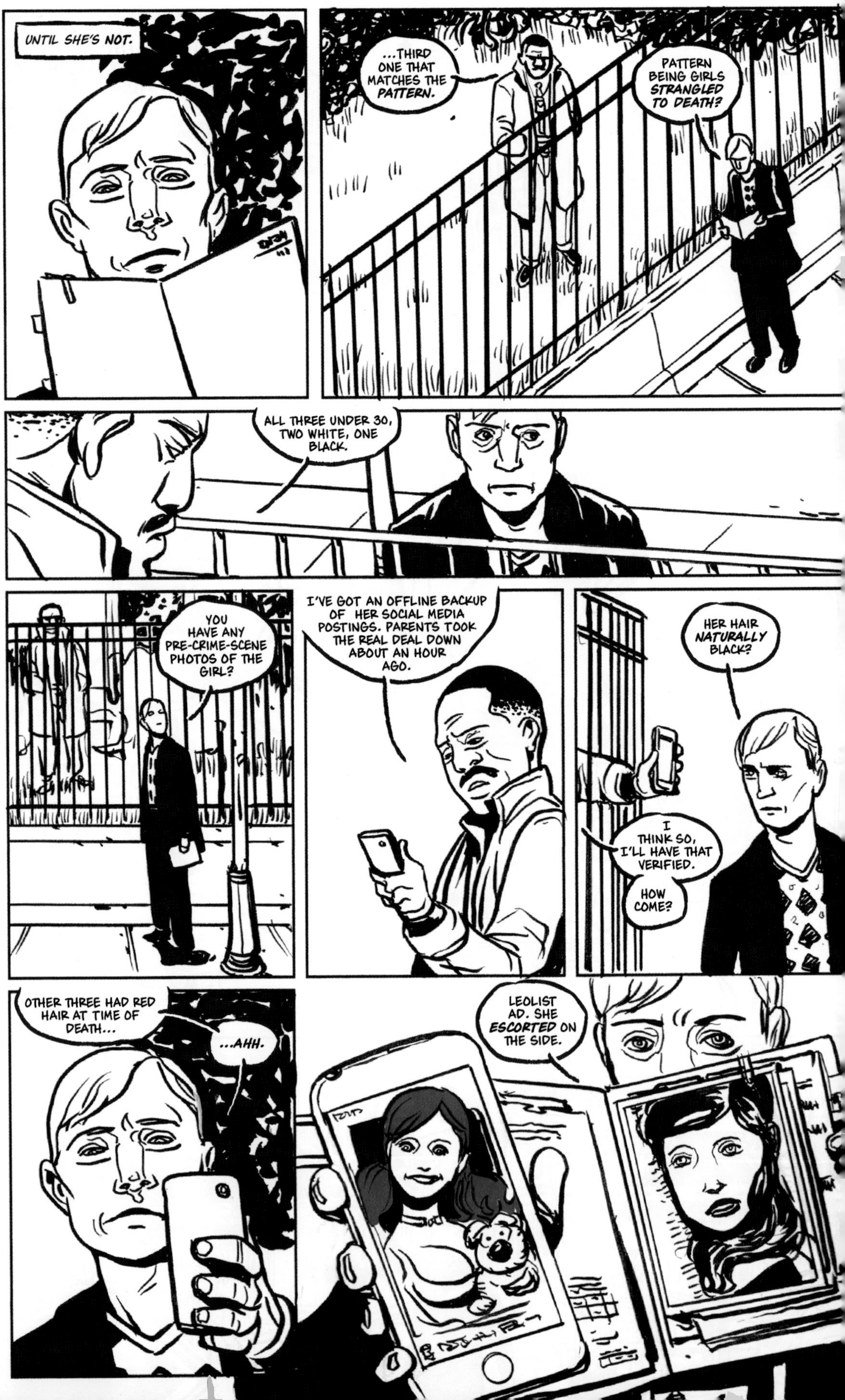
UNTIL SHE'S NOT.
...THIRD ONE THAT MATCHES THE PATTERN.
PATTERN BEING GIRLS STRANGLED TO DEATH?
ALL THREE UNDER 30, TWO WHITE, ONE BLACK.
YOU HAVE ANY PRE-CRIME-SCENE PHOTOS OF THE GIRL?
I'VE GOT AN OFFLINE BACKUP OF HER SOCIAL MEDIA POSTINGS. PARENTS TOOK THE REAL DEAL DOWN ABOUT AN HOUR AGO.
HER HAIR NATURALLY BLACK?
I THINK SO, I'LL HAVE THAT VERIFIED.
HOW COME?
OTHER THREE HAD RED HAIR AT TIME OF DEATH...
...AHH.
LEOLIST AD. SHE ESCORTED ON THE SIDE.

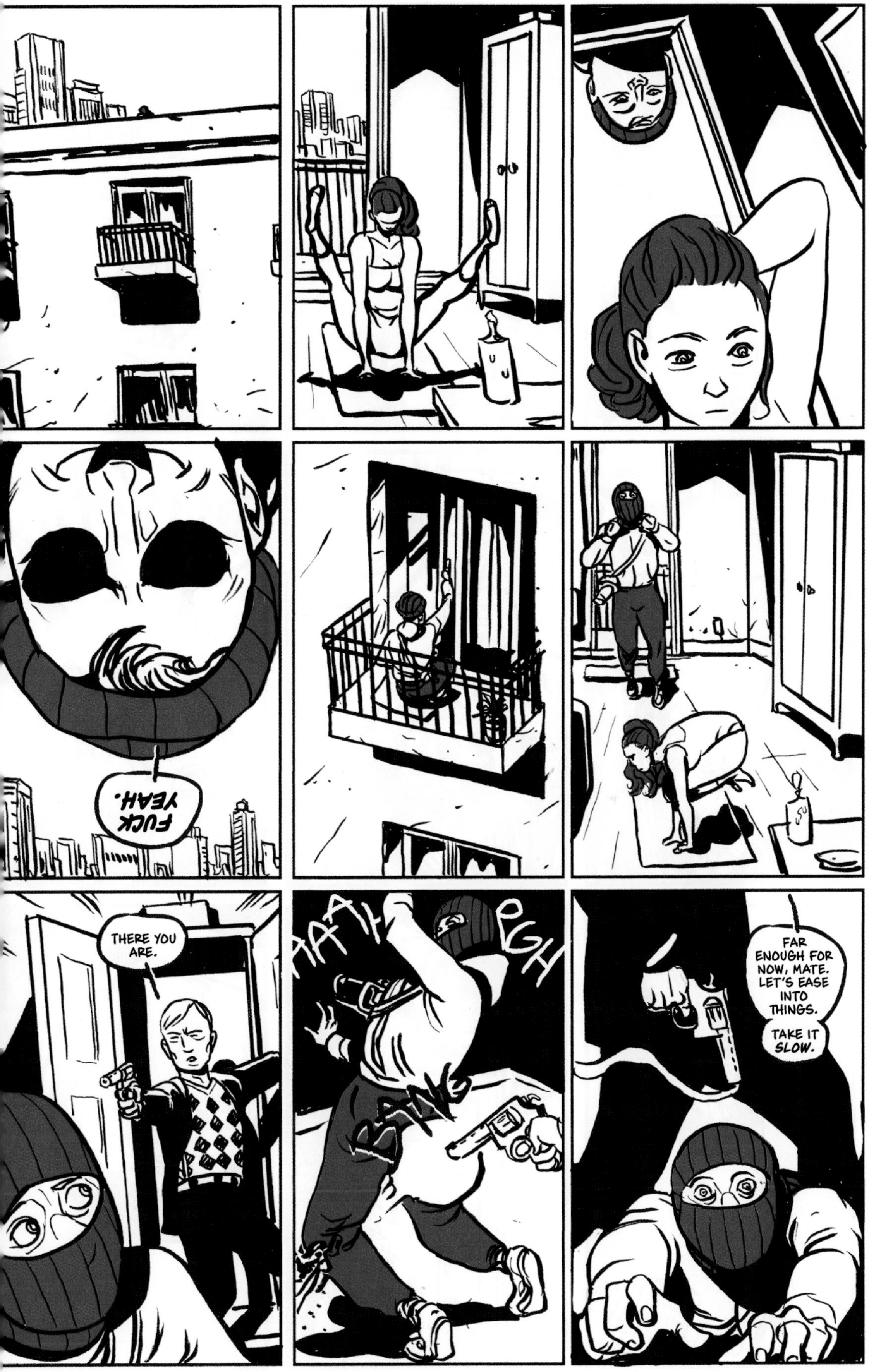
FUCK YEAH.
THERE YOU ARE.
FAR ENOUGH FOR NOW, MATE. LET'S EASE INTO THINGS.
TAKE IT SLOW.

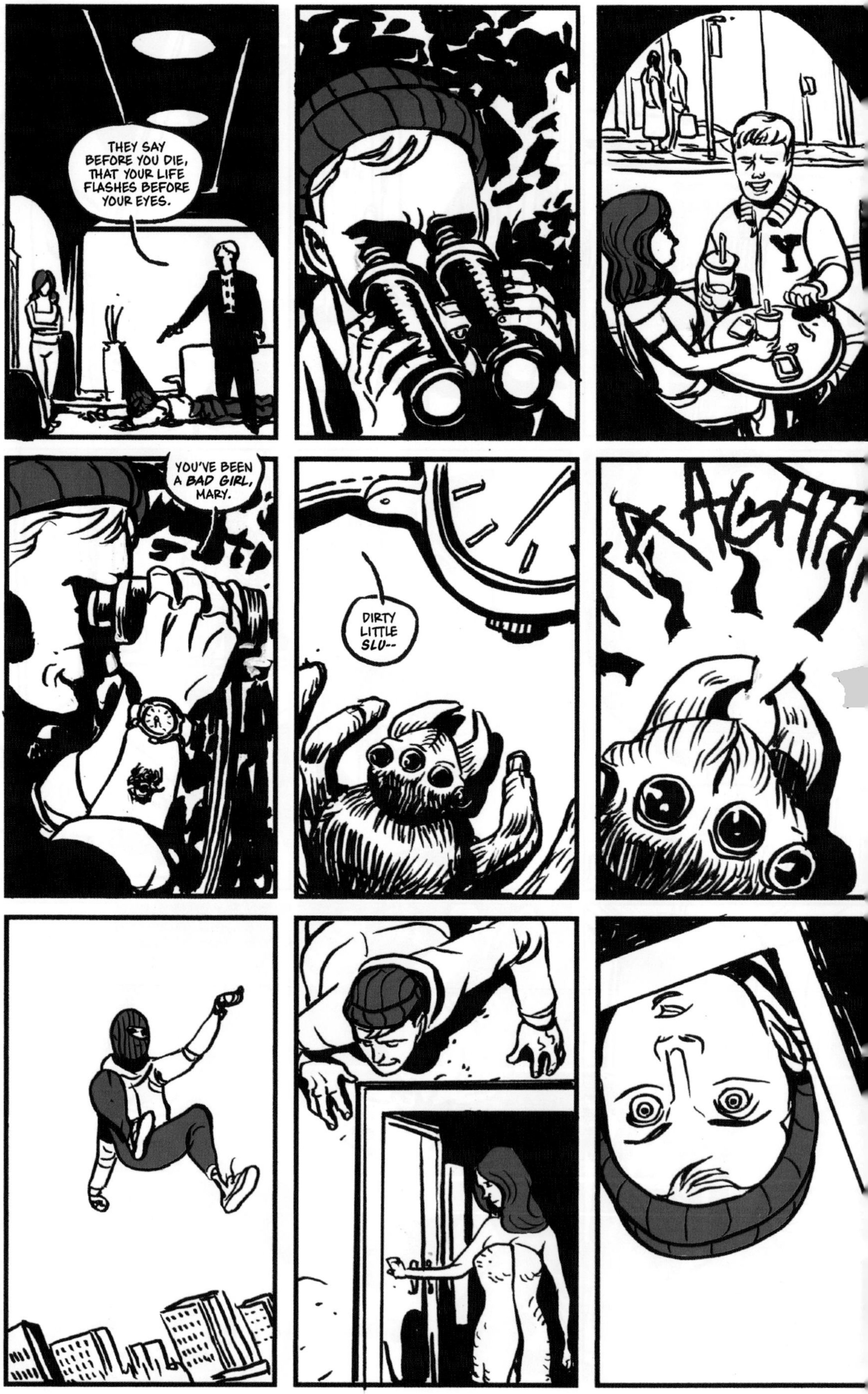

THEY SAY BEFORE YOU DIE, THAT YOUR LIFE FLASHES BEFORE YOUR EYES.
YOU'VE BEEN A *BAD GIRL*, MARY.
DIRTY LITTLE *SLU--*

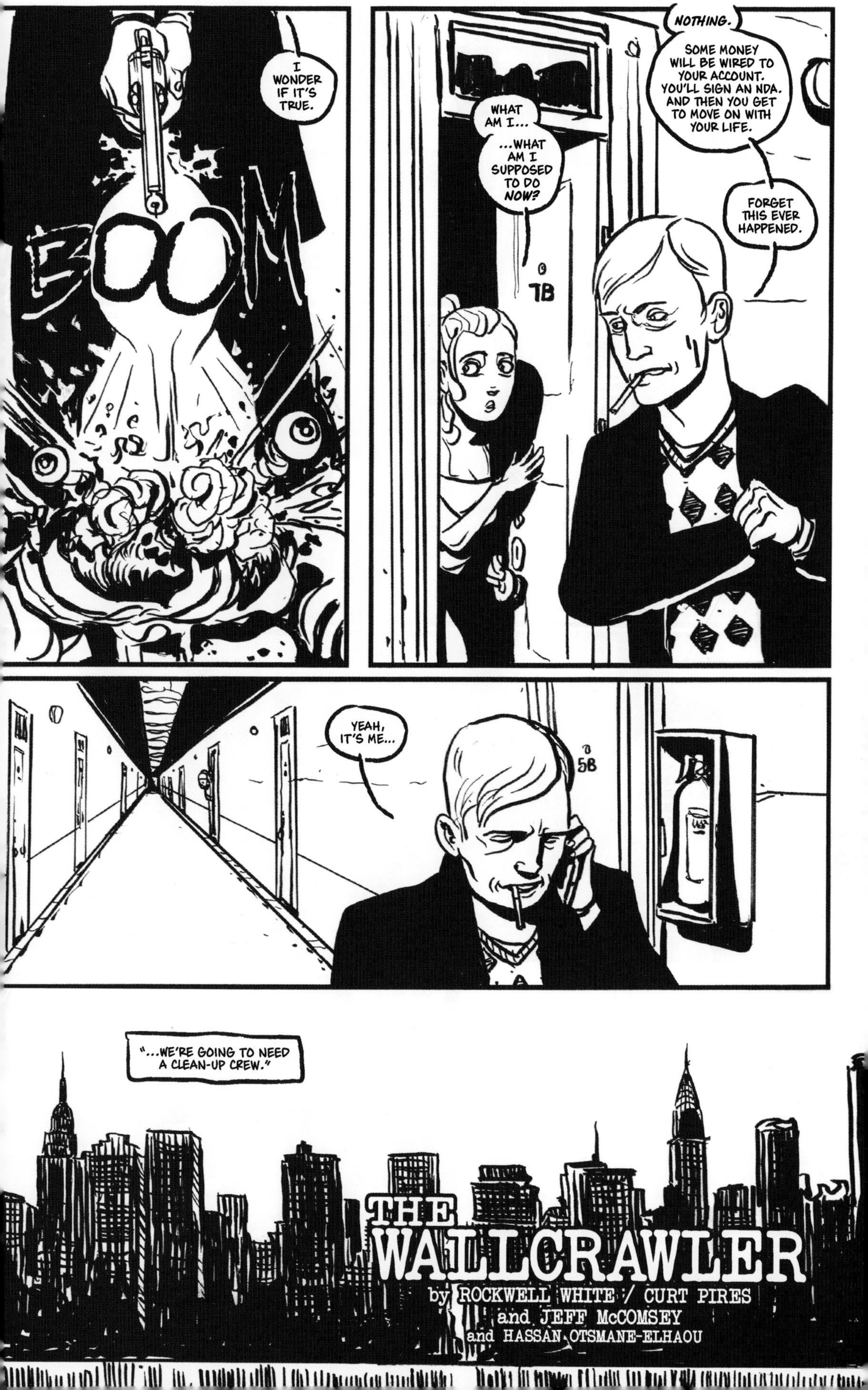

I WONDER IF IT'S TRUE.
BOOM
WHAT AM I...
...WHAT AM I SUPPOSED TO DO NOW?
NOTHING.
SOME MONEY WILL BE WIRED TO YOUR ACCOUNT. YOU'LL SIGN AN NDA. AND THEN YOU GET TO MOVE ON WITH YOUR LIFE.
FORGET THIS EVER HAPPENED.
7B
YEAH, IT'S ME...
5B
"...WE'RE GOING TO NEED A CLEAN-UP CREW."
THE WALLCRAWLER
by ROCKWELL WHITE / CURT PIRES
and JEFF McCOMSEY
and HASSAN OTSMANE-ELHAOU

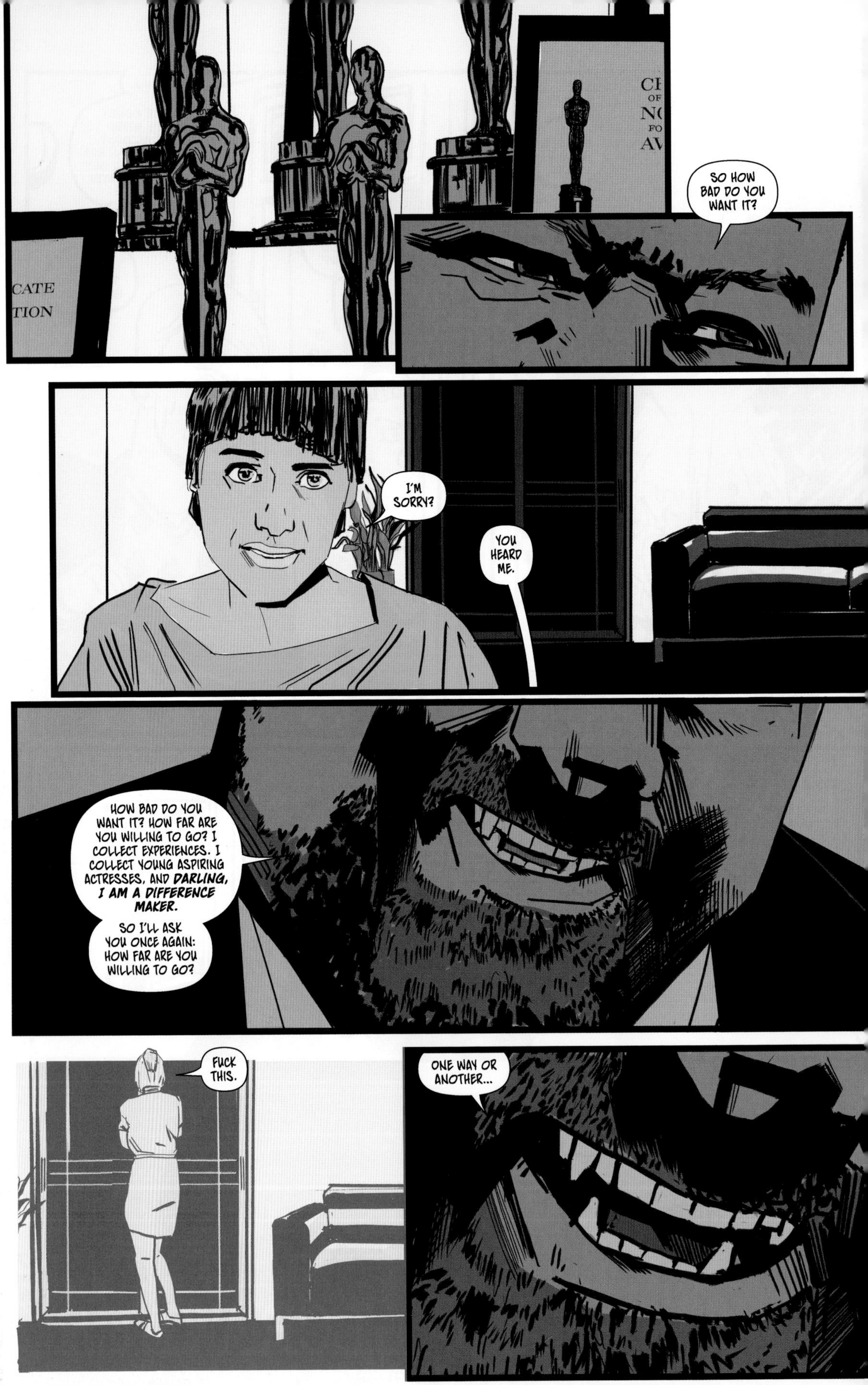
CATE
TION
SO HOW BAD DO YOU WANT IT?
I'M SORRY?
YOU HEARD ME.
HOW BAD DO YOU WANT IT? HOW FAR ARE YOU WILLING TO GO? I COLLECT EXPERIENCES. I COLLECT YOUNG ASPIRING ACTRESSES, AND ***DARLING, I AM A DIFFERENCE MAKER.***
SO I'LL ASK YOU ONCE AGAIN: HOW FAR ARE YOU WILLING TO GO?
FUCK THIS.
ONE WAY OR ANOTHER...

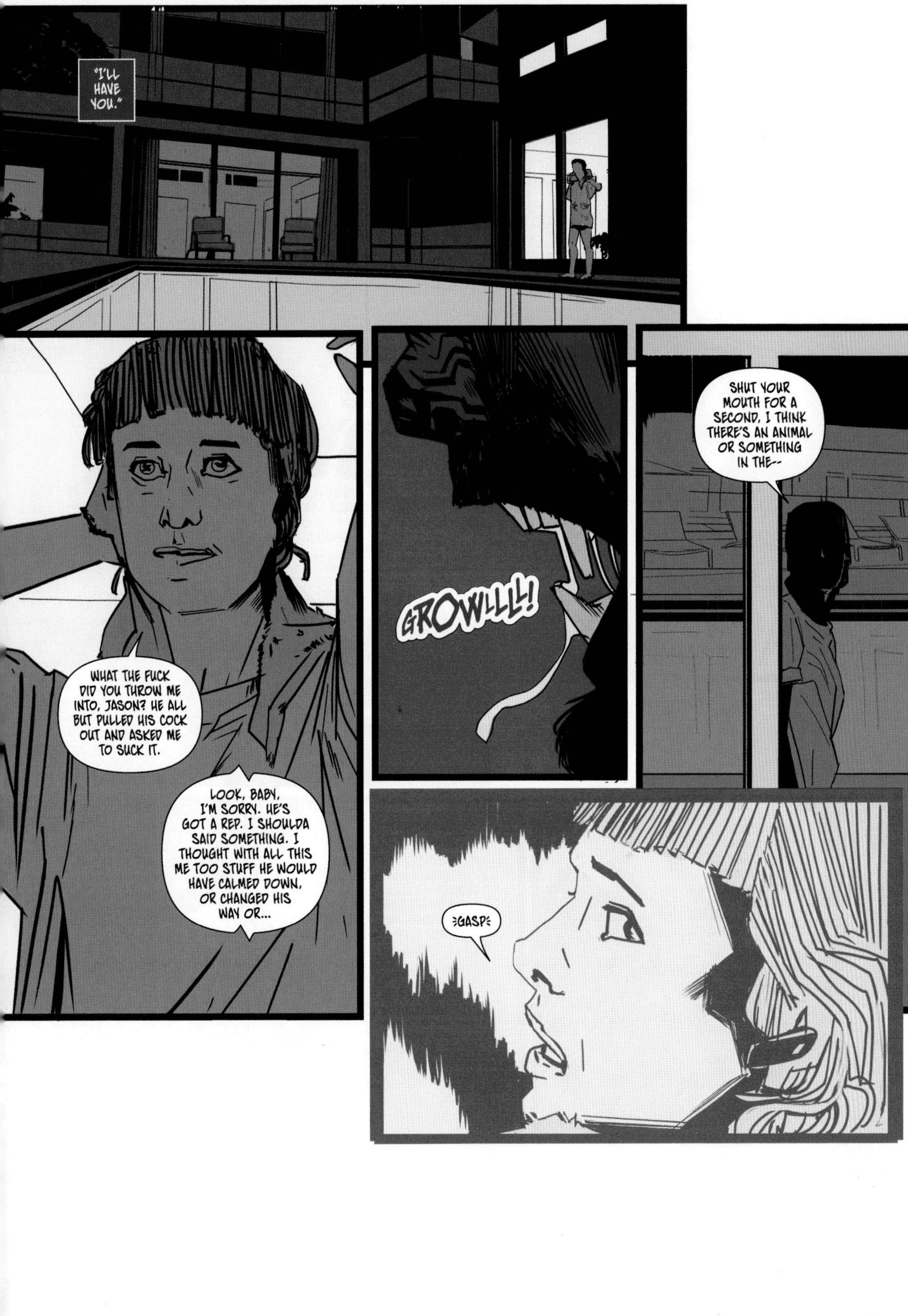
"I'LL HAVE YOU."
WHAT THE FUCK DID YOU THROW ME INTO, JASON? HE ALL BUT PULLED HIS COCK OUT AND ASKED ME TO SUCK IT.
LOOK, BABY, I'M SORRY. HE'S GOT A REP. I SHOULDA SAID SOMETHING. I THOUGHT WITH ALL THIS ME TOO STUFF HE WOULD HAVE CALMED DOWN, OR CHANGED HIS WAY OR...
GROWLLLL!
SHUT YOUR MOUTH FOR A SECOND, I THINK THERE'S AN ANIMAL OR SOMETHING IN THE--
GASP

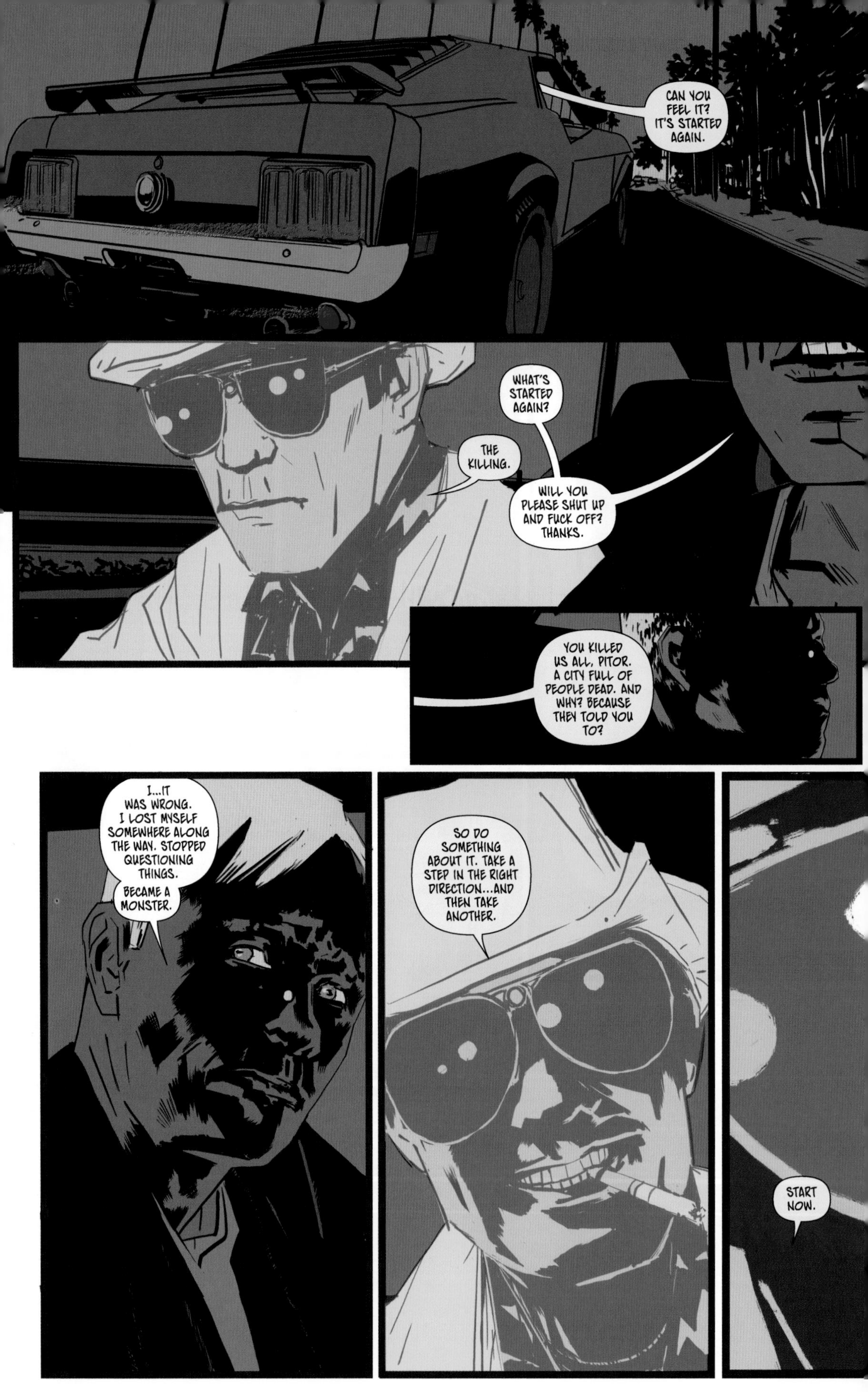
CAN YOU FEEL IT? IT'S STARTED AGAIN.
WHAT'S STARTED AGAIN?
THE KILLING.
WILL YOU PLEASE SHUT UP AND FUCK OFF? THANKS.
YOU KILLED US ALL, PITOR. A CITY FULL OF PEOPLE DEAD. AND WHY? BECAUSE THEY TOLD YOU TO?
I...IT WAS WRONG. I LOST MYSELF SOMEWHERE ALONG THE WAY. STOPPED QUESTIONING THINGS.
BECAME A MONSTER.
SO DO SOMETHING ABOUT IT. TAKE A STEP IN THE RIGHT DIRECTION...AND THEN TAKE ANOTHER.
START NOW.

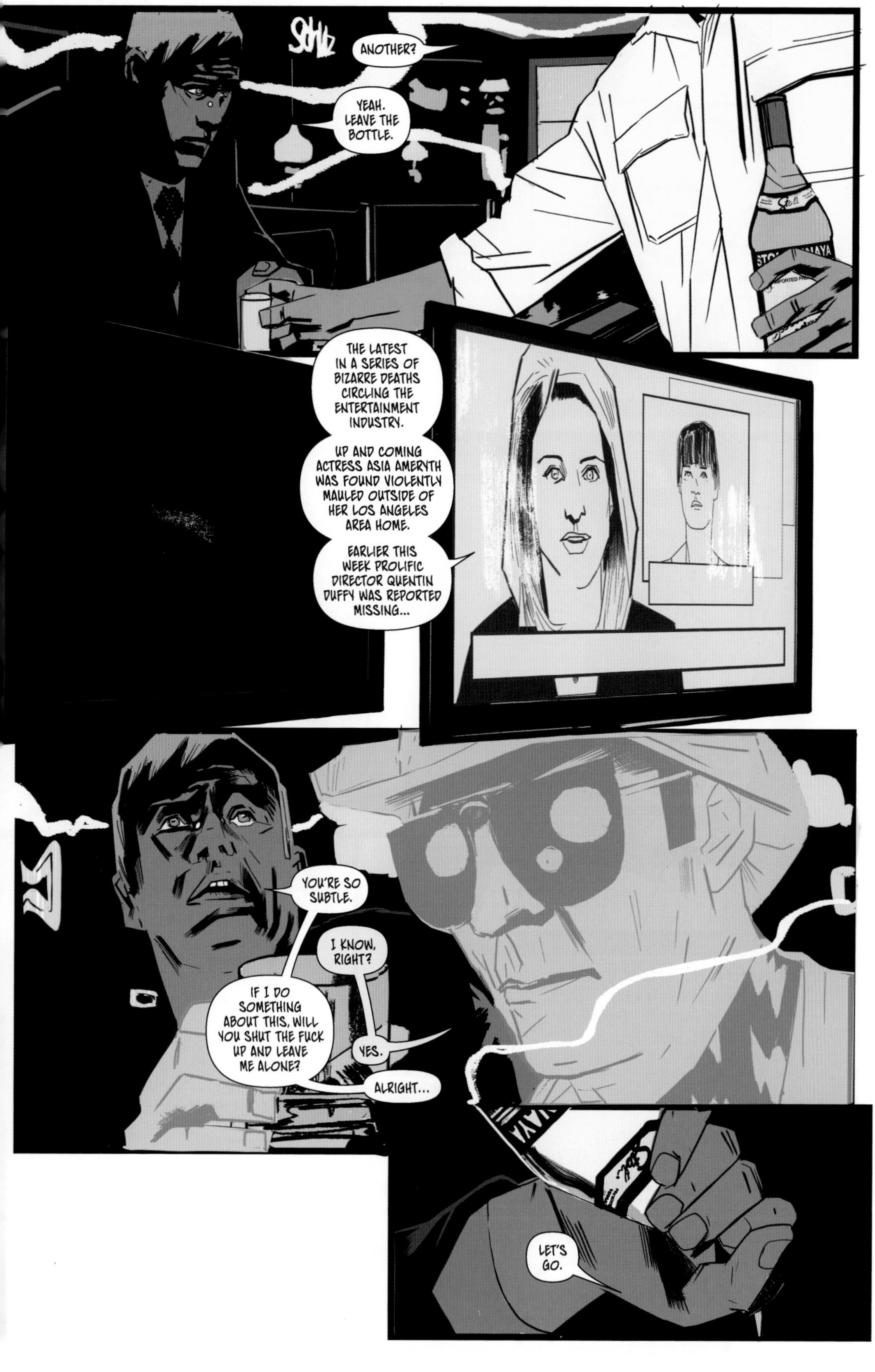

ANOTHER?
YEAH. LEAVE THE BOTTLE.
THE LATEST IN A SERIES OF BIZARRE DEATHS CIRCLING THE ENTERTAINMENT INDUSTRY.
UP AND COMING ACTRESS ASIA AMERYTH WAS FOUND VIOLENTLY MAULED OUTSIDE OF HER LOS ANGELES AREA HOME.
EARLIER THIS WEEK PROLIFIC DIRECTOR QUENTIN DUFFY WAS REPORTED MISSING...
YOU'RE SO SUBTLE.
I KNOW, RIGHT?
IF I DO SOMETHING ABOUT THIS, WILL YOU SHUT THE FUCK UP AND LEAVE ME ALONE?
YES.
ALRIGHT...
LET'S GO.

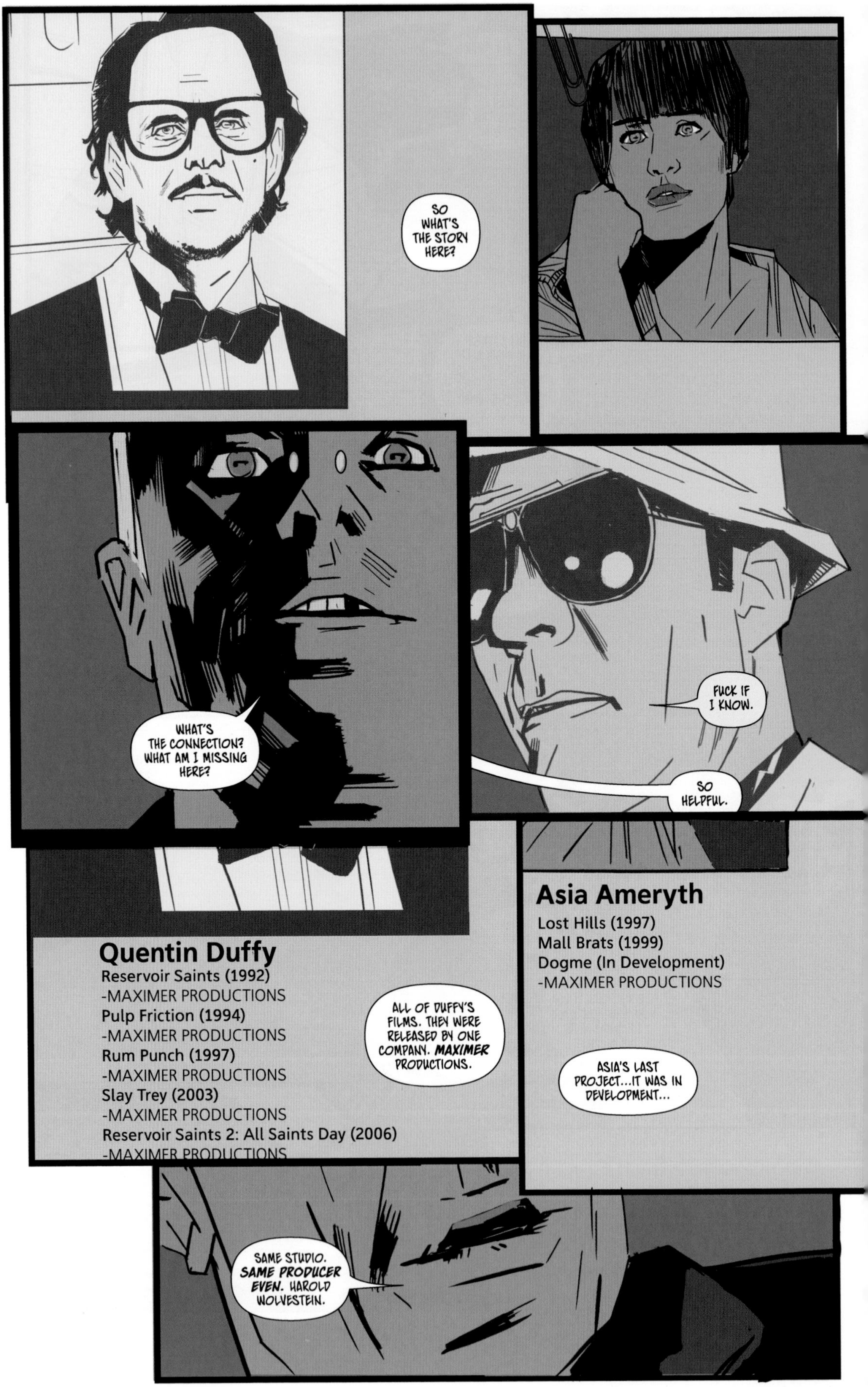
SO WHAT'S THE STORY HERE?
WHAT'S THE CONNECTION? WHAT AM I MISSING HERE?
FUCK IF I KNOW.
SO HELPFUL.
Quentin Duffy
Reservoir Saints (1992)
-MAXIMER PRODUCTIONS
Pulp Friction (1994)
-MAXIMER PRODUCTIONS
Rum Punch (1997)
-MAXIMER PRODUCTIONS
Slay Trey (2003)
-MAXIMER PRODUCTIONS
Reservoir Saints 2: All Saints Day (2006)
-MAXIMER PRODUCTIONS
ALL OF DUFFY'S FILMS. THEY WERE RELEASED BY ONE COMPANY. MAXIMER PRODUCTIONS.
Asia Ameryth
Lost Hills (1997)
Mall Brats (1999)
Dogme (In Development)
-MAXIMER PRODUCTIONS
ASIA'S LAST PROJECT...IT WAS IN DEVELOPMENT...
SAME STUDIO. SAME PRODUCER EVEN. HAROLD WOLVESTEIN.

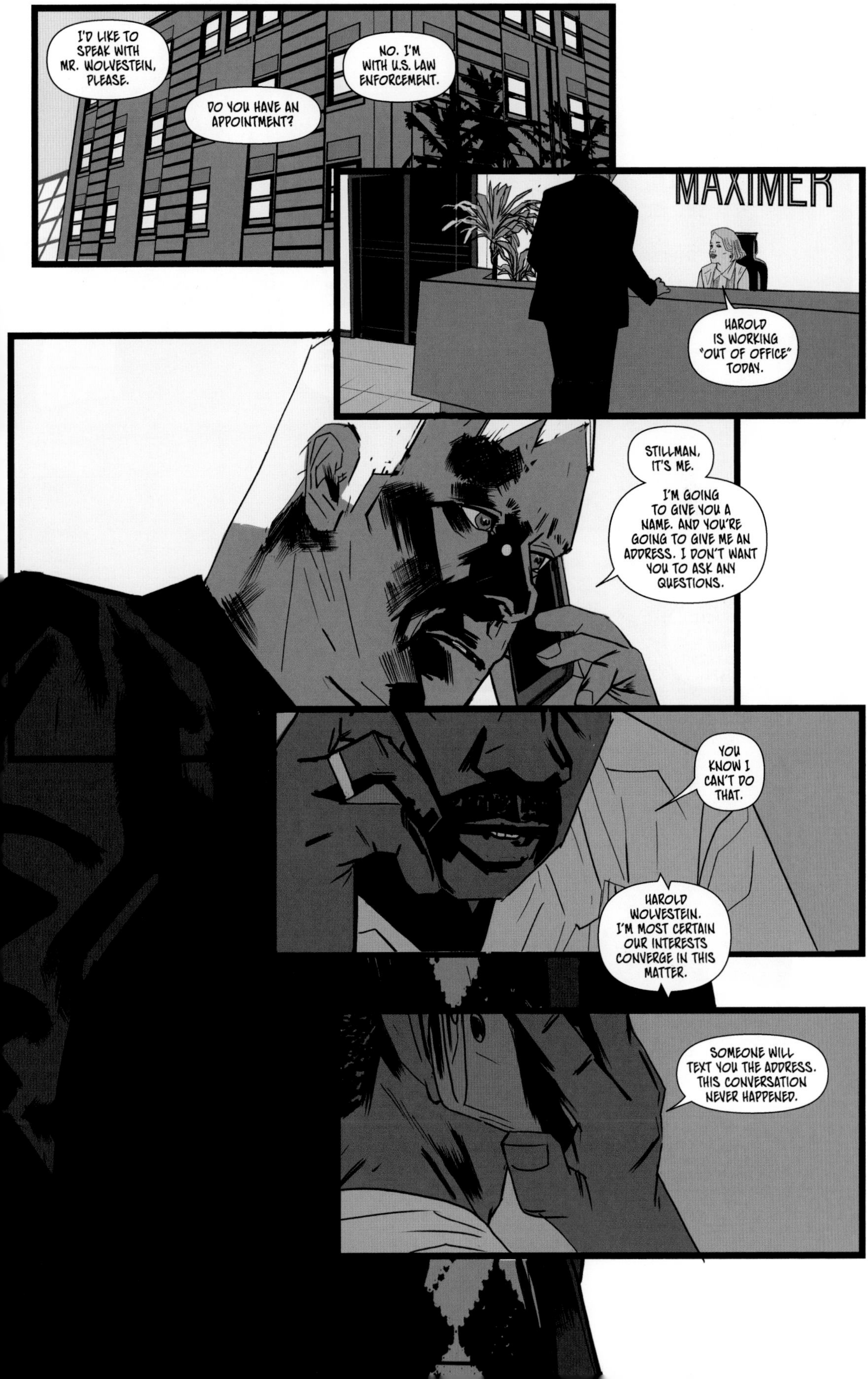
I'D LIKE TO SPEAK WITH MR. WOLVESTEIN, PLEASE.
DO YOU HAVE AN APPOINTMENT?
NO. I'M WITH U.S. LAW ENFORCEMENT.
MAXIMER
HAROLD IS WORKING "OUT OF OFFICE" TODAY.
STILLMAN, IT'S ME.
I'M GOING TO GIVE YOU A NAME. AND YOU'RE GOING TO GIVE ME AN ADDRESS. I DON'T WANT YOU TO ASK ANY QUESTIONS.
YOU KNOW I CAN'T DO THAT.
HAROLD WOLVESTEIN. I'M MOST CERTAIN OUR INTERESTS CONVERGE IN THIS MATTER.
SOMEONE WILL TEXT YOU THE ADDRESS. THIS CONVERSATION NEVER HAPPENED.

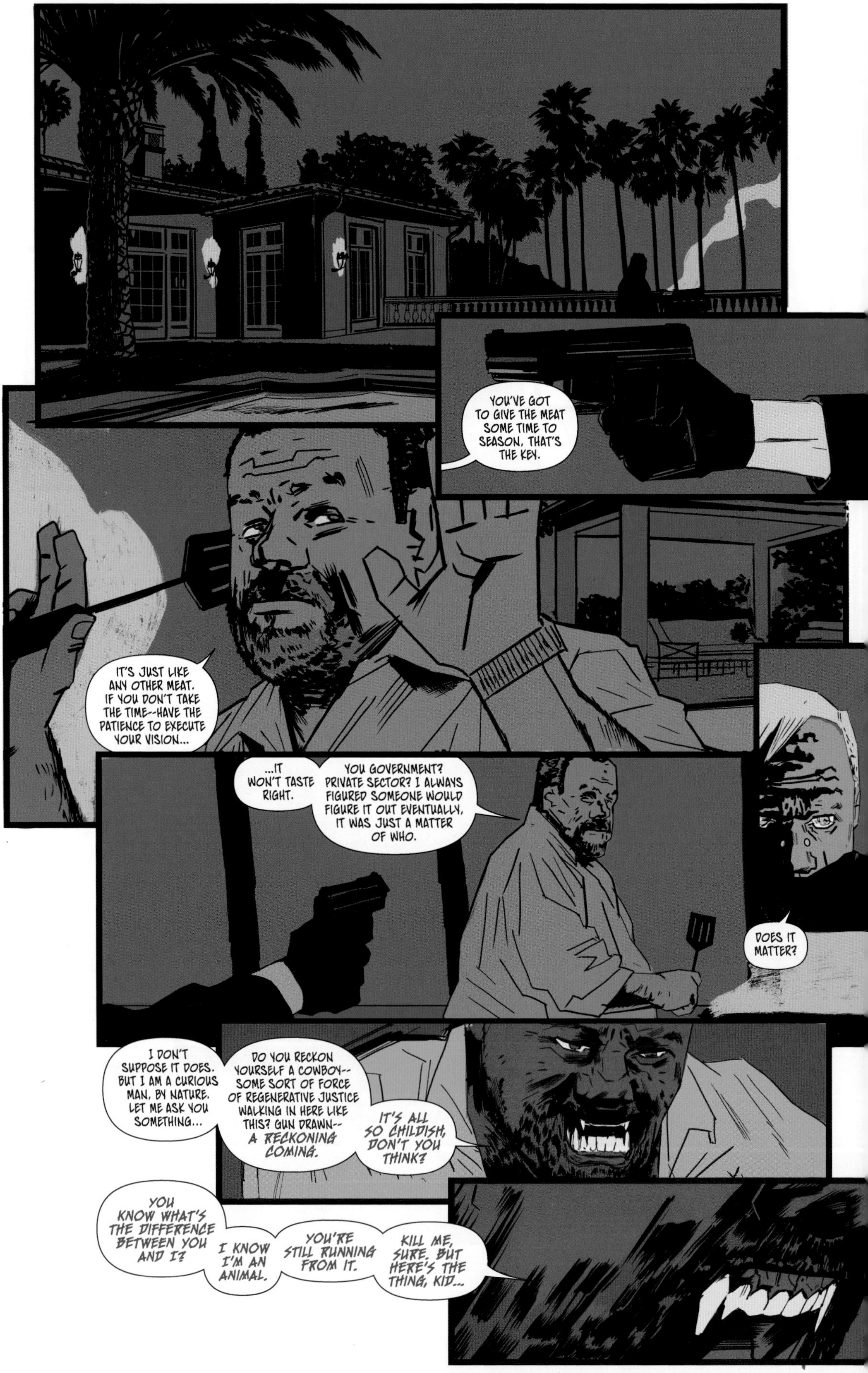
YOU'VE GOT TO GIVE THE MEAT SOME TIME TO SEASON, THAT'S THE KEY.
IT'S JUST LIKE ANY OTHER MEAT. IF YOU DON'T TAKE THE TIME--HAVE THE PATIENCE TO EXECUTE YOUR VISION...
...IT WON'T TASTE RIGHT.
YOU GOVERNMENT? PRIVATE SECTOR? I ALWAYS FIGURED SOMEONE WOULD FIGURE IT OUT EVENTUALLY, IT WAS JUST A MATTER OF WHO.
DOES IT MATTER?
I DON'T SUPPOSE IT DOES. BUT I AM A CURIOUS MAN, BY NATURE. LET ME ASK YOU SOMETHING...
DO YOU RECKON YOURSELF A COWBOY--SOME SORT OF FORCE OF REGENERATIVE JUSTICE WALKING IN HERE LIKE THIS? GUN DRAWN--A RECKONING COMING.
IT'S ALL SO CHILDISH, DON'T YOU THINK?
YOU KNOW WHAT'S THE DIFFERENCE BETWEEN YOU AND I?
I KNOW I'M AN ANIMAL.
YOU'RE STILL RUNNING FROM IT.
KILL ME, SURE. BUT HERE'S THE THING, KID...

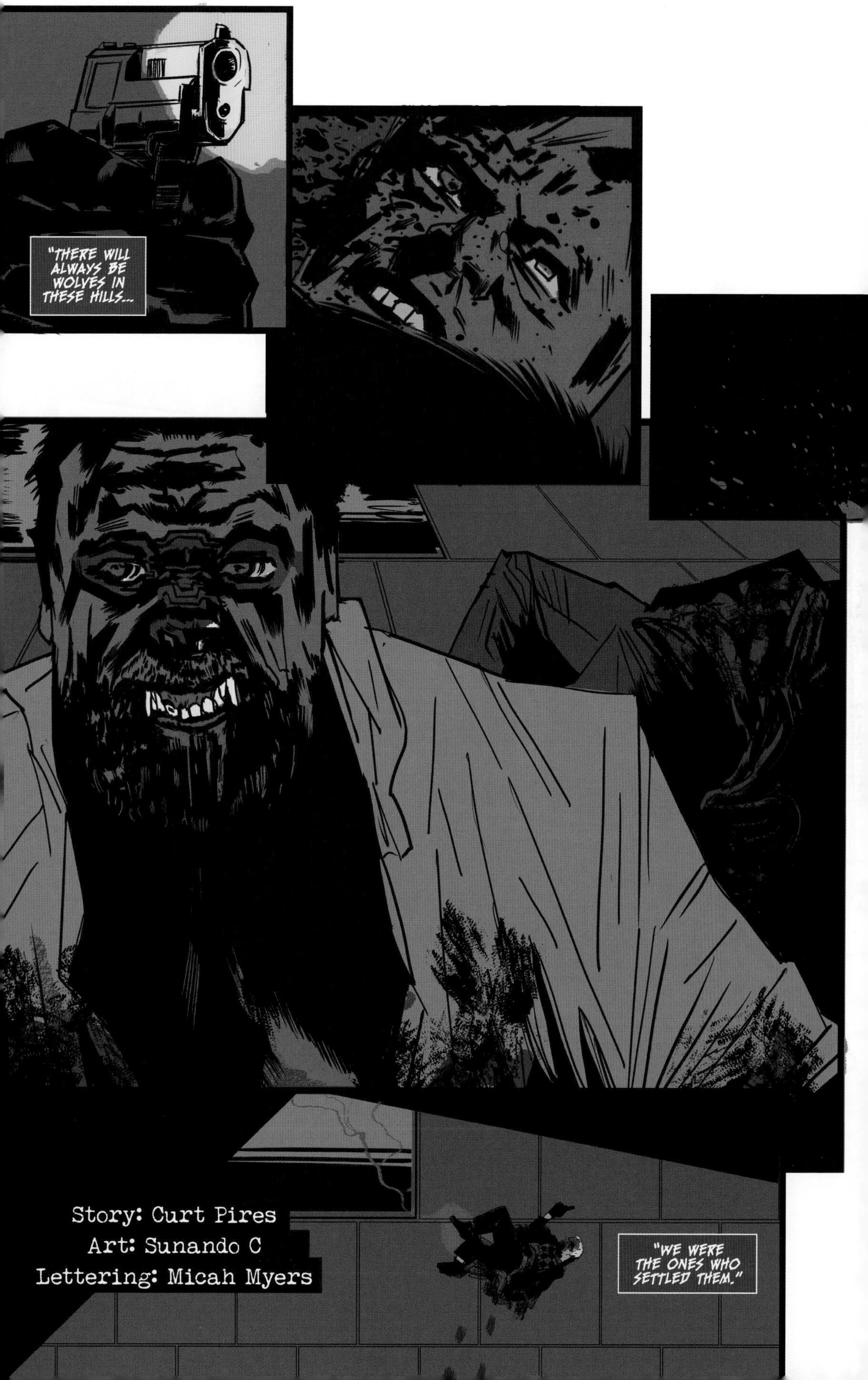
"THERE WILL ALWAYS BE WOLVES IN THESE HILLS...
Story: Curt Pires
Art: Sunando C
Lettering: Micah Myers
"WE WERE THE ONES WHO SETTLED THEM."

Illustration by Antonio Fuso

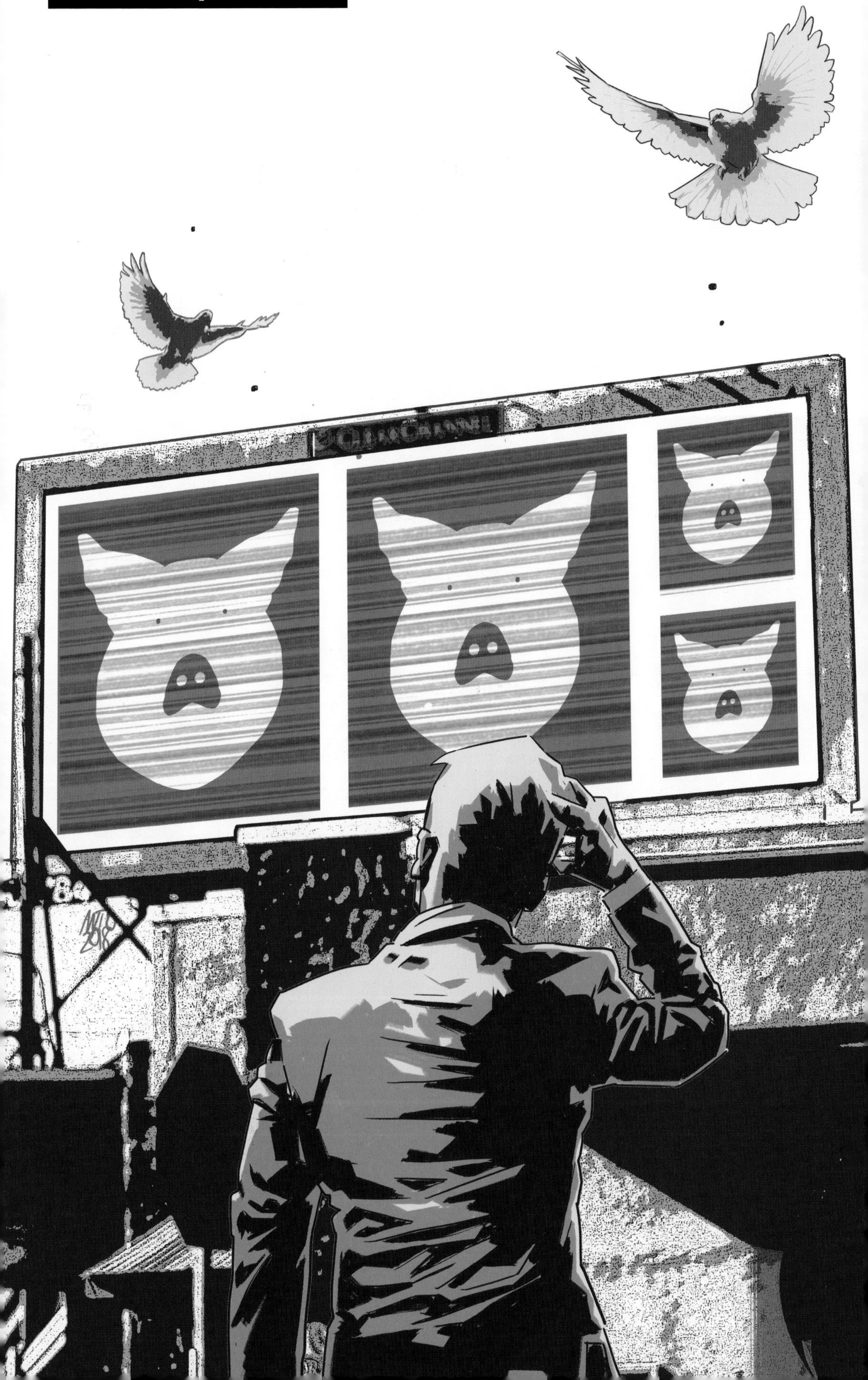

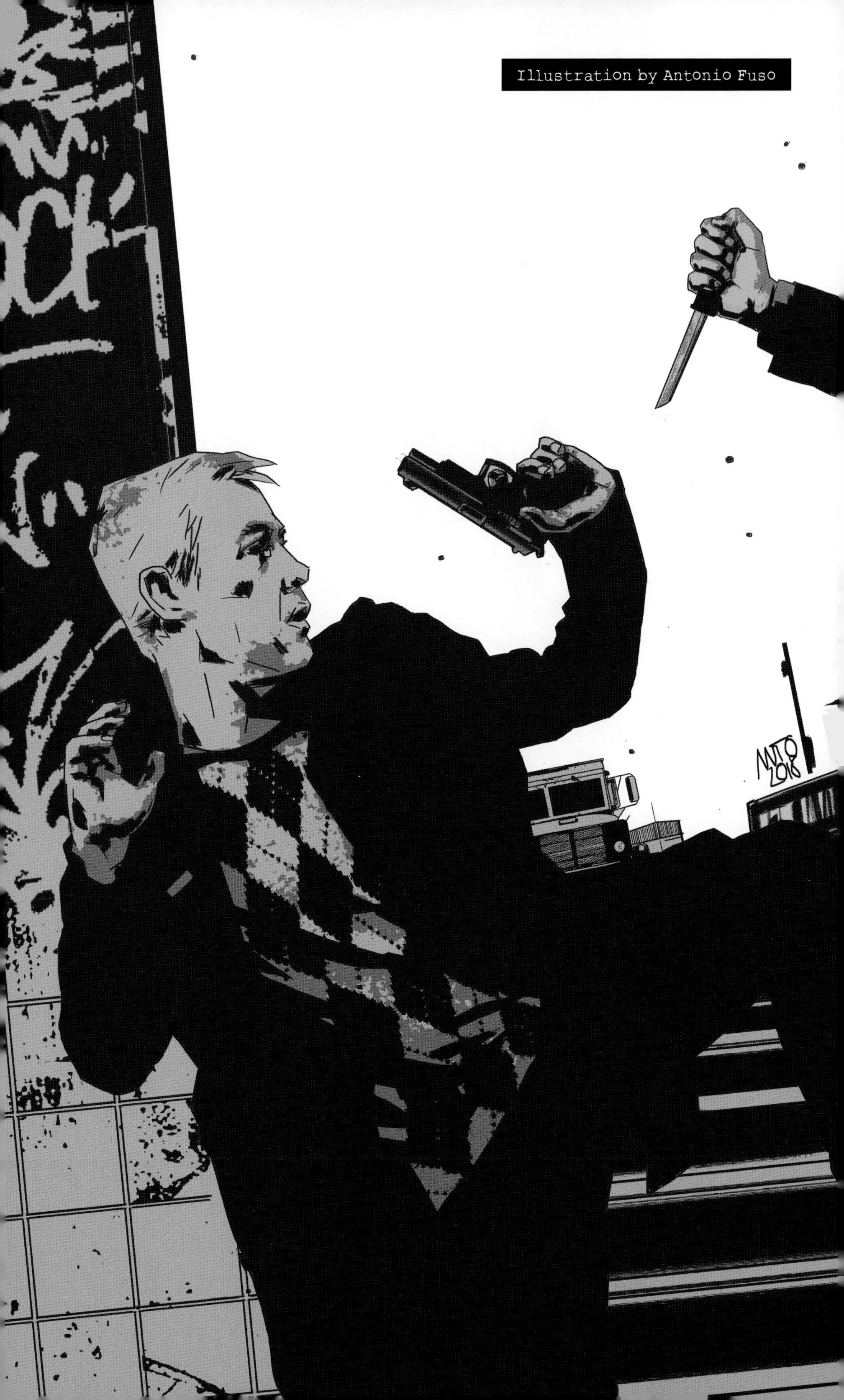

Illustration by Antonio Fuso

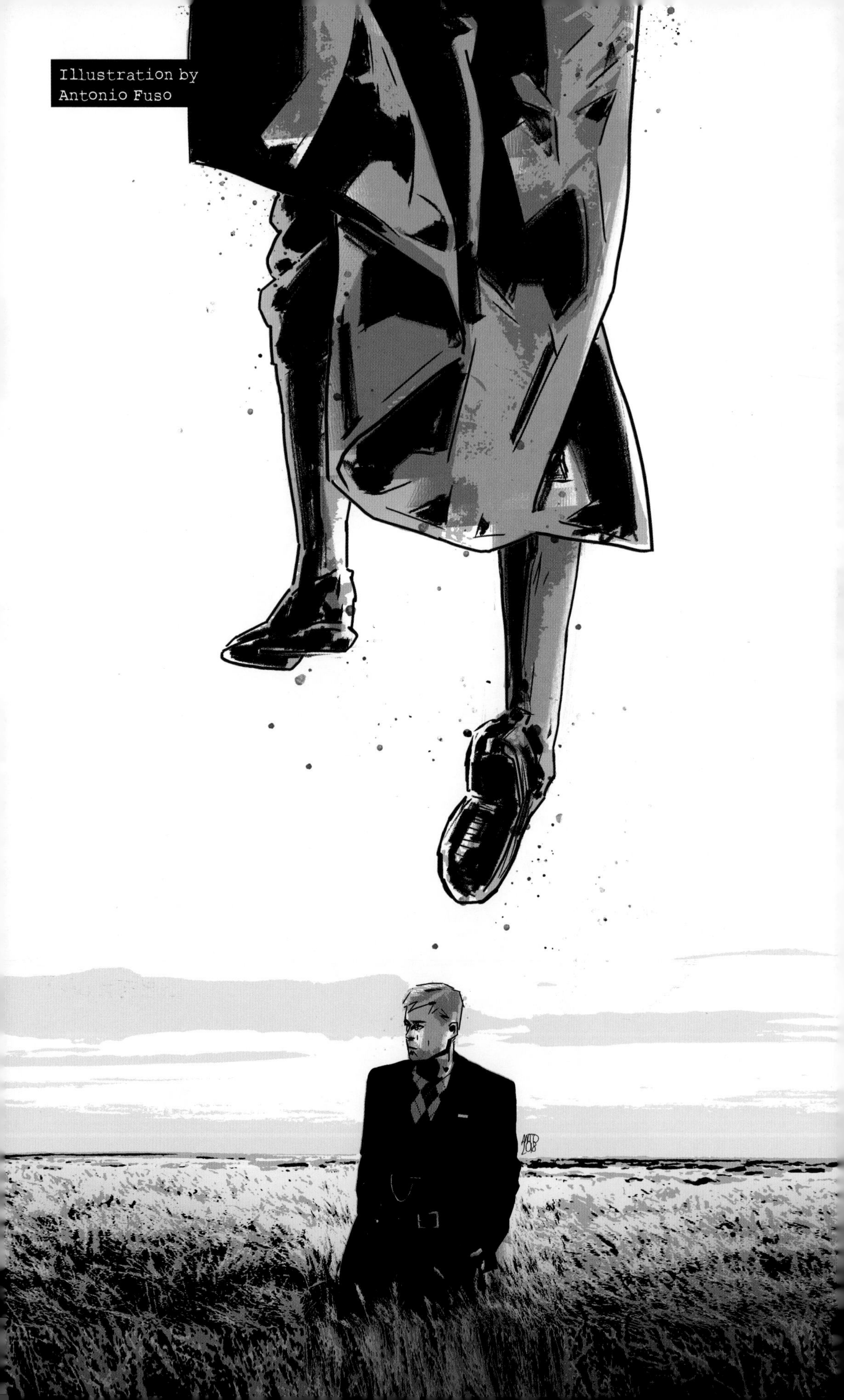

Illustration by
Antonio Fuso

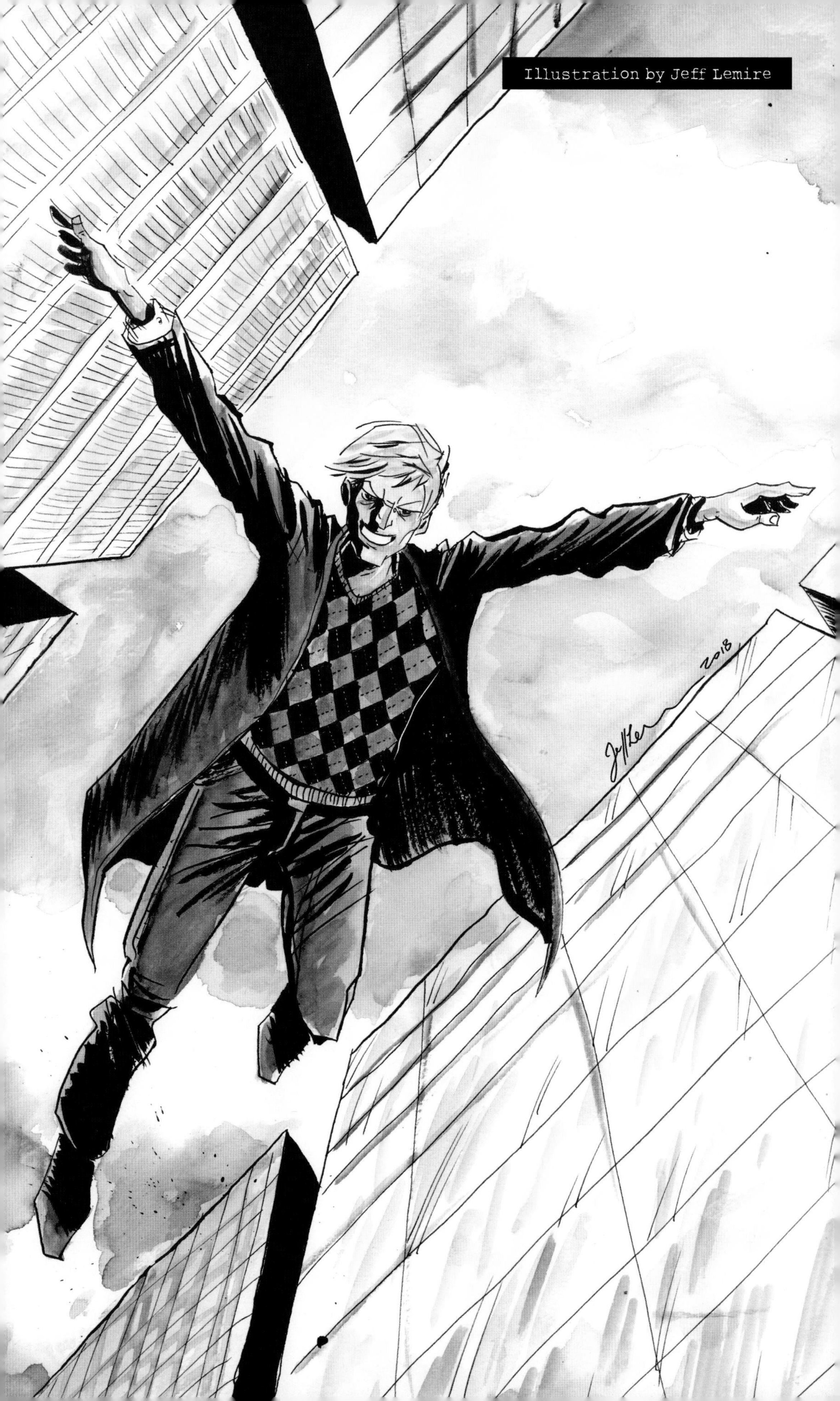

Illustration by Jeff Lemire

Illustration by
Rafael Albuquerque

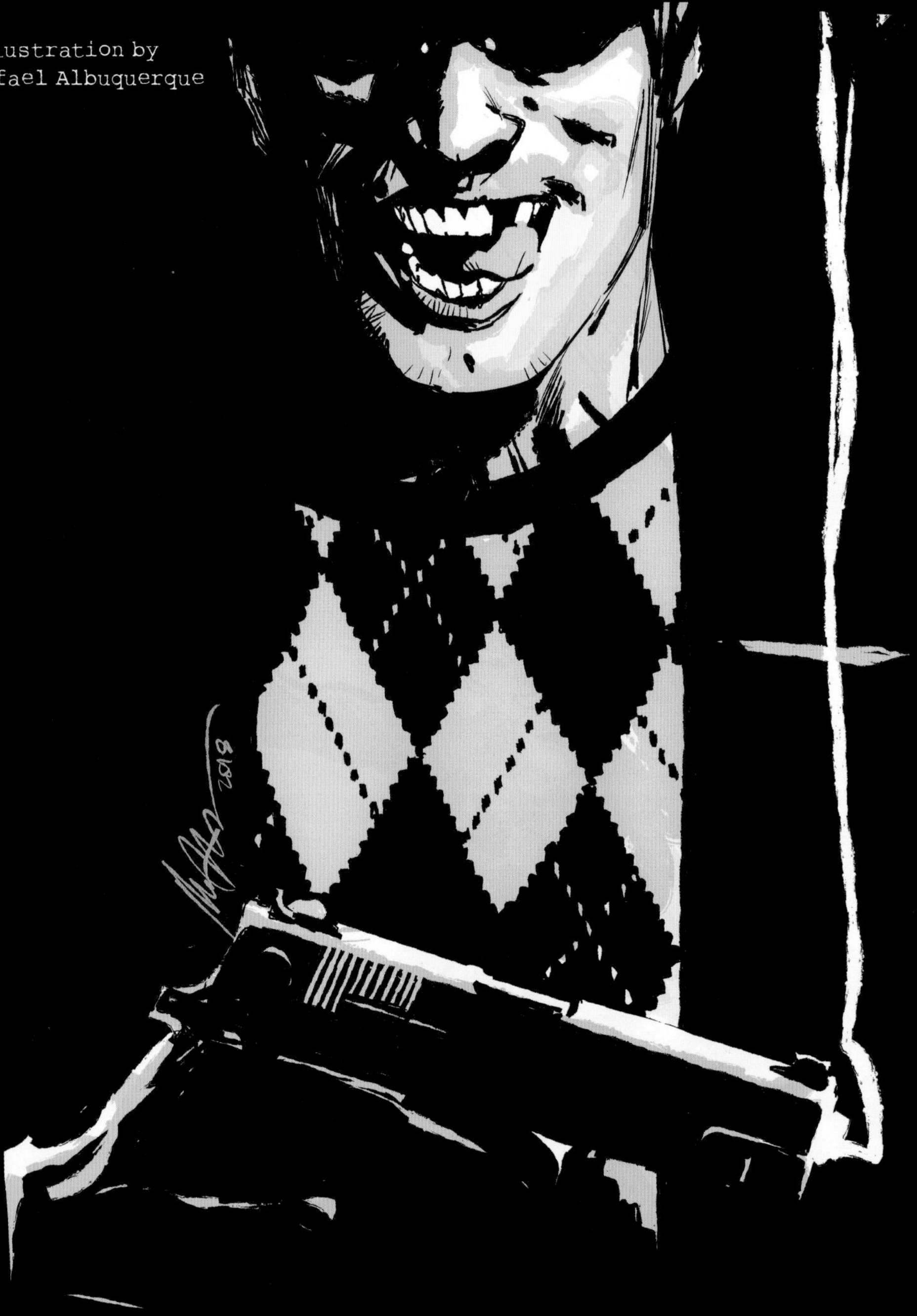

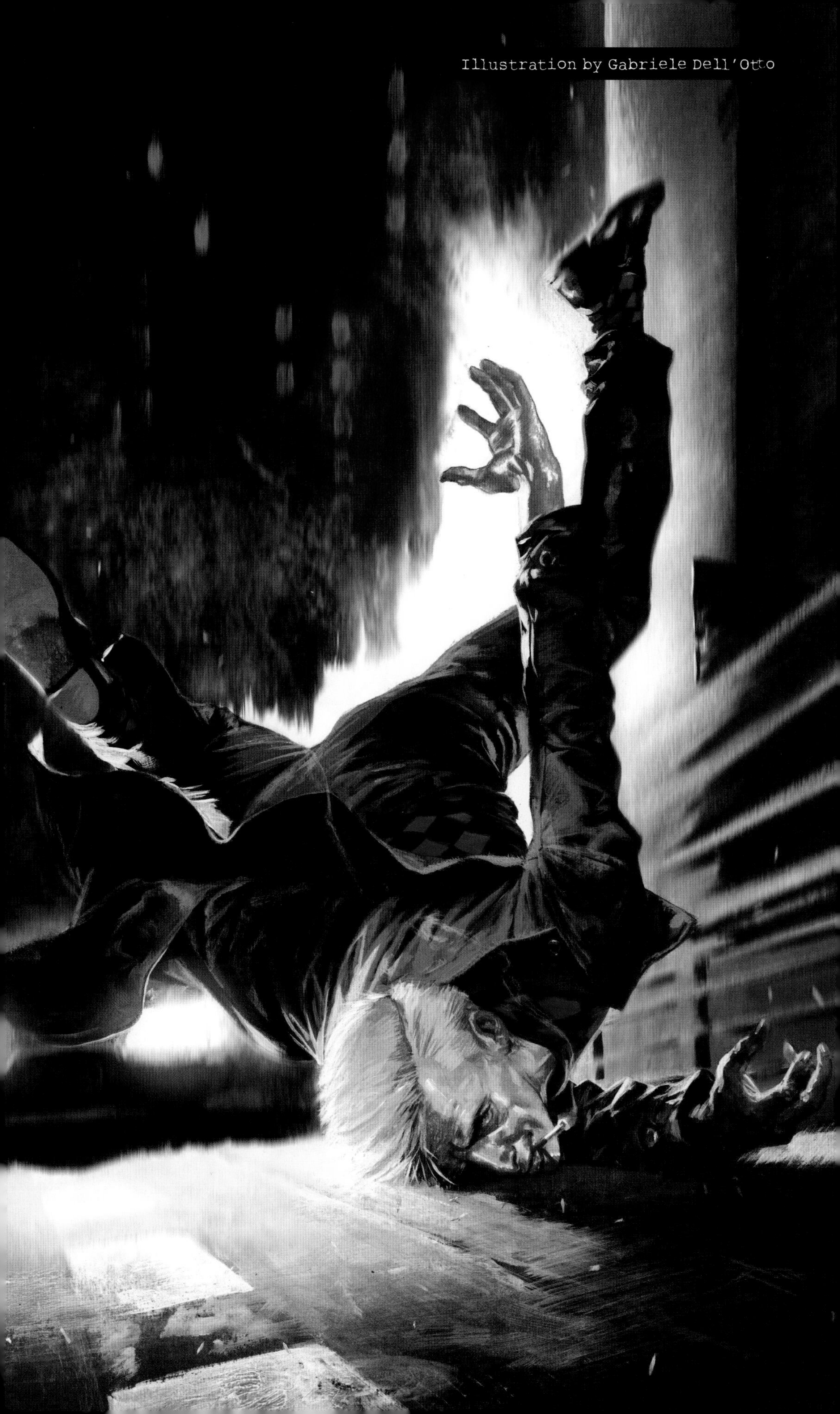

Illustration by Gabriele Dell'Otto

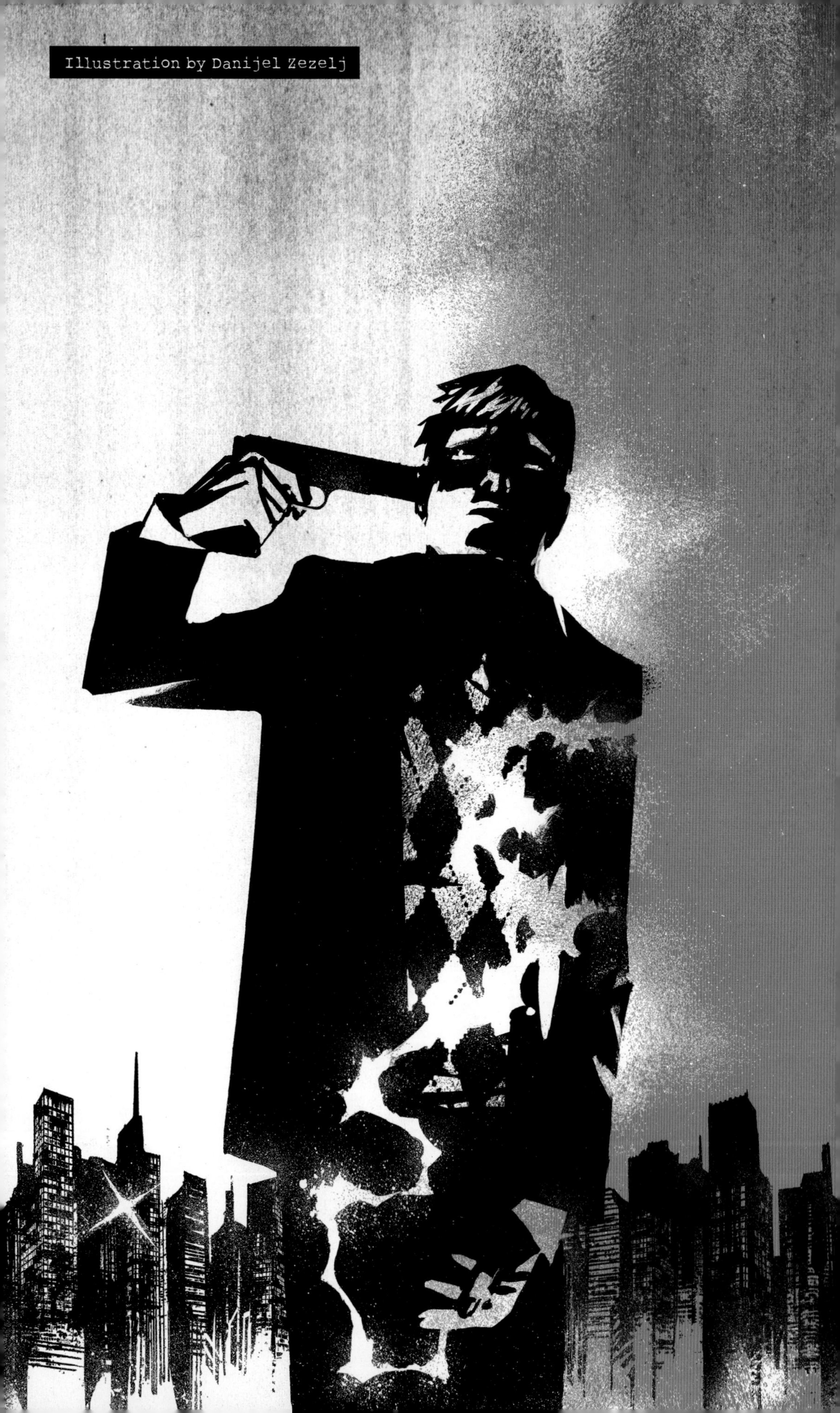
Illustration by Danijel Zezelj

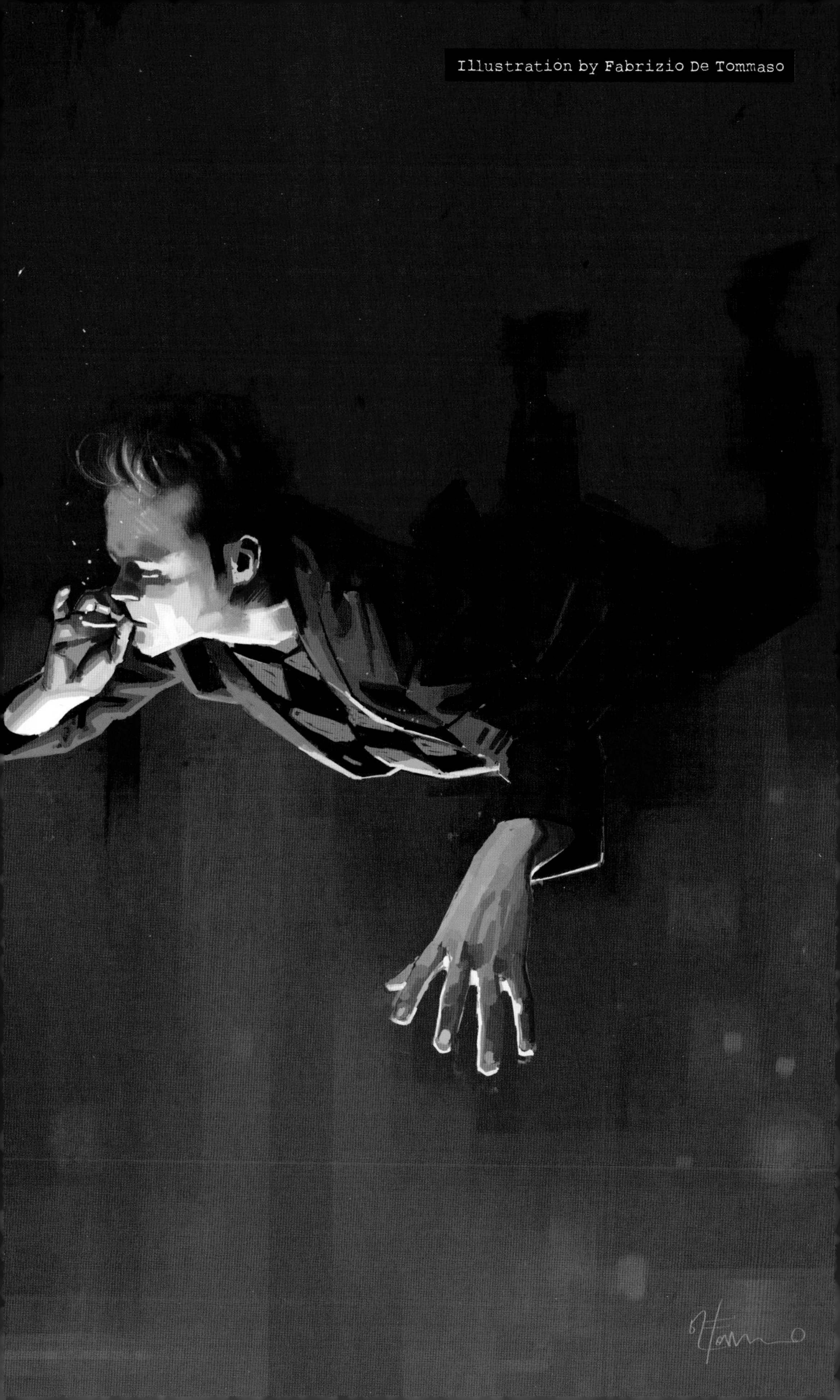

Illustration by Fabrizio De Tommaso

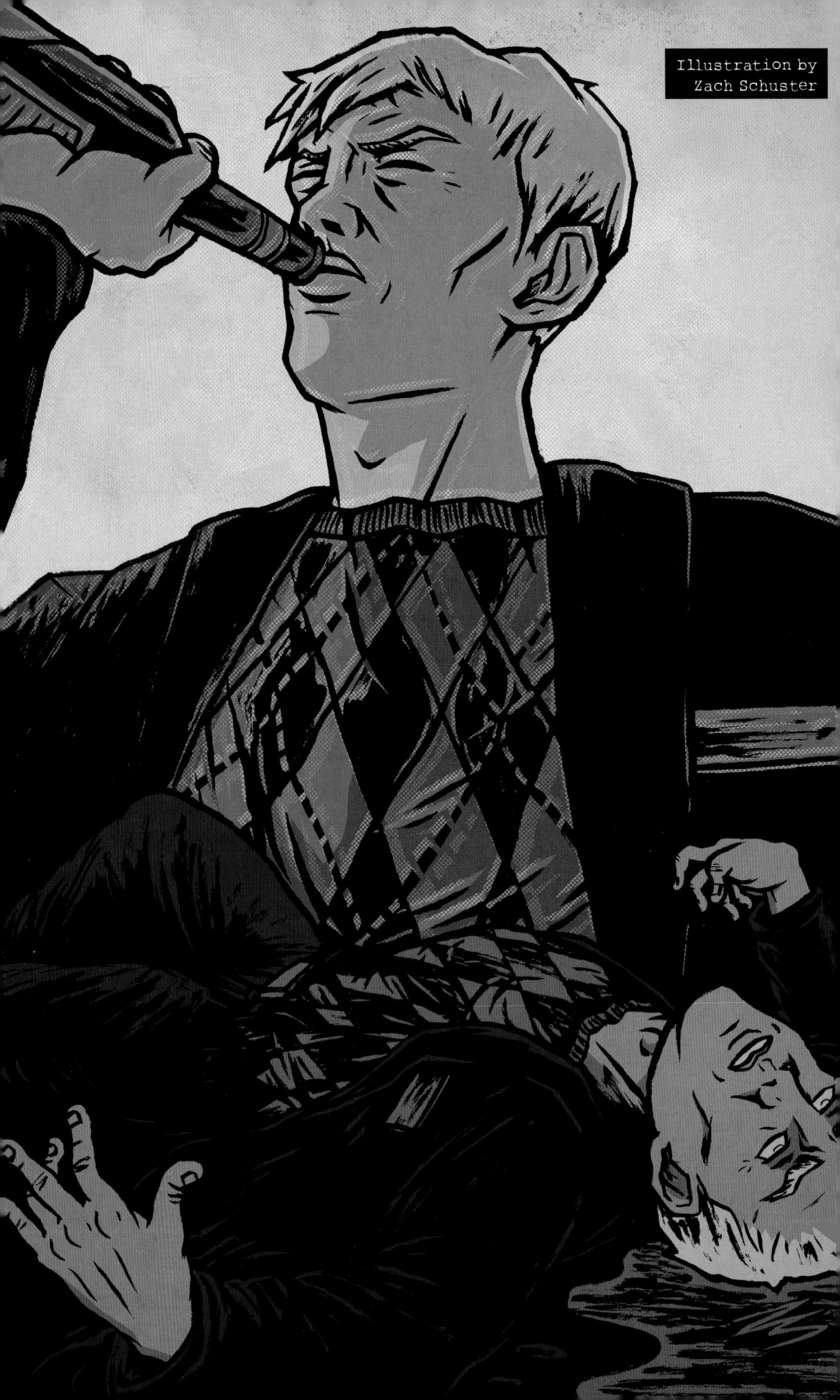
Illustration by
Zach Schuster

The following was originally published in PanelxPanel #20 - the comics craft magazine. You can find it at gumroad.com/panelxpanel, and this issue at gum.co/PXPNO20

CREATOR CHAT

The team behind Wyrd *- Curt Pires, Antonio Fuso, Stefano Simeone and Micah Myers - talk about bringing their creation to life.*

Wyrd opens by being familiar, prodding at us with references and connections to comics we've probably read in the past, and a lead character we've seen iterations of before. Which is just a very clever shorthand to get you immediately into the story, so it can tell you a whole, complex tale of everlasting life, superheroics, dark government activity, espionage, and European folklore in one issue. And again, by the end, it reveals another layer that separates *Wyrd* from those stories it immediately brings to mind.

And that's really the source of both its genius and its charm. By bringing you in with elements you recognize, it can subvert the traditions and the norms with a deeper story lingering throughout, one of not just of a cool, edgy character, but one with heartbreak, a life lost, and visions of being something else.

Wyrd's writer, Curt Pires, has talked before about building comics that give you bang for your buck, an interesting concept in a world of double-shipping and increasing single issue prices. It immediately calls to mind Warren Ellis's experimentations with bringing comics back to the model of newsstand comics, where you could pick up any issue in any order and get something satisfying from it. Every model has its own ups and downs, but there is something extremely fascinating about one-and-done stories with an undercurrent of a longer narrative. *Wyrd* manages it beautifully.

It's not Pires's first time approaching a character like this, but in *Wyrd,* with conspirators Antonio Fuso (art), Stefano Simeone (colors), and Micah Myers (letters), they find a delicate balance that makes *Wyrd* far more than the sum of its parts. We took an opportunity to ask a little more about the creation of *Wyrd,* and the work and themes behind it.

PanelxPanel: *I'd love to start with the two things that first struck me in the first issue. The cover design and that silent opening.*

With the cover design, it's likely the first thing you'll see with any comic, and with this issue, too. The Wyrd *covers are very striking, and the single-palette approach gives them a very designed look and feel, almost more akin to book covers. Antonio, what's your process for cover design? What are you aiming for, and how do you know when you've gotten there?*

Antonio Fuso [art/story]:   When I start thinking about a cover (and even more if I'm working on a sequence of covers for the same book), my first approach is a design approach. Because I studied at a design school and not a comics school, we can say I'm more of a designer who was loaned to comics.

Talking about covers, art is just an element with the same importance as the main title design, the publisher's logo, creative team's names . . . even bar code placement is important for the final composition. Everything must be balanced. Before starting a new series I always ask the editors if I can design book's main title logo as well, in order to have full control on composition and, luckily, they let me do it.

I think a plain and well designed cover pops better on the shelves. That's why we wanted the single palette approach, too.

PanelxPanel: *And once you're inside, the opening is this silent introduction to the world of the self-destructive Wyrd. Curt, why did you want to start with the silence?*

Curt Pires [writer]:   The opening was one of the last things to come to me, and that's sort of when I finally cracked the character and the larger story of *Wyrd* became clear to me.

As for the silence, I think one of the big problems I encounter when reading comics, is this thing where writers always need to be scripting—

writing over everything. This idea that if there' no caption boxes or internal monologue, tha you're not doing your job? I wanted to move way past that. And just sort of have total confidence to have a purely visual communication of the story—and trust the team to deliver. I think it's bit that I'm trying to draw from film technique now, too. That idea of a cold open . . .

PanelxPanel: *As a writer, how different is crafting something entirely visually and action based with something sculpted with dialogue? D you tend to approach them in different ways?*

Curt Pires: I find a lot of it is mostly jus getting out of the way. Clear instructions of what' happening, and what needs to be communicated but just trusting the team to execute. Which they always do.

But yeah, script for something like this is a lo more sparse, than, say, for the stuff later in the issue.

PanelxPanel: *I love the way Wyrd gets hit b the car. There's the panel of him standing in the lights of the car, arms outstretched, almost god-like And then the splash that seems unceremonious b comparison, him flipping in the air is very matter-of-fact.*

How visual do you tend to be in your scripts? Ar you doing emotional directing, visual directing, o a mix of both?

Curt Pires: That's a moment that actually i inspired by something I witnessed in real life Though, there's no way in hell I'm about to share the story [laughs].

I think I mostly go for the emotional beats, bu there are times when I have specific visual cue in mind—that I'll normally reference, or include links to in the script. I think the big thing for me is the emotional moments, if there's something I'm trying to land in a scene, communicating it in the script, so Antonio can embed this into the artwork.

PanelxPanel: *And Antonio, what are you aiming to capture in your layouts when turning the script into the page? Is it a focus on particular key images, or trying to balance everything across a whole page, or something else?*

Antonio Fuso: Second one! I think about the page as a single art piece and not a sum of panels. For example, if we have lots of black in the last panel on the bottom right corner of the page, you can be sure I will find a way to add black to the first panel on the top left corner. Obviously in practicality it is not that simple, but it sells the idea.

What I said about covers works for interior art, too. Composition comes before storytelling, in my opinion. I'm not the kind of artist who thinks storytelling should necessarily be easy to read, and I don't think my readers are six years old, so they can be focused on a panel more than one second to understand what is happening. Reality is messy, and what I try to do is to choreograph that mess.

PanelxPanel: *There's a lot of very playful visuals in* Wyrd. *I love the bone breaking panels early on, overlapping panels.*

Antonio Fuso: Ah, the bone breaking panels. I must admit I stole the idea from *Desolation Jones,* by Warren Ellis and J.H. Williams III!

PanelxPanel: *In the second issue, the page of Wyrd and Cameron fighting, the panels themselves start to replicate the movement and action, and it's like you're directly wanting to use the page composition itself as storytelling. When do you know you can get away with a design like this, and when do you feel the need to restrain?*

Antonio Fuso: Oh, I never feel the need to restrain. Composition and page layout are always part of the storytelling.

If we have a sequence with two people talking, then the page layout and the panel shapes will be regular and simple. As the action grows even panels and layouts starts to go crazy, too!

PanelxPanel: *Curt, it feels like* Wyrd *is a commentary on the broken white male archetype, the self-destructive bad-boy who, at the end of the day, still fixes everything. It's the end of the first issue, the flashback, that seemed to indicate this wasn't just a pulpy, cold war superheroic thriller, but also a discussion and dissection of that. What is it about that hard-boiled archetype that initially pulled you in, and why did you want to explore it with* Wyrd?

Curt Pires: I mean, to me *Wyrd* works on a couple of levels. If you show up just wanting a fix of this very typical spy/detective narrative, and want to engage on the work on just a simple level— that's all there for you. Each issue is a case. But the larger story—the bigger sort of narrative at play—is a more post-modern meditation on identity, violence, performative masculinity, all these things that tie into the genre. To me that's where the heart of the book is, that larger narrative/exploration.

PanelxPanel: *When I saw the end of the first issue, I had to go back to the start of it. The juxtaposition between this image of love and connection, compared to an opening of self-destructive violence, was incredibly interesting. You mentioned performative masculinity, and that is throughout* Wyrd. *It's portrayed as something that only seems to end in power, greed, and destruction. The super soldier as the villain, Cameron's need and hunger for power, and even Wyrd's tendencies. Do you see this grasp for power and destruction as something specifically masculine?*

Curt Pires: I don't specifically tie this need for power and the greed and destruction that comes with it to masculinity, no. I think it's a larger issue and conversation that can transcend gender.

I think what *Wyrd* really tries to explore is the angles of these stories that we don't often see. It's true, figures of power and politicians, and sort of these bureaucratic figures, are depicted as having a negative impact on the world around them. I think that's a bit of my bias bleeding into it, and just sort of observing the world and asking the question, can people who seek power over their fellow man act justly and benevolently, or do they all sort of give into and yield to the corruption and evil of the system.

That splash when Wyrd breaks Cameron's neck, and he says: "I hate politicians." That's me sort of letting the character speak for me.

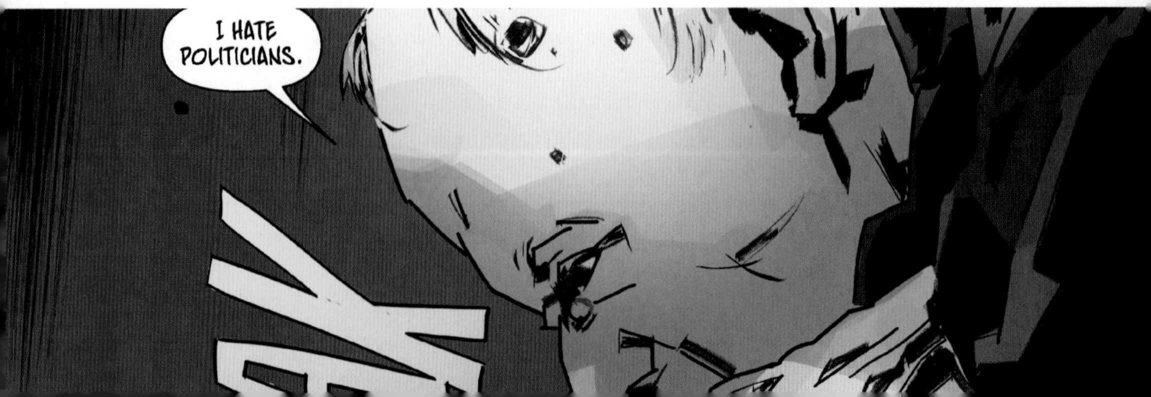
I HATE POLITICIANS.

PanelxPanel: I really do love the approach, because we're given this story that, initially, is one thing, before revealing more of the heart. The second issue is a strong example of it. Ending with this winky nod to the reader, after an issue of in-your-face fantasy and politics, then suddenly taking a turn into historical thriller-romance, one that feels infinitely more grounded. When did this come up as structure for the book? And do you find a need to create a kind of tonal balance between them?

Curt Pires: I think when I was writing the first issue, I came up with it. I didn't just want to end on Wyrd coming home to LA and getting the money. I knew I needed to set up the larger scope and mystery of the story. I also just wanted a bit of hope and optimism in the book.

The characters are, in a lot of ways, just embodiments of this internal argument I am constantly having about the nature of the world. Is it good? Is it evil? What's the point of participating? What's really the value in any of this? I'm not going to shy away from the dark impulses of Wyrd— that suicidal ideation and extreme nihilism is just as much a part of the internal conversation I'm pulling out of myself. They're impulses I think a lot of us struggle with, and I think it's what makes Wyrd so unique. That a lot of what the book is about, is the mental health of its title character.

I've been watching *Patriot* on Amazon, and that definitely motivated and inspired me to push that angle.

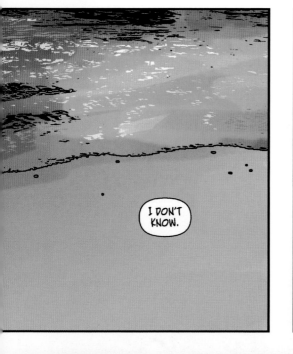

I DON'T KNOW.

LOOK AROUND US. AT ALL OF IT. THE INEVITABLE DECAY. THE DISINTEGRATION AND VIOLATION OF ALL GOODNESS. HOW IN GOOD CONSCIENCE COULD WE BRING A CHILD INTO THIS?

HOW COULD WE NOT?

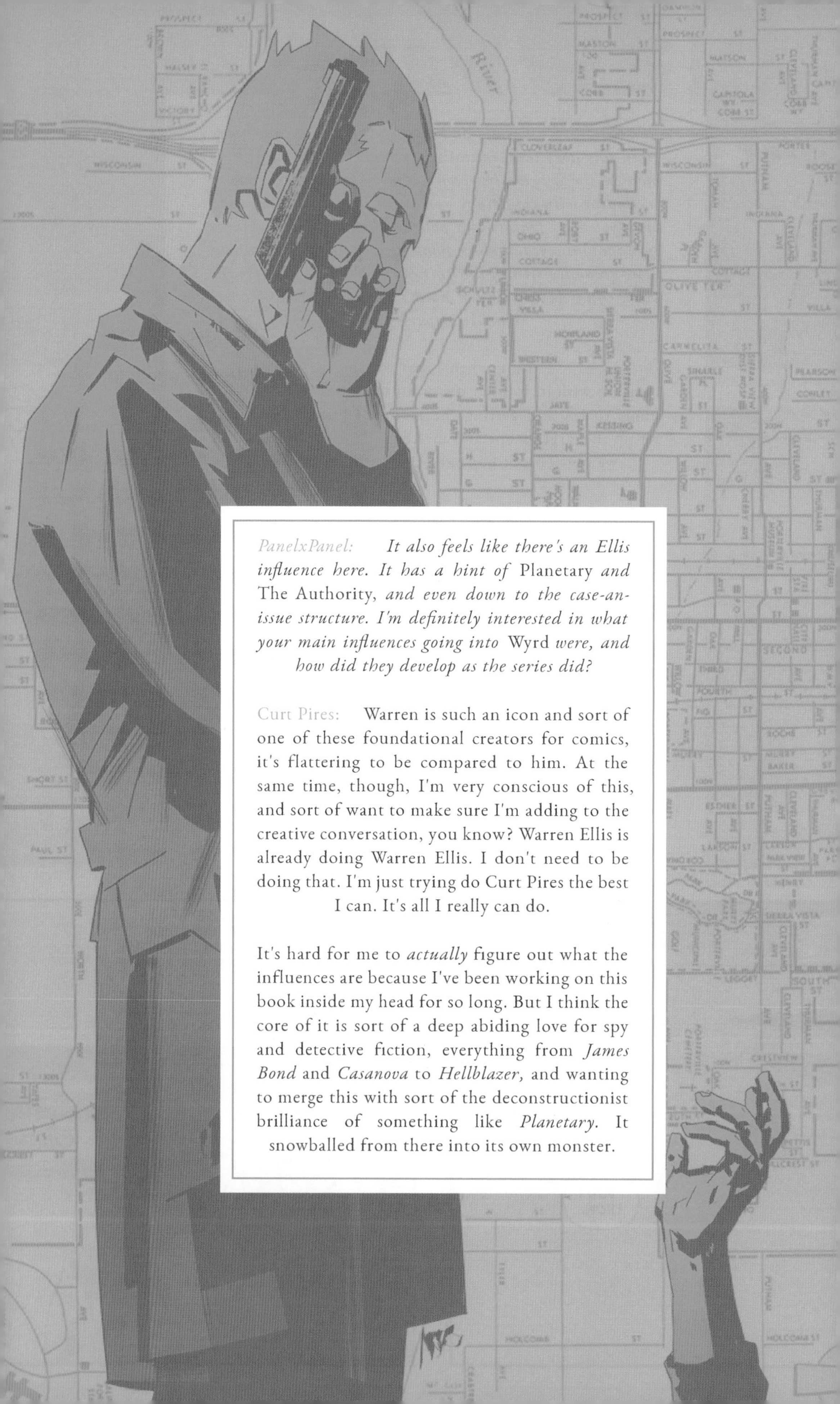

River
PROSPECT
CLOVERLEAF
WISCONSIN
INDIANA
OHIO
COTTAGE
OLIVE TER
CARMELITA
SECOND
ROCHE
SIERRA VISTA
CRESTVIEW
HOLCOMB

PanelxPanel: It also feels like there's an Ellis influence here. It has a hint of Planetary *and* The Authority, *and even down to the case-an-issue structure. I'm definitely interested in what your main influences going into* Wyrd *were, and how did they develop as the series did?*

Curt Pires: Warren is such an icon and sort of one of these foundational creators for comics, it's flattering to be compared to him. At the same time, though, I'm very conscious of this, and sort of want to make sure I'm adding to the creative conversation, you know? Warren Ellis is already doing Warren Ellis. I don't need to be doing that. I'm just trying do Curt Pires the best I can. It's all I really can do.

It's hard for me to *actually* figure out what the influences are because I've been working on this book inside my head for so long. But I think the core of it is sort of a deep abiding love for spy and detective fiction, everything from *James Bond* and *Casanova* to *Hellblazer,* and wanting to merge this with sort of the deconstructionist brilliance of something like *Planetary.* It snowballed from there into its own monster.

PanelxPanel: It's also got a strong touch of the cold war espionage, something that I guess we'd typically associate with seventies political thrillers, but is really coming back to be more and more pertinent to discussions today. The second issue also focuses again very directly on politics. It feels like it's impossible to evade at the moment, with turmoil in the US and in Britain. Why was it that you wanted to balance these realities in your fiction?

Curt Pires: I mean, I'm honestly not trying to have too much of a political conversation with this book, but like you say it's inevitable. Part of it is, I think this concept of recurrence, us as a species is very on my mind these days. It's hard not to look at America right now and think about Germany pre-World War II, and how this slow cooking hate and anger eventually boiled over into a genocide—a world war. Maybe some of it's a longing for a time when Nazis were just fucking villains, end of discussion, and not talking heads on Fox News. I don't know.

The angle of Wyrd's parents and their role in the story sort of comes from the concept of the Americans whisking away Germans post-WWII to work on their rockets, their science. I'm not going to say any more on that though because the story needs to unfold.

PanelxPanel: I've read you mentioning the idea of immersion in comics in other interviews, really trying to make each single issue be something worth that time and investment. But what does that idea mean to you, of immersion in comics? And how do you work to craft that?

Curt Pires: You know, I remember being really obsessed with that idea, and I think in a way I still am. I still like the design and everything to feed into each other, but more and more I find myself letting go of factors like that, and wanting the story just to speak for itself. Although, there's a care and attention to detail that is always there, I guess.

PanelxPanel: How does the collaboration between you and Antonio tend to work?

Curt Pires: It's really fluid, hence going with the storytellers credit as opposed to breaking things down as "writer and artist." I write the scripts, try to include all relevant information about plot, emotion, and any specific visual references I have, and then I like to let Antonio run wild.

Sometimes he adds panels, sometimes he stays true to the script, but I always rewrite after I see the art and try and improve the interaction between the words and the pictures—because that's really what it's all about. The bone-breaking thing in the first issue, which is one of the best parts of it? All Antonio. But I found a way to bring it back for issue four, in a new subversive way, so everything on this book is a full circle feedback loop. I feel like we're pulling our best work out of one and other.

PanelxPanel: Antonio, what's the process for character design for you?

In Wyrd *especially there's a balance between the natural and supernatural, and still keeping it grounded, so how to do you build that in the world and character design?*

Antonio Fuso: The first thing I think whe designing a character is that I'll have to draw for a hundred pages (more or less), so it should b easy to draw—according to what is easy for me draw. Every artist is different. I know it's not s evocative or inspiring to say, but doing comics is job and I have to be fast and productive.

Then I think about the look: Wyrd is a rotte secret agent, so he dresses in black, as all secre agents do since James Bond, but also an ol sweater, a couple of piercings on the sides of h nose, and last but not least, he has a tooth missir in his mouth. Wyrd wants to die, so I don't thin he would take care of his teeth!

PanelxPanel: When it comes to Stefano's color how aware are you of what choices he's going make? The palette and your visuals seem so wel defined, so is there much back and forth on th color work, or any decision making as a team?

Antonio Fuso: Stefano and I share a studi in Rome with six other amazing artists, and w work together on several projects, so he knows m and I know I can trust him. Also, he's just a des away, with no oceans in the middle, so if I need t ask him something or he has a question, the onl thing we need to do is to turn off the radio for while and talk each other.

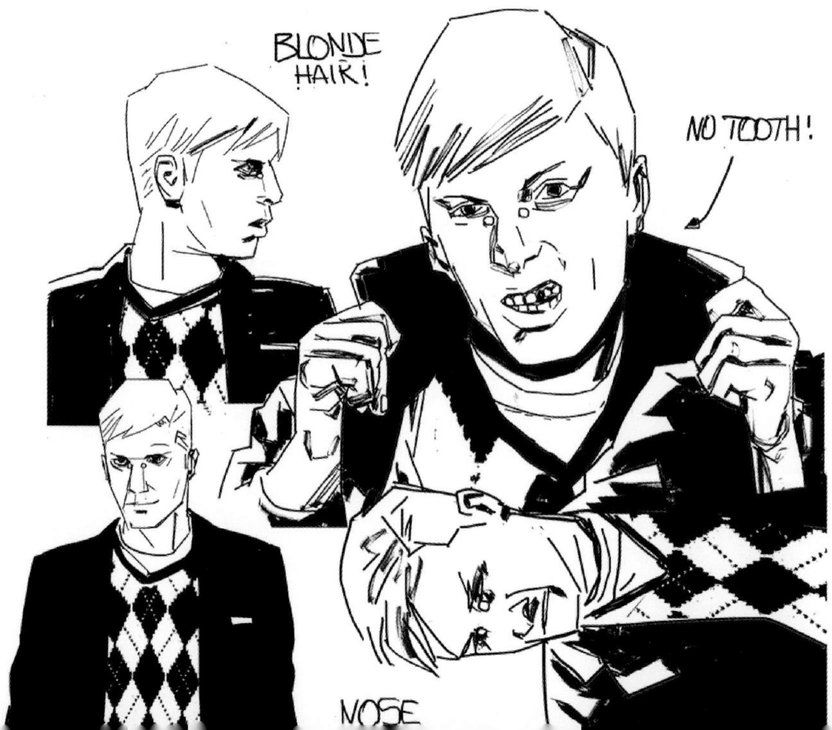
BLONDE HAIR!
NO TOOTH!
NOSE

PanelxPanel: Stefano, your palettes are gorgeous. I love how limited they tend to be, even across the whole issue. How do you come to develop a look and palette for a series? What questions and decisions are you working through until you get to a place where you're happy?

Stefano Simeone [colors]: First of all, I look at the composition. If Antonio has decided a type of equilibrium for the page, my goal is to keep it, adding colors and atmosphere. I think colors have to add information to the storytelling, so I first concentrate my work on the context. I do this by reading the script, maybe if there's an important element in the page I'll make a note.

Then, I don't care about realistic colors, because colors are just a physical reaction of the human eyes to a material, but I give more significance to light, which is the way we understand volumes. For the colors I choose, I think they are a direct consequence of the movies I like, or the TV series I'm watching, the frames I look at. I really care about being in and working on the modernity.

PanelxPanel: Do you tend to build palettes through scenes or across whole issues? The heavy purple and orange feels quite present throughout the opening, for example.

Stefano Simeone: I proceed step-by-step, looking at the real timing of each issue. I like to focus on the passage of time, for example, when two people are talking for the entire page, I usually change the shadows a bit from panel to panel, because I imagine the sun is slowly moving.

So I change my palettes in reaction of this reason, not really caring too much about the look of the whole issue as I work though it initially, but that's something I change in my final revision, in order to avoid the "rainbow effect."

PanelxPanel: It's such an interesting look, because there's a mix of gradients, hard-edged coloring and lighting, but also these brushy moments, where it feels like it's been digitally painted. How do you get a feel for when to make a stylistic decision like that? And what quality did Antonio's work have that specifically drew you to this look and feel?

Stefano Simeone: I usually work on a digital painting effect only when I know very well the artist I'm working with. Elsewhere, I avoid the "drawing with the colors" look on the pages. Me and Antonio, we work in the same studio, and have done for years, so we know each other very well and we're constantly talking about color approach. So I know what he likes, most of the time. I try to use a different look for each project, because every inked page, I think, has its specific way to be colored.

PanelxPanel: Micah, what's your process for getting the look on the lettering that works for the book?

Micah Myers [letters]: For the main story, the dialogue font was picked to match the art style. The captions would styled to look similar to the logo, which is that look of government paperwork with redacted parts, giving everything a consistency.

The time I broke that was for backup in the second issue, which had such a different art style. It was like a drug fever dream, so the lettering style and font had to change to match in that case.

PanelxPanel: *And why did this particular story have to be told as a comic? What was it about the medium that makes it right for telling* Wyrd?

Curt Pires: I think that really it just comes down to I love espionage comics, and there was sort of a vacancy, a gap in the specific flavor I like, so I decided to make one! Like everything I do creatively it's a bit selfish. I'm always trying to make what I want to read.

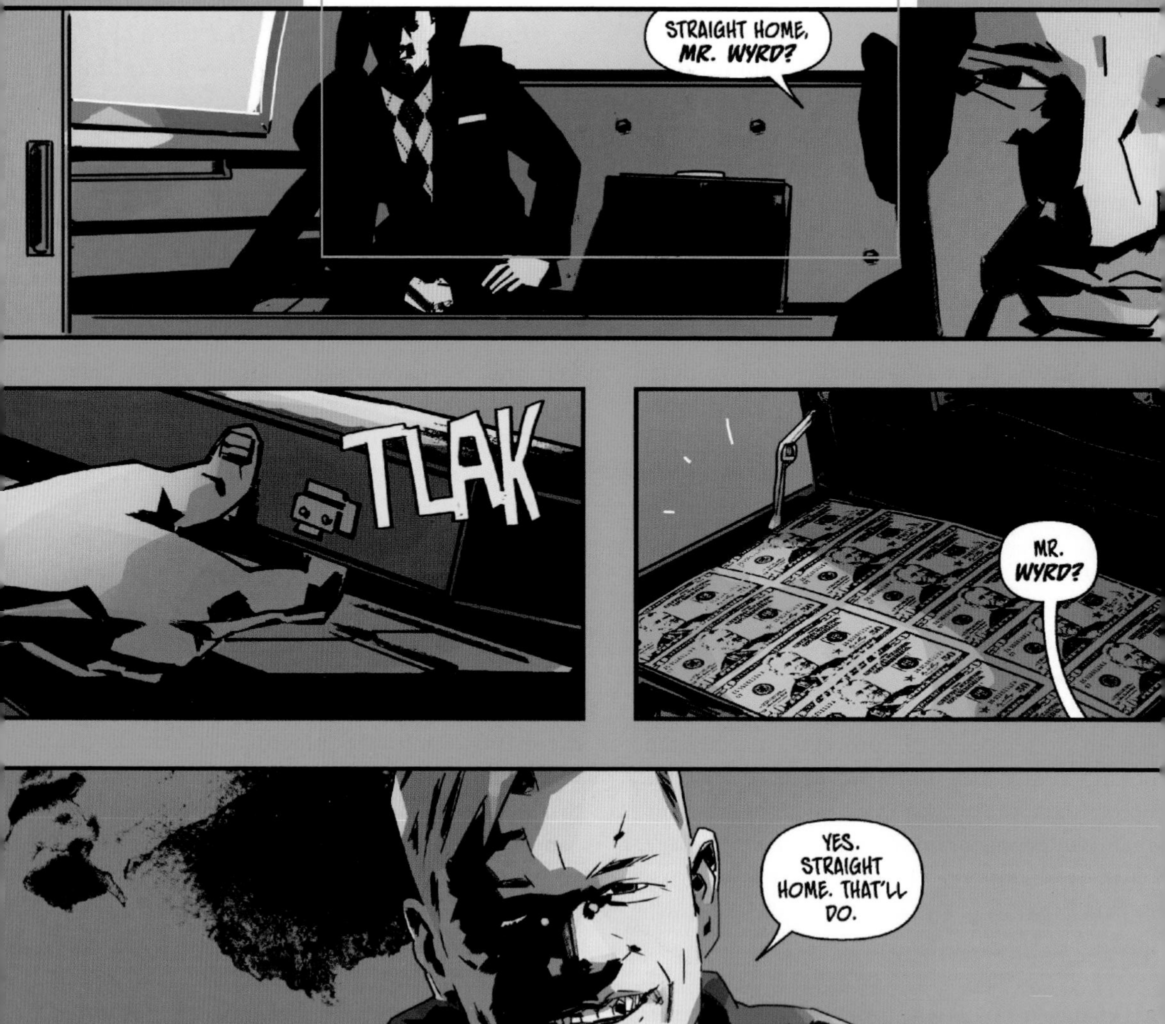

STRAIGHT HOME, MR. WYRD?
TLAK
MR. WYRD?
YES. STRAIGHT HOME. THAT'LL DO.